The Psychology of Paranormal Belief

A researcher's handbook

In loving memory of
Robert L. Morris
1942–2004

Koestler Chair of Parapsychology
University of Edinburgh
1985–2004

The Psychology of Paranormal Belief

A researcher's handbook

HARVEY J. IRWIN

University of Hertfordshire Press

First published in Great Britain in 2009 by
University of Hertfordshire Press
Learning and Information Services
University of Hertfordshire
College Lane
Hatfield
Hertfordshire AL10 9AB

British Library Cataloguing in Publication Data
A catalogue record for this book is available from the British Library

ISBN 978-1-902806-93-8

Design by: Heavens and Earth Art, IP12 3DB
Printed in Great Britain by: Charlesworth Press, WF2 9LP

Contents

Foreword

Dr Caroline Watt, Koestler Parapsychology Unit, University of Edinburgh
Professor Richard Wiseman, Department of Psychology, University of Hertfordshire

The term 'paranormal belief' tends to be carelessly used as if it were referring to a monolithic belief in phenomena for which science has no explanation. Those of us who conduct research in this area are often approached by members of the public, journalists, even fellow academics, expressing their interest in 'the paranormal'. In response to such enquiries, we first have to begin to unpack what particular aspect of the paranormal has piqued their curiosity. As Irwin demonstrates in this book, the paranormal is not a unitary concept. The term 'paranormal belief' encompasses different varieties of beliefs, including beliefs in psychic abilities such as extrasensory perception, precognition, and psychokinesis; beliefs in all-powerful deities and the power of prayer; beliefs in survival of the soul after death and the ability to communicate with the deceased; superstitious beliefs; beliefs that organisms can be healed, or harmed, through the direct action of mental intention; and beliefs that the earth is visited by intelligent alien life forms.

Parapsychologists, anthropologists, sociologists and psychologists have explored these beliefs from their own individual academic perspectives. Those from the first group tend to focus on beliefs in psychic abilities, and do not rule out the possibility that psychic abilities may be genuine. For this reason, part of their research investigates the relationship between belief in psychic ability and actual performance on controlled laboratory tests of psychic ability. Anthropologists and sociologists, in contrast, are not concerned with the ontological reality of paranormal beliefs. Rather, their interest focuses on the social and cultural function that such beliefs serve. Psychologists are perhaps the most sceptical about the accuracy of paranormal beliefs, and some of their work has proceeded on the assumption that such beliefs are basically misguided and maladaptive. Others retain a more open mind about the possibility that our current scientific understanding may be incomplete. Their work instead explores how such beliefs have arisen, and what psychological function they may serve. In this book, Irwin gives us a comprehensive overview of these different approaches to paranormal belief, before focusing on the question of the origin and psychological function of paranormal belief.

Not only do paranormal beliefs, *plural*, come in many different shapes and sizes, but in looking at the research it quickly becomes apparent that the different kinds of beliefs serve different functions. For instance, culturally supported beliefs, such as traditional religious beliefs, serve a different function from beliefs in extraordinary human capabilities such as mind-reading and mind over matter. Some beliefs may be functional, others dysfunctional. Perhaps due to the complexities surrounding the topic of paranormal belief, much of this work has proceeded in little self-contained bubbles, with scant reference to the other perspectives or bodies of work. This leads to pockets of understanding that address one facet of belief, but ignore others. What is needed is a piece of work to set out and synthesise these different approaches, and this is what Irwin seeks to achieve with this monograph.

Those of a sceptical bent may question why so many researchers are apparently wasting their time investigating the causes and consequences of beliefs that are evidently false. If so, they miss the point. Paranormal beliefs are very widely held in the population: around the world, surveys consistently show that about 50 per cent of people hold one or more paranormal beliefs and, of these, about 50 per cent believe that they have had a genuinely paranormal experience. Regardless of whether these beliefs and experiences are 'correct', they are clearly an important part of what it is to be human. Paranormal beliefs occur in every culture around the world. Therefore academics have a responsibility to attempt to understand what causes these beliefs, and the consequences to individuals and to society of holding them. This much-needed book does just that.

Acknowledgments

Much of this monograph was written during a year of study leave. I thank my employer, the University of New England, for granting me leave of absence from my teaching duties, and thank Professor Malcolm Cooper for providing office facilities during this period at the Wide Bay campus of the University of Southern Queensland.

The monograph was originally to be published by the Parapsychology Foundation. The financial constraints under which the Foundation has recently operated prompted repeated delays in its publication program, and now Lisette Coly of the Parapsychology Foundation has kindly allowed me to negotiate publication of the monograph with University of Hertfordshire Press. I would like to thank employees of the Foundation for their support of the original project. In particular, I wish to acknowledge the constructive editorial input from Dr Debra Weiner; Debra's incisive queries did much to sharpen the exposition.

Since the manuscript has been placed in the hands of University of Hertfordshire Press I have benefited from the enthusiastic and sympathetic support of my editor, Jane Housham. Jane's assurances during the transition between publishers and her professionalism throughout the publication process were greatly appreciated. The ultimate form of the book benefited greatly from Jane's thoughtful and creative input. Thanks are due, too, to Professor Richard Wiseman for his assistance in putting me in touch with University of Hertfordshire Press.

I acknowledge with gratitude some suggestions offered by Dr Tony Lawrence in preliminary correspondence about the form of this monograph. His generous encouragement to proceed with the project was much appreciated. The structure of the monograph was also influenced by an earlier review compiled by the author (Irwin, 1993); this strategy was undertaken with the gracious permission of the editor of the *Journal of the American Society for Psychical Research*.

For their permission to reproduce the questionnaire measures of paranormal belief included in the Appendix to the monograph, acknowledgment is given to the respective authors and the original publishers. Specific acknowledgments are given at the end of each questionnaire in turn. Chris Lisle is also thanked for his assistance in generating the computer graphic for Figure 1. The photograph of Professor Bob Morris was kindly provided by Professor Peter Mulacz.

Finally, I would like to take this opportunity to thank the many hundreds of people who participated in my empirical studies of paranormal belief over the past twenty-five years. Without their freely given time and effort this monograph would never have been realised.

Harvey J. Irwin
Research Fellow, School of Psychology, University of New England, Armidale, Australia
February, 2009

Chapter 1: Introduction

The fundamental purpose of this monograph is to examine paranormal belief from a psychological perspective. More specifically, the objective here is to explore the origins and psychological functions of paranormal beliefs. Chapter 1 sets the scene by considering what the term 'paranormal belief' may signify and by identifying the psychological and cultural significance of scientific research into these beliefs.

The definition of paranormal belief

It would perhaps be an overstatement to describe paranormal beliefs as ubiquitous, but they certainly are shared by many people. Rigorously solicited poll data suggest that a majority of the American population embraces at least one paranormal belief. A 2001 Gallup poll (Newport and Strausberg, 2001) reported the following levels of endorsement.

	per cent
Psychic or spiritual healing	54
Extrasensory perception (ESP)	50
Haunted houses	42
Ghosts	38
Telepathy	36
Visits to Earth by extraterrestrial beings	33
Clairvoyance	32
Astrology	28
Spirit communication	28
Witchcraft	26
Reincarnation	25
Spirit possession	15

In addition, an earlier Gallup poll (Gallup, 1997) indexed support for some other paranormal beliefs: psychokinesis ('mind-over-matter' effects): 17 per cent; the existence of the devil: 56 per cent; diabolic possession: 42 per cent; UFOs (unidentified flying objects, or 'flying saucers'): 48 per cent; and being at least 'somewhat superstitious': 25 per cent.

By way of independent confirmation, a Southern Focus poll conducted in 1998 (Institute for Research in Social Science, 1998) also identified substantial endorsement of selected paranormal beliefs:

	per cent
God answers prayers	86
God	84
Life after death	73
Heaven or hell	68
Biblical account of creation	62
ESP	60
Diabolic possession	55
Psychic or spiritual healing	55
Ghosts	41
UFOs	39
Extraterrestrial beings' visits to Earth	34
Astrology	33
Being at least somewhat superstitious	25
Reincarnation	25

Some account here should also be taken of the degree of conviction, because the rejection of even the less widely endorsed paranormal beliefs may be unequivocal in only a minority of the population. For example, Hamilton (2001) found that while there was considerable scepticism toward astrology, only 25 per cent of her sample said they had 'no belief at all' in astrology. In short, some degree of conviction in paranormal beliefs is very common in the general population.

Apart from documenting the frequency of paranormal beliefs in contemporary America, the above data also serve to instantiate some specific paranormal beliefs. A few readers may be surprised by some of the categories included in these polls. This surprise is not due merely to some trivial conceptual fuzziness in the notion of 'the paranormal'. Rather, we have the curious situation that in the sense in which the term is used both by many professional researchers and the general public, 'paranormal belief' in fact encompasses rather more than belief in paranormal phenomena. Strictly speaking, paranormal phenomena are scientifically impossible events or, as Broad (1949) argued, they are phenomena that violate the 'basic limiting principles' of current scientific understanding.[1] Not all of the above beliefs relate to paranormal phenomena as thus defined; it may reasonably be argued that in a strict sense the existence of UFOs or the existence of God, for example, is not 'scientifically impossible'.

There is a fundamental dilemma here that requires at least tentative resolution. One option would be to implement from the outset a definition of paranormal belief as belief in scientifically impossible phenomena and henceforth to exclude discussion of any belief (e.g., the existence of UFOs or God) that does not meet this criterion. Although this option is logically defensible, at this point of the exposition it would be tactically injudicious. There is a substantial quantity of research on these 'paranormal' beliefs that do not pertain to scientifically impossible phenomena and it would be premature to discard this knowledge without examining its potential implications for paranormal belief as more widely conceived. If belief in scientifically impossible phenomena were to be found to differ from the other beliefs that researchers have classified as paranormal, there will be ample opportunity in the final chapter of the monograph for some conceptual house-cleaning in relation to the 'paranormality' criterion.

Thus I now aim to construct a *working definition* of 'paranormal belief' that accommodates the common broad usage of this term by most researchers and lay people. Under this approach paranormal belief cannot viably be defined simply as belief in scientifically impossible phenomena and, indeed, even a minor modification of Broad's (1949) definition of paranormality would not suffice for this purpose. As will become evident, the formulation of a working definition is not a straightforward task, but the following critical scrutiny of various definitional issues may help to clarify the nature of the concept of paranormal belief as it is popularly applied.

Instances of paranormal belief

In discussing the definition of paranormal belief a useful starting point is to provide a contextual background, namely, a list of some broad categories of belief that might generally be recognised as 'paranormal'. Unless otherwise indicated, there is a reasonable consensus among researchers that each of the following categories does qualify as a paranormal belief; such consensus would be signified, for example, by the inclusion of the belief category in measures of paranormal belief that have been designed for research purposes (see Chapter 3).

Superstitions. The majority of questionnaires surveying paranormal beliefs include some items relating to superstitions. Indeed, superstitious belief was the first context in which paranormal belief was scientifically studied (Dresslar, 1907; Minot, 1887; see also Ch. 3). Traditional superstitions commonly relate to omens of unspecified good or bad luck (e.g., breaking a mirror, finding a horseshoe). Other superstitions convey more specific predictions (e.g., 'If your right hand itches, you will receive money'), information about distant events ('If your ears burn, someone is talking about you'), or counsel on actions that will be advantageous ('Cross your fingers when you make a wish').

Some superstitious practices are now little else than a social custom (Knowlson, 1930/1998), their original purpose having long been forgotten; examples include giving decorated eggs at Easter and hanging mistletoe at Christmas. Indeed, many superstitions are thought to be very ancient (Knowlson, 1930/1998), although others do have a recent origin. The belief that Friday the 13th is in some way fateful, for example, arose in the twentieth century (Hirschfelder, 2001), as did the belief that carrying a rabbit's foot brings luck (Ellis, 2002). Thus it seems new superstitions are still springing up (e.g., superstitious attributions about computer crashes). Even today superstitious behaviours reportedly play an important role in various professional and collegiate sports (Bleak and Frederick, 1998; Burger and Lynn, 2005; McClearn, 2004; Todd and Brown, 2003; Womack, 1992). Some traditional superstitions incorporate elements of other paranormal beliefs (e.g., divination), but if these are eliminated the core element of superstitions appears to be a belief in (good and bad) luck (Irwin, 2007).

Psi processes. Experimental parapsychologists apply the scientific method to the investigation of fundamental paranormal processes designated collectively as psi (see Irwin, 1999a). Nominated psi processes include various forms of extrasensory perception (telepathy, clairvoyance, precognition or ESP of future events and retrocognition or ESP of events in the distant past) and psychokinesis (PK, or the direct influence of mind over matter). As these hypothetical processes are posited to underlie psychic and other paranormal phenomena, belief in psi is a particularly basic form of paranormal belief. Current global measures of paranormal belief typically include items on psi belief and focused measures of psi belief have also been constructed; several of these measures are reviewed in Chapter 3 and some are included in the Appendices to this monograph.

Divinatory arts. Endorsement of various prophetic practices is generally regarded as a type of paranormal belief. Divinatory practices include the reading of Tarot cards, astrology, numerology, palmistry, other forms of fortune-telling (e.g., reading tea leaves) and diverse esoteric rituals of divination (e.g., hieromancy, or prophesying the future from the entrails of a sacrificed animal). In shamanistic or other traditional settings these divinatory arts are embedded in an extensive magico-religious framework (Frazer, 1911; Seligman, 1948/1975), but this epistemological context may not always be so profound in the contemporary fortune-telling rituals used in Western countries; some of the latter rituals, for example, are constructed simply as a psychic process.

Esoteric systems of magic. Divination is only one facet of esoteric systems of magic; other rites are designed to intervene more directly in human affairs. Thus, some of the magical rituals of witchcraft (including neo-pagan Wicca), sorcery, Vodoun (voodoo) and shamanism are designed to achieve a change in the physical or social world that is desired by the specially gifted exponent of the ritual or by the person whose wishes are represented by the practitioner (Hutton, 2000, 2007; Maxwell-Stuart, 2001). Paranormal beliefs encompassed by this category include belief in the effectiveness of magical spells, potions and talismans (charms).

New Age therapies. The New Age movement encompasses a diffuse set of groups variously in pursuit of human transcendence, world peace and environmentalist objectives. The philosophical outlook of these groups may loosely be described as eclectically 'holistic' (Houtman and Mascini, 2002) and as advocating the person's obligation to assume the fundamental responsibility of plotting his or her own destiny (Redden, 2002). Some of the activities of the New Age movement reflect beliefs that researchers may construe as paranormal. Under this category there falls a variety of alternative health practices and therapies such as aromatherapy, aura drainage, crystal power, homeopathy, iridology, naturopathy, psychic healing, 'pyramid power', reflexology and Reiki.

Spiritism. Another domain of paranormal belief encompasses beliefs in the world of spirits, the intervention of spirits in the mundane world and the existence of the spirit in living persons. Spiritism includes belief in mediumistic communication with spirits of the dead and in other phenomena of the séance room; belief in ghosts, haunted houses and poltergeists; and belief in astral travel or out-of-body experiences as an instance in which the spirit of a living person is temporarily released from the physical body. In the broadest use of the term spiritism is not confined to the tenets of the formalised religious movement known as Spiritualism, although certainly the general philosophy of Spiritualism is consistent with spiritism.

Eastern mystico-religious beliefs. Certain elements of Eastern mysticism and religions are recognised by most commentators as types of paranormal belief. The most notable example would be the belief in reincarnation but others include belief in the law of Karma and the endorsement of such practices as the I Ching and Feng Shui. Some of these beliefs, of course, can be endorsed outside the context of Eastern mysticism (Walker, 2000; Walter and Waterhouse, 1999) and may even be modified to suit the cultural setting (Edwards, 1996; Lang and Ragvald, 1998).

Judeo-Christian religious beliefs. Perhaps the most contentious category of paranormal belief is religious belief. This category encompasses such metaphysical tenets as the existence of God, the devil, heaven, hell and angels; belief in the power of prayer; and more extreme views such as creationism (the belief that at a single point in time God created the Earth and its inhabitants), the literal truth of the Bible and other religious texts, the divine status of certain prophets, the Virgin birth and other elements of Judeo-Christian and non-Christian fundamentalism (Almond *et al.*, 2003; Brasher, 2001). Broadly speaking, these beliefs are traditional in Western societies and at least in this respect they may be differentiated from Eastern mystico-religious beliefs. Thus, this facet of paranormal belief is termed 'traditional religious belief' by Tobacyk and Milford (1983).

As might be expected, many sceptical commentators (Alcock, 1981; Goode, 2000a; Tobacyk and Milford, 1983) see no need to distinguish traditional religious beliefs from nonreligious instances of paranormal belief. On the other hand, some writers (Fitzpatrick and Shook, 1994; Hergovich *et al.*, 2008; Kristensen, 1999; Lawrence, 1995; Sullivan, 1982; Williams *et al.*, 1989) have disputed the classification of religious tenets as paranormal beliefs either on philosophical or on tentative empirical grounds. Religious beliefs are included here for two principal reasons. First, the supernaturalism implied by some of these beliefs (e.g., the existence of angels, the occurrence of miracles) appears at least superficially to be cognate with that of other paranormal beliefs (the existence of ghosts and the effectiveness of magical rituals, respectively). Second, at this relatively early stage of scientific research into paranormal belief it is advisable not to exclude precipitately a category of belief that still is regarded as paranormal by many commentators, even if others may hold a different view. This is not to say that religious beliefs will necessarily exhibit the same properties as other paranormal beliefs; this certainly remains a matter for empirical resolution. In the meantime, however, it is appropriate to look for a definition of paranormal belief that will include the category of traditional religious belief.

Extraterrestrial aliens. Recent space probes have provided clear evidence of the existence of primitive life forms (e.g., algae) on other planets and it is at least feasible that more complex forms of life may exist in other galaxies. On the other hand, a conviction in the existence of intelligent extraterrestrial aliens living in a sophisticated civilisation on a distant planet is regarded by the general public and by some commentators as a paranormal belief. Although some researchers (e.g., Thalbourne and French, 1997) explicitly discount the notion that a belief in extraterrestrial aliens is a form of paranormal belief, items about UFOs appear sufficiently often in measures of paranormal belief (see Chapter 3) for the category to be provisionally included here.

Despite being unified by the theme of extraterrestrial life this paranormal belief may be relatively heterogeneous (Saunders, 1968; Simón, 1979); the category includes belief in UFOs as alien spacecraft, visits to Earth by extraterrestrial aliens, abduction of people by aliens and that some seemingly inexplicable phenomena (ranging from the construction of the Egyptian pyramids to crop circles) are evidence of alien visitations.

Cryptozoological creatures. Strange creatures need not be confined to other planets. Sightings of mysterious animals in isolated forests, lakes and other sparsely populated regions are occasionally reported. Now, some of these sightings prove to be linked to feral animals or zoo escapees or to remains that are difficult to identify because of decomposition (Carr *et al.*, 2002; Kuban, 1997). One must be mindful, too, that new species of animals are still being discovered (The Word Cryptozoology, 2002). On the other hand, some people believe in the existence of life forms that are not recognised by orthodox zoologists; the study of these possible life forms is known as cryptozoology (Bauer, 1996; Coleman and Clark, 1999). Contemporary examples of such animals include the Loch Ness monster of Scotland, Bigfoot and the Ogopogo in North America, the Yeti (Abominable Snowman) of the Himalayas and the Mokele-Mbembe of the African Congo. Belief in cryptozoological creatures, or so-called 'cryptids' (Coleman and Clark, 1999), is nominated as another category of paranormal belief. The category also includes belief in such legendary monsters as unicorns, mermaids, sea serpents and dragons.

The foregoing categories are offered as a working list to facilitate further discussion in this chapter. In addition, these examples serve at the outset to establish the remarkable diversity of what researchers have classified as paranormal beliefs, from frankly crackpot ideas and faddish 'cosmobabble' to concepts that receive at least some serious scientific scrutiny. It must be stressed, however, that the above list certainly is not intended to be a definitive taxonomy of paranormal belief and it should not be used for that purpose. As a taxonomy the list would clearly be deficient. The categories are not mutually exclusive; several of the categories overlap to some extent and a fundamental belief in ESP, for example, might reasonably be held to underlie beliefs in several other categories (e.g., superstitions about distant events, divinatory and other occult rituals, some séance phenomena and the process of prayer). Further, the set of categories is not exhaustive; not explicitly mentioned are some traditional folkloric beliefs (e.g., fairies, leprechauns, werewolves, vampires), beliefs advocated by small single-issue groups (e.g., a cargo cult, the Flat Earth Society) and beliefs associated with paranormal fads that briefly emerge from time to time (e.g., the Bermuda Triangle). Indeed, given the multiplicity of paranormal beliefs (see Stein, 1996), it is difficult for any categorisation to be comprehensive. On the other hand, as far as I am aware, the above list does include all of the major types of paranormal belief that have attracted the attention of researchers.[2]

Having provided this contextual background I now address a series of focal questions to help define the construct of paranormal belief.

Are paranormal beliefs really beliefs?

A viable definition of paranormal belief must subsume a shared understanding of the term 'belief'. Unfortunately, the differentiation between beliefs and attitudes has been something of a conceptual minefield for psychologists. In their highly influential work Fishbein and Ajzen (1975) advocated the use of 'belief' to refer to the purely cognitive representation of a proposition independent of emotion-laden associations. That is, 'attitudes' were deemed to have cognitive, affective (or emotional) and behavioural components, with the cognitive component referred to as a 'belief'. Other writers opted to use 'belief' for the cognitive component of a proposition and 'attitude' for its affective component (Oskamp, 1977). While continuing to recognise the three components, contemporary usage tends not to draw such a sharp distinction between beliefs and attitudes. Most importantly, the imputation of an emotional facet of beliefs is now generally accepted. Thus, Reber (1995, p. 90) defines a belief as 'an emotional acceptance of some proposition, statement or doctrine'.

Under this approach the question of whether paranormal beliefs are really beliefs or attitudes is of little consequence. It is therefore appropriate to continue to use the expression 'paranormal belief'. In doing so, however, we should still be mindful of the three components just discussed (Lewis, 1974). A paranormal belief therefore is deemed to have not only a cognitive component (e.g., 'reincarnation occurs'), but also an affective component ('I feel more secure in the knowledge that I will be reincarnated' or 'I feel very strongly about the doctrine of reincarnation') and possibly a behavioural component ('During my current lifetime I act in ways that will enhance the prospects for my next incarnation' or 'I try to convert others to a belief in reincarnation').

At the same time it is reasonable to differentiate beliefs from values (Scheibe, 1970). A value is an ideal or an abstract principle that society holds in high regard (Reber, 1995, p. 834). A value is thus an expression of preference rather than of belief. So-called beliefs in freedom, justice, democracy and similar principles therefore are values rather than beliefs. Similarly, there are grounds for distinguishing between beliefs and opinions. Although in the past some writers (e.g., Oskamp, 1977) equated these terms, Reber (1995, p. 514) distinguishes them on two grounds. First, whereas beliefs are embraced on a relatively sustained basis, opinions are held only tentatively and may quickly be revised or discarded in light of additional information. By way of illustration, a so-called belief in the basic goodness of people is actually an opinion rather than a belief, because it might readily be revised after exposure to a detailed account of the acts of a sadistic psychopath. Second, whereas beliefs have the three components described above, opinions are fundamentally intellectual propositions. Paranormal beliefs therefore will not be regarded here as opinions. This is not to deny that a person may have an opinion about a paranormal belief. To continue the example employed in the previous paragraph, one may have the opinion that a belief in reincarnation is nonsensical (e.g., because a person's memories are necessarily grounded in neural activity and thus could not survive the death of the brain).[3]

In summary, paranormal beliefs are beliefs with cognitive, affective and (sometimes) behavioural components; they are not an abstract value or statement of preference and they are more durable than mere opinions. It is stressed, however, that believers themselves might not conceptualise their paranormal beliefs in these terms. As Zusne and Jones (1982, pp. 196–7) insightfully remarked, 'Rarely are beliefs even thought of as beliefs. Instead, they comprise an individual's sense of reality and truth.' This characterisation is particularly apposite to paranormal belief.

Are paranormal beliefs necessarily consensual?

Poll data such as those cited at the beginning of this chapter do indicate that paranormal beliefs are widespread in our society. At the same time it is pertinent to consider if the sharing of a paranormal belief is one of the defining characteristics of this construct. That is, is it necessary that a paranormal belief be consensual?

In at least one sense it is difficult to conceive of a paranormal belief being peculiar to one person; thus, an idiosyncratic belief in some anomalous concept (e.g., 'I am a Martian') would more typically be regarded as pathological than as paranormal. The relationship between paranormal and pathological beliefs nevertheless is conceptually distinct from the issue of consensus and is addressed more fully in another section of this chapter. The present question therefore may be reframed as follows: should an apparently *nonpathological* belief that was peculiar to one person ever be admissible as a paranormal belief? The view advocated here is that it should not; that is, a belief must attract a degree of consensus before being eligible for definition as a paranormal belief. Paranormal beliefs therefore are construed as cultural representations (Sperber, 1990; see also Chapter 2).

This position is consistent with the fact that the categories of paranormal belief identified earlier in this chapter are not idiosyncratic but, rather, they have substantial (although far from universal) endorsement within the general population. Such data nevertheless are evidentially weak for the present case, simply because a paranormal belief that was peculiar to one person is unlikely to have been documented in the literature. The basic reason for requiring a paranormal belief to be consensual is that this criterion ensures there is some testimony to the cultural meaningfulness of the belief. By contrast, there is no independent evidence that an idiosyncratic belief has significance in the broader cultural context.

Perhaps a more pragmatic rationale for the consensualist criterion is that it is very difficult to study idiosyncratic beliefs. Empirical research into paranormal belief relies fundamentally on the development of effective measures of this construct (see Chapter 3) that can be applied to the general population and unless the researcher is able to identify a number of common (shared) instances of the construct, the breadth of a respondent's endorsement of paranormal beliefs cannot readily be gauged. At least for the present, it seems reasonable to assume that at least certain core elements of paranormal beliefs are consensual.

Are paranormal beliefs a type of delusion?

Sceptical commentators (e.g., Rawcliffe, 1959) sometimes refer to paranormal beliefs as 'delusions', although typically such statements are primarily for rhetorical purposes rather than to specify the technical status of paranormal belief. One widely used questionnaire measure of delusional ideation (Peters, Joseph and Garety, 1999) nevertheless includes such items as, 'Do you ever think that people can communicate telepathically?', 'Do you ever feel that you are especially close to God?' and 'Do you believe in the power of witchcraft, voodoo or the occult?'. It is appropriate therefore to consider if paranormal beliefs are a type of delusion.

Although current definitions of delusion are alleged to be both conceptually and clinically deficient (Jorgensen, 1995; Leeser and O'Donohue, 1999; Maher and Spitzer, 1993; Sedler, 1995), in essence a delusion is a persistently held false belief, often with bizarre or absurd content. Delusional thinking is a cardinal symptom of schizophrenia and other psychiatric disorders and thus sceptics' association of paranormal beliefs with delusion is in part an attempt to impute psychopathology among paranormal believers. In fact, however, delusional thoughts are found also in the nonpsychiatric population. Delusions therefore are not necessarily pathognomic of a psychological or organic disorder (Manschreck,

1995). More generally, delusions are not a severe symptom that a person either does or does not exhibit. Rather, delusional tendencies are a dimensional attribute which varies across the population from very low to very high levels and which is marked by variations in both the degree of conviction and the time one spends preoccupied with the belief (Appelbaum *et al.*, 1999; Chadwick and Lowe, 1990).

There is no doubt that paranormal concepts may be integrated into a person's delusional system (Fisman and Fisman, 1999; Greyson, 1977; Morrison and Wells, 2003; Page, 1935; Persinger, 1987). Paranoid schizophrenics, for example, commonly believe they are being spied upon and the patient may depict this in terms of other people's use of ESP to gain information about his or her actions and thoughts. Another common psychotic symptom is so-called 'thought insertion', the belief that other people are putting ideas into one's mind; again, the patient may formulate this belief in terms of telepathy. The presence of paranormal concepts in some delusional thinking is nevertheless not evidence that paranormal beliefs themselves are delusory.

Are paranormal beliefs then 'persistently held false beliefs, often with bizarre or absurd content'? Most researchers would agree that paranormal beliefs are persistently held. As noted earlier, such beliefs are not mere opinions that are readily modified as further relevant information comes to hand. Further, although there is some evidence to suggest that the strength of paranormal beliefs can be diminished by educational processes (see Chapter 6), such effects are usually marginal and their interpretation equivocal; broadly speaking, paranormal beliefs are relatively resistant to the influence of counterargument, just as delusions typically are.

The notion that paranormal beliefs often have bizarre or absurd content is more contentious. The absurdity of a belief admittedly is a subjective judgment, but while some instances of paranormal belief may reasonably be regarded as absurd (e.g., some superstitions), it is difficult to sustain this view for every paranormal belief. A person may, for example, thoughtfully reject a belief in God, but even the most ardent atheist would be hard pressed to demonstrate in a conclusive way the bizarreness or absurdity of this matter of faith.

Even more problematic is the proposition that like delusions, paranormal beliefs are false. Experimental research can never *disprove* the ESP hypothesis, for example; at best, the data may fail to support the hypothesis. For this reason it is not legitimate to claim that psi belief is false. Similarly, religious belief cannot validly be said to be false; in most instances such a metaphysical belief is purely a matter of faith that is not accessible to disproof (nor indeed to proof). In this context it is interesting to note that a widely used guide to psychiatric diagnosis, the *Diagnostic and Statistical Manual of Mental Disorders, Fourth Edition* (DSM-IV; American Psychiatric Association, 1994) explicitly excluded from classification as a delusion any belief for which there is some cultural or subcultural consensus and, in particular, any 'article of religious faith' (p. 765). Research by Jones and Watson (1997) and by Peters *et al.* (1999) also casts doubt on the view that religious beliefs in themselves are delusory in the strict technical sense.

Some readers might also object that paranormal beliefs are much more common than delusions. On the other hand, it is not a simple matter to document this opinion. In addition, we must be mindful of the existence of so-called *collective delusions*, that is, a situation in which there is a rapid community-wide spread of a false belief or false interpretation of a situation. Bartholomew (2001) cites as putative instances of a collective delusion reported sightings of cryptids and UFOs and visions of the Virgin Mary. Such a construction is of course not uncontentious, but Bartholomew's analysis does raise the possibility that some paranormal beliefs may well result from collective delusions. Be that as it may, this still does not constitute a case for defining all paranormal beliefs as collective delusions. As demonstrated in Chapter 2, the development of many paranormal beliefs is quite unlike the rumour-spreading processes that instil collective delusions.

Some paranormal beliefs evidently are absurd by any reasonable standard of scrutiny and the absurdity of most paranormal beliefs is widely professed by sceptical commentators. In some instances paranormal concepts may also be incorporated into a person's delusional system. Notwithstanding these circumstances the available evidence does not demonstrate that all paranormal beliefs are delusory in a technical sense. It is concluded that paranormal belief therefore should not be intrinsically defined as a type of delusion.

Are paranormal beliefs irrational?

Paranormal beliefs might not necessarily be false but they could still be irrational, that is, in violation of the conventional rules of logic. Indeed, even a valid conclusion may be reached through invalid deductive processes. I now address the possibility that paranormal beliefs should be defined as instances of irrational belief.

The irrationality of paranormal beliefs has been widely asserted since the early research into superstitiousness during the first few decades of the twentieth century. Wagner (1928) described superstitions as irrational beliefs and Dresslar (1907, p. 141) went further by actually defining superstitiousness as an inclination 'to believe in certain causal relations, which have not and cannot be proved to exist through a course of reasoning, through revelation or through direct observation'. More recently, Vyse (1997, p. 195) also concluded that most paranormal beliefs are irrational, although he did concede that this might not invariably be the case.

In order to pursue a more incisive analysis of the rationality of paranormal beliefs three distinct phases are addressed in turn: the formation of a paranormal belief, the maintenance of a paranormal belief and the decision to act upon a paranormal belief.

The rationality of paranormal-belief formation. Sperber (1990) proposed a basic dichotomy of beliefs defined by their different modes of formation. The first kind he termed *intuitive* beliefs which are formed through 'spontaneous and unconscious perceptual and inferential processes' (Sperber, 1990, p. 35) or what Goode (2000a) called an everyday or 'commonsensical' style of cognition. In the course of mundane perceptual experience a person sometimes will make an unconscious inference about the nature of the world. The subsequent verbal formulation of this inference may be informed by concepts and other relevant background acquired through the media, communication with others and similar sociocultural influences, but the initial inference is fundamentally intuitive. By way of illustration, consider the possible processes underlying intuitive beliefs in terms of a commonly cited context for the formation of a belief in telepathy. While thinking of a long-lost friend a person may unexpectedly receive a phone call from that friend, unconsciously infer the occurrence of direct mind-to-mind contact, consciously realise that this experience is what people call 'telepathy' and henceforth embrace a belief in telepathy. The unconscious nature of the inferential process in intuitive belief formation nevertheless creates opportunities for logical flaws in such beliefs (Gilovich *et al.*, 2002; Kahneman and Tversky, 1972). As Goode (2000a, p. 55) remarks, 'common sense often works, but its wisdom is highly fallible'. Thus, in the above example the inference of telepathy could be erroneous; the case might have been due to coincidence, synchronicity, an error of perception or recollection, or any one of several other factors (Irwin, 1999a).

The second kind of belief in Sperber's (1990) dichotomy is the *reflective* belief. Reflective beliefs generally are based on intuitive inferences but they involve an additional reflective process whereby the inferences are validated through explicit (conscious) reasoning and in light of the affirmations of a respected authority. A belief in an afterlife, for example, might arise in this manner. Thus, an observation of the grief of bereaved people or of the mutilated death of a wild animal may successively instigate an intuition of the dreadfulness of death, a reflection that it would be nice never to die and in light of the assurances of religiously inclined authority figures, a reflective belief in an afterlife. Because reflective beliefs involve some validation they are less susceptible to irrational influences, although a person's reflective processes and their choice of authority figures may still be flawed.

There is therefore at least some scope for the formation of paranormal beliefs to be irrational to some extent. The role of irrational processes in the formation of these beliefs nevertheless remains a matter for empirical scrutiny rather than for definition. There seem to be no *a priori* grounds for assuming the formation of every paranormal belief to be intrinsically and invariably irrational.

The rationality of paranormal-belief maintenance. Conventional rules of logic might be contravened not only during the formation of a belief but also during its maintenance once formed (Alcock, 1981, p. 33). The persistence of paranormal beliefs might therefore be due in part to some logical deficit that impedes or prevents the believer from revising the beliefs in light of further critical analysis and further evidence as this becomes available. One possible such deficit identified by Langdon and Coltheart (2000) is an inability to suspend natural biases against alternative beliefs. This is the essence of dogmatism, that is, an unwillingness to address counterarguments and instead to maintain a belief without subjecting it to further critical scrutiny. This tendency could fairly be deemed irrational.

Despite the evident importance of belief maintenance in accounting for the persistence of a belief, relatively little is known about this process in the context of paranormal belief or, indeed, in regard to beliefs in general. Perhaps some indications of the nature of belief maintenance in paranormal believers can be found in personality characteristics. There are reports that dogmatism as a personality trait is a correlate of belief in witchcraft, traditional religious concepts (Thalbourne, Dunbar and Delin, 1995; Tobacyk and Milford, 1983) and psi (Alcock and Otis, 1980), although a statistically nonsignificant association for global paranormal belief was found by Auton *et al.* (2003). This suggests a rigid tendency to resist any attempt to assess critically the bases of one's paranormal beliefs. On the other hand, there is as yet a dearth of evidence for an association between dogmatism and other forms of paranormal belief. Data for the related trait of authoritarianism also are mixed (Heard and Vyse, 1998; Randall, 1991). Again, there do not appear to be adequate grounds for defining the maintenance of paranormal beliefs to be intrinsically irrational (see also Leeser and O'Donohue, 1999).

The rationality of acting upon paranormal beliefs. Another way to address the rationality of paranormal beliefs is to consider if it would be uniformly irrational to act in accordance with a paranormal belief. Following Vyse (1997) I assess this issue in terms of the utility of such actions.

Despite Vyse's (1997) view that paranormal beliefs usually are irrational, he does acknowledge that there can be exceptions to this rule. By way of illustration, when faced with a desperate situation (e.g., dying from cancer) a person's decision to seek paranormal intervention (e.g., through prayer or an alternative healing practice) — no matter how small the probability of that intervention's efficacy — might fairly be deemed to be rational, according to Vyse. What Vyse essentially seems to be arguing here is that if there is any possibility that a paranormal belief could enhance the well-being of the believer, then this belief does have rational appeal. It is possible to concur with this view without assuming that it would obtain only in exceptional circumstances. Evidence surveyed in subsequent sections of the monograph (particularly Chapter 7) suggests that many paranormal beliefs could well have the effect of enhancing their adherents' *psychological* well-being. A belief in an afterlife, for example, might be very reassuring for many people, irrespective of the validity of this belief. Under the criterion of utility it would therefore be inappropriate to depict the behavioural component of paranormal beliefs as uniformly irrational.

In summary, there are insufficient grounds for defining paranormal beliefs generically as irrational beliefs and, indeed, in some respects it can be argued that they may serve rational purposes. It must be stressed that this stance in relation to the *definition* of paranormal belief does not of itself obviate the possibility that believers in paranormal phenomena have irrational tendencies. Empirical findings that bear on the latter issue are surveyed in Chapter 6.

As a footnote to this analysis of the irrationality of paranormal beliefs, mention may be made of some beliefs that may actually be precluded from classification as 'paranormal' on the grounds that they are specifically designed to appeal to minds too immature to be capable of properly rational analysis. These are the beliefs of childhood, such as belief in Santa Claus, the Easter Bunny and the Tooth Fairy. Such beliefs, if widely endorsed by adults, might well be classified as paranormal, but as they are peculiar to early childhood most observers would be inclined to accept them simply as developmentally immature beliefs. Admittedly, the distinction between immature beliefs and paranormal beliefs remains moot, given that developmental perspectives on paranormal belief have not been given due attention by researchers. In any event, it seems that paranormal beliefs cannot legitimately be defined as irrational and that the people who endorse them might normally be expected by society to be capable of rational thought.

Are paranormal beliefs scientifically unacceptable?

A paranormal belief is intrinsically a proposition enunciating the existence of an underlying paranormal phenomenon. Now, in most contemporary societies science is generally deemed to be the ultimate arbiter of knowledge. In the scientific view any proposition that is not attested by empirical evidence lacks credibility. Indeed, under a more extreme *scientistic* perspective any proposition that is inaccessible to empirical scrutiny is dismissed as patent nonsense or undeserving of any attention (Appleyard, 1992). The scientific status of paranormal beliefs therefore requires some discussion.

One position on this issue is that paranormal beliefs pertain to phenomena that are scientifically inexplicable; that is, no current scientific theory nor body of scientific knowledge can possibly accommodate the alleged phenomena. This is a popular construction of the term 'paranormal' (see Braude, 1978) and is noteworthy in that it implies that some beliefs might not be regarded as paranormal forever. On the other hand, at best this framework accommodates only some of the categories of paranormal belief identified earlier in this chapter. Extraterrestrial aliens and cryptozoological life forms, for example, are not scientifically inexplicable. If an unknown monstrous creature were to be washed up on the shores of Loch Ness, for example, biologists would be quick to find a phylogenetic place for it. The purported scientific inexplicability of some other paranormal phenomena also is moot. Although Scriven (1962) once described parapsychology as a collection of facts (or experimental findings) without a theory, there are now many theories of psi processes that meet the requirements of a scientific account (for a review see Irwin, 1999a). Paranormal beliefs therefore are not limited to inexplicable phenomena.

A second and more radical position on the scientific perception of paranormal beliefs is that such beliefs pertain to phenomena that actually *contravene* scientific understanding. Thus, in Lindeman's (1998) view paranormal beliefs espouse processes that 'contravene some fundamental and well-founded assumptions of science' (p. 257). Consider the superstition that breaking a mirror will bring bad luck. The causal process presumed to link these two events is of a kind that is not merely inexplicable but contrary to that allowed under a mechanistic scientific philosophy. Many of the other paranormal beliefs listed earlier also implicate scientifically unacceptable causal mechanisms. The violation of scientific principles by hypothesised psi processes has been subject to particular attention in the literature (Broad, 1949). Precognition, for example, might be held to be incompatible with a basic scientific law of causation, namely, that a cause must precede its effect (Broad, 1937; McMullen, 1978); in precognition a cause (the future event) seems to *follow* its effect (perception or knowledge of that event). Similarly, the more general notion of extrasensory perception may be deemed to contradict the scientific tenet that (external) information can be conveyed to a person solely through the recognised human senses. On such grounds Alcock (1981, p. 191) has lamented, 'if psi exists, science as we know it can not'. In this sense some sceptics evidently view paranormal beliefs as *antiscientific*, a dangerous threat to the scientific worldview.

It must be acknowledged that on philosophical grounds other commentators have questioned whether backward causation, as seemingly implied by precognition, would necessarily contravene scientific principles (Beloff, 1977). More recently, scientific models of psi processes formulated within a quantum mechanical framework have also challenged traditional perceptions of the scientific inadmissibility of psi processes (for a review see Irwin, 1999a). The scientific establishment nevertheless continues to regard psi as an inherent impossibility. Be that as it may, the fact remains that some other paranormal beliefs do not implicate scientifically impossible processes. Many of the metaphysical beliefs of spiritism and religion are not a literal violation of scientific tenets. The existence of spirits and of heaven, for example, is not precluded by science. It is therefore not appropriate to define paranormal beliefs in terms of the contravention of scientific principles by paranormal phenomena.

Another view of the scientific status of paranormal belief is that these propositions are *inaccessible* to science; that is, belief in the paranormal is purely a matter of faith and its validity cannot be assessed through scientific methods of empirical investigation (Kelly, 1998; Leeser and O'Donohue, 1999; Novella and Bloomberg, 1999). This view can certainly be sustained for the case of some traditional religious beliefs: no amount of controlled experimental research could demonstrate, for example, the existence of God. Not all propositions underlying paranormal beliefs, however, are inaccessible to empirical scrutiny. Hypothesised psi processes have been subjected to considerable scientific investigation (see Irwin, 1999a), even if the outcomes of this research effort are still contentious in academic circles. Similarly, the efficacy of New Age therapies and esoteric magical rituals is certainly accessible to scientific evaluation and cryptozoological hypotheses also can be investigated empirically. Generally speaking, therefore, we cannot legitimately say that paranormal beliefs are based on scientifically untestable propositions.

Although there appears to be no single principle under which all paranormal beliefs can be considered scientifically unacceptable, the fact remains that these beliefs are scientifically unaccepted. In some instances this may seem little else than unabashed prejudice. The *a priori* assumption that paranormal beliefs 'must be groundless' is characteristic among mainstream scientists (Coll and Taylor, 2004) and has been demonstrated to be particularly salient among the scientific elite (McClenon, 1982). Be this as it may, it is still the case that paranormal beliefs are beliefs in propositions that are not part of conventional scientific wisdom. As indicated in the foregoing discussion the scientific unacceptance of paranormal beliefs appears to have a multifaceted basis, but the essential theme appears to be that *paranormal beliefs pertain to phenomena that have not been empirically attested to the satisfaction of the scientific establishment*. This has been termed the *rationalist* view of paranormal beliefs; under this view 'there is no distinction between believing in leprechauns, alien abductions, ESP, reincarnation, or the existence of a god — each equally lacks objective evidence' (Novella and Bloomberg, 1999, p. 45).

It is proposed that the above criterion has the potential to define paranormal belief, subject to some additional minor qualifications. It must be acknowledged that not all empirically unattested propositions are paranormal. Some concepts are couched within an explicitly scientific framework and are awaiting due scientific investigation for their acceptability to be properly determined. These clearly are generated as scientific hypotheses; that is, they are (presently) not accepted by science only in the sense that they are still undergoing the procedures required for such acceptance. Such is not the case for paranormal beliefs. Under this qualification I therefore concede that not all scientifically unattested propositions are necessarily paranormal.

An additional qualification of slightly greater importance is that the propositions encompassed by paranormal beliefs originally were not formulated with any scientific scrutiny in mind. Rather, they arose within the broader community as a nonscientific, commonsense endeavour to account for anomalous experiences and phenomena. Even the concept of psi initially was generated not by scientists as a hypothesis for investigation but by lay people as an attempt to make sense of everyday events. Psi and some other paranormal beliefs may subsequently have been refined as scientific hypotheses with the aim of facilitating empirical investigation, but the underlying belief does have its fundamental origins in the broader community.

With these collective observations in mind I proceed to the enunciation of a working definition of paranormal beliefs.

A working definition of paranormal belief

As the concept is popularly used, a paranormal belief is defined on a working basis as a proposition that has not been empirically attested to the satisfaction of the scientific establishment but is generated within the nonscientific community and extensively endorsed by people who might normally be expected by their society to be capable of rational thought and reality testing. For these people, the belief is phenomenologically a part of their sense of reality and truth rather than 'a proposition they endorse'. Like other types of belief, a paranormal belief will be either intuitive or reflective; will have cognitive, affective and (sometimes) behavioural components; will be distinct from a value or simple statement of preference; will be relatively stable and thus somewhat resistant to the influence of counterargument; and will be dimensional, that is, marked by various degrees of endorsement between the poles of extreme scepticism and extreme gullibility.

By way of a minor elaboration, note that endorsement of a belief is here termed 'extensive' in the sense that the belief is clearly associated with a social or cultural system. The belief therefore is neither idiosyncratic nor limited, for example, to a particular interpersonal relationship. The poll data cited at the beginning of the chapter might be taken to suggest that a paranormal belief is endorsed by at least 10 per cent of the population, but it is unnecessary to provide a quantitative specification of the term 'extensive'. The essential point is that a paranormal belief must be at least reasonably common and shared.

The above definition encompasses all of the major categories of paranormal belief listed at the beginning of this chapter plus such minor instances as some traditional folkloric beliefs (e.g., fairies), beliefs of single-issue groups (e.g., those of the Flat Earth Society) and beliefs associated with popular paranormal fads (e.g., the Bermuda Triangle). None of these beliefs has a scientifically endorsed empirical foundation. At the same time the definition excludes idiosyncratic beliefs (as these are not 'extensively endorsed'), demonstrably psychotic delusions and developmentally immature beliefs (as florid psychotics and young children are not regarded as 'capable of rational thought and reality testing') and scientific hypotheses awaiting empirical evaluation (as these are not 'generated within the nonscientific community').

The definition also admits the cultural and temporal relativity of paranormal beliefs. Thus, a paranormal belief that is widely embraced in one culture (or subculture) might not be endorsed in a different cultural setting and in the latter context the proposition therefore fails to meet the criterion of extensive endorsement.[4] Similarly, a proposition that is deemed paranormal at one time might not be so regarded at another time, either because the proposition becomes empirically substantiated to the satisfaction of mainstream science or it is no longer extensively endorsed within the community.

In addition, the definition carries a minimum of theoretical baggage. Most important, the definition is atheoretical to the extent that in itself the definition does not preclude any major theoretical options. This is notably the case in the following respects. The specification of paranormal phenomena as outside mainstream scientific knowledge should not be taken to imply that belief in the paranormal is an inappropriate topic for scientific scrutiny. On the contrary, research into the bases of paranormal belief need not presume the truth of these beliefs; to a large extent the belief in psi, for example, can be studied irrespective of the reality of parapsychological phenomena. Similarly, the definitional requirement that believers normally be regarded as 'capable of rational thought and reality testing' does not proscribe investigation of the hypothesis that some paranormal beliefs may be associated with a subclinical degree of deficient (irrational, pathological, or immature) thought processes. More generally, the definition has minimal implications for the supposed nature of paranormal believers. The comprehensiveness of the definition, for example, does not necessarily imply that paranormal beliefs are homogeneous and hence there is no intrinsic assumption that a person will be undiscriminating in his or her paranormal belief, either accepting every paranormal belief or rejecting them all (Irwin, 1997; Schriever, 1998; Taylor *et al.*, 1995).

The present definition therefore is sufficiently sensitive to admit the types of belief that warrant consideration in this monograph as 'paranormal' yet it does not precipitately rule out any substantial theories about the psychological origins and functions of paranormal belief. The definition nevertheless is intended to function only on a working basis; there are some residual concerns about this definition. One of these concerns is the issue noted earlier, that religious beliefs and belief in extraterrestrial aliens are identified as being paranormal beliefs under the definition, yet some researchers dispute this categorisation. Another concern is the problem of ensuring definitional specificity, that is, its capacity *not* to admit beliefs that would generally be regarded as not paranormal. As far as I am aware, common nonparanormal beliefs (excluding values and opinions) do not meet the criteria of the definition, but this cannot be universally guaranteed. One extensively researched belief (Lerner, 1980) that warrants particular consideration in this context is the so-called 'just world' belief, or the view that while bad things can happen to anyone, in the long run 'good people' will receive their just rewards and 'bad people' will get their just desserts. This is a widespread belief for which there is no empirical foundation (Lerner, 1980) and which meets the working definition for a paranormal belief. While some readers may object to the classification of the 'just world' belief as paranormal, I am comfortable that it should be so; this belief seems, for example, to have a good deal in common with the Eastern paranormal belief known as the law of Karma and with Judeo-Christian notions of God's reward and punishment of human behaviour. At the same time, this example signals that the working definition of paranormal belief may lack the specificity that some people would prefer. I will revisit the definition of paranormal belief in Chapter 8.

Having established the general subject matter of the monograph I now turn to the psychological and cultural significance of scientific research into paranormal belief.

The significance of research into paranormal belief

Although the nature of paranormal belief has been investigated by academics representing a wide range of attitudes toward the paranormal, the rationale for this research has been most vigorously expounded by commentators with an unreservedly sceptical perspective. For this reason it is expedient to begin with sceptical views of the psychological and cultural significance of research into paranormal belief.

Goode (2000a, p. 40) supported the study of paranormal beliefs on the grounds that it is important to determine if a paranormal claim is true. As noted above, however, the bases of paranormal belief can be investigated irrespective of the ultimate truth of the individual beliefs. Indeed, most sceptics work from the premise that paranormal beliefs are patently false and thus the sceptical rationale for research into paranormal belief typically does not include Goode's objective of authenticity. In general terms, sceptics promote research on this topic because they hold that paranormal beliefs have highly undesirable social and psychological consequences.

Several such consequences have been cited (Alcock, 1981; Beyerstein, 1998; Horne, 1996; Näyhä, 2002; Vyse, 1997). First, paranormal beliefs may predispose people to misinterpret normal events as paranormal (Ayeroff and Abelson, 1976; Benassi *et al.*, 1979; Jones and Russell, 1980; Singer and Benassi, 1981) and thereby impede their capacity to think and act in a critical fashion. Second, paranormal believers may be deceived and cheated by charlatans offering psychic readings or alternative therapies. Third, the health of paranormal believers may be endangered if they become anxious when superstitious beliefs are activated or if they neglect orthodox medical treatment in favour of alternative healing practices. Fourth, believers' preoccupation with the paranormal may distract them from constructive action about the major social and economic problems faced by their community. According to one elite scientist interviewed by McClenon (1984, p. 246), 'Psi has no rational, physical, scientific basis and diverts attention from reality and real problems of world concern'. This preoccupation could become extensive, leading some people to become destructively addicted to the paranormal, cautions Horne (1996). Fifth, people may be socially stigmatised if they embrace absurd beliefs. Sixth, those who are seduced into joining a sect may become psychologically and morally damaged by pressures put on them to respect the tenets of the sect. Seventh, immersion in paranormal beliefs may make people antagonistic to science and, in particular, to the mechanistic view of humanity; according to Gross and Levitt (1994), there is a growing view that objectivity is an illusion and that intuition is the best way to solve a problem. Eighth, believers who elect to undertake parapsychological research may be so pressured by the need for vocational success that they become careless or even fraudulent, at great professional and personal moral cost. On these collective grounds sceptics view paranormal beliefs as a personal and social threat. Empirical research into these beliefs therefore is promoted by sceptical commentators as a means to inform society's efforts to discourage the spread of paranormal belief. Indeed, Singer and Benassi (1981) have even proposed that the prevalence of paranormal belief in the general population be rigorously estimated and used as an index of the inadequacy of the US's program of science education.

Other researchers do not evaluate the research in this area predominantly under the premise that paranormal beliefs are false. Parapsychologists, of course, are generally open to the possibility that at least some paranormal beliefs may have an evidential foundation (Schmeidler, 1971). In any event, parapsychologists have long supported research into the belief in psi on the ground that it may influence participants' performance in experimental tests of ESP (Palmer, 1971; Schmeidler and McConnell, 1958). Indeed, psi belief may also be a factor in an experimenter's success in conducting ESP experiments and even some sceptics (e.g., Kurtz, 1985a) have recognised this as a legitimate rationale for research into psi belief.

Parapsychological interest in the study of other paranormal beliefs has been slower to develop (see Chapter 3), but research on the broader topic is now commonly reported in parapsychological journals. Apart from the relationship between psi belief and ESP-test performance, there are several reasons for parapsychologists to promote research on paranormal belief. An understanding of the bases of these beliefs might help to account for the ambivalence some parapsychologists feel when they obtain positive results in psi experiments (Inglis, 1986; McConnell and Clark, 1980). Additionally, research on paranormal belief — and disbelief — may illuminate the belligerence of many critics to parapsychology as an academic discipline (Irwin, 1989, 1999a). In a survey of members of the American Association for the Advancement of Science, McClenon (1982) found disbelief in ESP was a predictor of the view that parapsychological research is not a legitimate scientific undertaking. The study of paranormal belief therefore may enhance parapsychologists' understanding of the sociology and the psychology of the reception of parapsychological research among other academics (Hess, 1993).

The value of empirical research into the bases of paranormal belief should nevertheless be established beyond the narrow agendas of special interest groups such as sceptics and parapsychologists. In the broader context such research is warranted fundamentally because paranormal belief is a nontrivial feature of the human condition. That is, a plausible case can be made to the effect that this topic of research is important to an adequate appreciation of what it is to be human. The popularity of paranormal beliefs suggests that they do serve some significant cultural and personal functions in contemporary society and research into the nature of these functions would therefore hold the promise of revealing a significant facet of human psychology. Any serious student of human behaviour should therefore concede at least the legitimacy of such research. On a more pathological note, the influence exerted by some cults over its members (see Chapter 2) also points to potentially negative consequences of paranormal belief and an insight into the bases of this influence may have both clinical and broader social value. Each of these issues can be studied, of course, whether paranormal beliefs are valid or invalid. In summary, for behavioural scientists and lay people alike, the bases of paranormal belief constitute a research question of interest in its own right.

The remainder of this monograph systematically surveys the available empirical findings pertaining to the psychology of paranormal belief. Chapter 2 examines the sociocultural factors that govern the specific form of a person's paranormal beliefs. Chapter 3 describes the scientific development of measures of paranormal belief and what these measures tell us about the structure of paranormal belief. Four successive chapters then are devoted to the identification of some key theories of the psychological functions of paranormal beliefs and to a comprehensive review of their empirical support. The final chapter offers a theoretical integration of these analyses.

Notes

1. More recently Lindeman (e.g., Lindeman and Aarnio, 2006, 2007; Lindeman and Saher, 2007; Lindeman *et al.*, 2008) has defined paranormality in terms of 'core knowledge violations', an approach that perhaps could be deemed a refinement of Broad's definition. Consideration of the work of Lindeman is deferred until Chapter 6 (for reasons that will become evident in that context).

2. Brief mention might be made of an intentional omission from the set listed here. Goode (2000a) has proposed that parapsychology is a paranormal belief. A detailed rebuttal of this suggestion is presented elsewhere (Irwin, 1999c), but in this context it will suffice to point out that parapsychology, the scientific investigation of hypotheses about paranormal processes, is not a belief but an academic discipline. For this and other reasons, Goode's suggestion is not incorporated in the present working set of examples of paranormal belief.

3. This example may also serve to signal the theoretical possibility that some paranormal beliefs could develop from an initial opinion, although the reader is cautioned against any presumption that this developmental course is the norm.

4. Note that Northcote (2007) has argued that the term 'paranormal' is fundamentally a Western ontological category.

Chapter 2: Sociocultural influences on paranormal belief

To most readers it will seem to be stating the obvious to say that paranormal beliefs are to some extent a product of the sociocultural environment of the believer. For example, a child growing up in a given culture is not likely to develop religious beliefs that are unrepresented in that cultural setting. Further, some people believe in paranormal phenomena that they themselves have not personally experienced (Patry and Pelletier, 2001). Paranormal beliefs (and disbeliefs) therefore may be acquired partly through a process of socialisation. It must be conceded, however, that paranormal beliefs probably do not spring solely from environmental influences. Several authors (e.g., Alcock, 1995; Kurtz, 1999; Schumaker, 1990) have argued that paranormal beliefs fundamentally arise from innate predispositions. Indeed, Cohn (1999) reported evidence that among Scottish families the belief that one has psychic ability ('second sight') conformed to a genetic model. Similarly, a study by Waller *et al.* (1990) comparing twins raised apart with twins raised together found evidence to suggest that religiosity has a strong genetic basis; that is, early separation did not substantially affect the similarity of twins' religiousness. Later research, however, indicates that while the strength of religious attitudes is moderately influenced by genetic factors, religious affiliation is essentially a culturally transmitted phenomenon (D'Onofrio *et al.*, 1999). In short, paranormal beliefs may well appeal to people with certain innate needs and personality characteristics but the actual *form* that paranormal beliefs take is primarily moulded by cultural and subcultural processes. This chapter addresses sociocultural influences on the form or identity of paranormal beliefs.

Relatively little research effort has been devoted to the study of the acquisition of paranormal beliefs through social learning and other social processes. Indeed, when Goode (2000a) undertook a specifically sociological analysis of paranormal belief he was evidently unable to locate information on the social sources of these beliefs. Without citing any supportive data he merely acknowledged in a cursory and sweeping manner the role of 'early socialization… educational background, social class position, the social networks in which one is involved and interacts, major life commitments and emotional investments and life situation' (p. 232). Mazur's (2008) commentary offers a little more detail but still the coverage is descriptive rather than empirically founded. As Markovsky and Thye (2001) remarked, sociocultural influences on paranormal belief are seemingly so evident that they have generally been taken for granted by researchers. The available research literature is also very narrow in scope, focusing predominantly on the acquisition of traditional religious beliefs and beliefs advocated by cults and sects and even here much of the evidence comes from individual case studies and interviews with believers rather than systematic quantitative research. On these grounds the nature of the data invites considerable caution in regard to the implied validity and generality of conclusions we draw from them. The following review of sociocultural factors reflects the fact that this topic is in many respects an unfortunate lacuna in the literature on paranormal belief.

An appreciation of sociocultural influences on paranormal belief should take account of two fundamental social processes in the acquisition of beliefs. The previous chapter mentioned Sperber's (1990) classification of beliefs in terms of their modes of formation. In one mode an unconscious 'commonsensical' inference is made about the nature of the world and the conscious (verbal) representation of this inference is informed by concepts and other relevant background acquired through social communication. Sociocultural processes therefore may be involved in providing people with very basic concepts and terminology (such as 'extrasensory perception') by which they can enunciate their interpretations of everyday experiences. The dissemination of concepts therefore is one social mechanism that should be accommodated in an analysis of sociocultural processes in the formation of paranormal beliefs. The other mode to which Sperber referred involves a reflective validation of a proposition through critical reasoning and the affirmations of a respected authority figure. Thus, the formation of paranormal beliefs also depends on social influences by authority figures and associated cultural institutions.

Although these two proposed sociocultural mechanisms in the formation of paranormal beliefs are both plausible and consistent with findings summarised in this chapter, there have been only a few direct attempts to test for their occurrence. The role of exposure to basic concepts is supported by Conklin's (1919) observation that some people report they have not been 'taught' superstitious beliefs but have merely heard of superstitions as an element of cultural tradition. In regard to the role of a perceived authority, Sparks and Pellechia (1997) found that credence in a journalistic report about a UFO was enhanced when the investigators inserted in the story a supportive statement from an alleged 'scientific authority'. In a study by Markovsky and Thye (2001) participants initially were told that a pyramid-shaped structure could preserve objects contained in it. After then hearing the credulous judgments of a confederate of the experimenters who was posing as another participant, people rated the freshness of bananas in a pyramidal box to be greater when the confederate was introduced as a high-status person (viz., university professor). A similar effect for ESP belief was found in an unpublished study by Raven *et al.* (1962, cited by Zusne and Jones, 1982, pp. 338–9): when the experimenters' confederate was introduced as an ESP adept, participants' ratings of their own psi abilities were enhanced. Somewhat less directly, Schriever (2000) observed that in an interview people often would justify their views on the paranormal by citing the authority of a perceived expert or someone they held in high regard.

Several social entities have been implicated in the acquisition of paranormal beliefs. Each of these will be addressed in turn.

Parents

Some people appear to have adopted much the same paranormal beliefs as their parents had. The psychological process of absorbing parental perspectives on life is known as *internalisation* (Reber, 1995). Internalisation may sometimes be a rather passive process whereby parental beliefs are absorbed by children as if by osmosis: the parents' behaviour is a readily available model that the child unwittingly imitates. On the other hand, internalisation can be a much more active process in which parents earnestly strive to inculcate their own beliefs in their children; this may involve an explicit program of instruction and positive encouragement and perhaps even some coercion and punishment of noncompliance. Thus, via the process of internalisation the paranormal beliefs of parents may become assimilated in the child's own frame of reference.

The internalisation of parental paranormal beliefs is widely acknowledged by commentators, particularly in regard to traditional religious belief and the beliefs associated with sects (Argyle, 2000). Although often internalisation is offered as merely a plausible assumption, empirical support occasionally is cited. Case material from anthropological research documents parental transmission of shamanistic rituals and beliefs (Eliade, 1964). Cosgel (2001) also reported that the strength of a person's commitment to a religious sect is correlated with kinship bonds within the sect. The statistical correlation between parents' beliefs and those of their children has been calculated as about .6 for religious observance (Cavalli-Sforza *et al.*, 1982; Erickson, 1992; Martin, White and Perlman, 2003) and statistically significant also for superstitious belief (Okamoto, 1988). This observed relationship may be due in part to parental transmission of beliefs to their children, but other factors may well be involved. The latter could include genetic influences on temperament and personality, as well as other environmental effects either on beliefs (e.g., exposure to additional advocates of the belief when the family attends religious services) or on psychological dispositions to paranormal belief (Makasovski and Irwin, 1999).

Another source of evidence entails believers' ratings of the relative contribution of their parents to the development of their paranormal beliefs. Such ratings typically are moderately high for religious belief, particularly in regard to the contribution of the respondent's mother (Gunnoe and Moore, 2002; Hunsberger, 1985; Ozorak, 1989; Westman *et al.*, 1992), an effect that may be traced back in turn to the person's grandmother (Copen and Silverstein, 2008). The consistency between the religious beliefs of the two parents also seems to be particularly important in this regard (Dudley and Dudley, 1986). Similarly, the recollection of a strong parental emphasis on religion during a person's childhood is a predictor of the likelihood that the person will not abandon their religious beliefs in adulthood (Altemeyer and Hunsberger, 1997). At least in terms of the believer's perceptions, then, parental influence on religious belief appears to be substantial. At the same time, it is possible that these findings were confounded by such extraneous variables as parental attachment (Granqvist and Hagekull, 1999; Granqvist *et al.*, 2007) and family values (Reiss, 2000).

Evidence for parental transmission of nonreligious paranormal beliefs is meagre. Early research on superstitiousness (Conklin, 1919; Emme, 1940; Maller and Lundeen, 1933) found that parents commonly were cited as a source of belief in superstitions. In qualitative studies Bennett (1987) and Preece and Baxter (2000) reported some support for parents as a source of paranormal beliefs more generally. In Schriever's (2000) interviews of paranormal believers and disbelievers, interviewees often justified their stance on the basis of their parents' views. Despite the limited documentation, there can be no doubt that some parents are vehemently antagonistic to any beliefs or practices associated with mysticism, superstition, the occult, or the New Age movement. Cohn (1999), for example, observed that some parents forbid discussion of psychic ability within the family. At the other extreme, some parents may enforce children's compliance with occult beliefs and participation in allied rituals. These contrasting childhood environments may well have different consequences for the person's willingness to embrace paranormal beliefs later in life.

In summary, there is a degree of empirical support for the hypothesis of parental transmission of paranormal beliefs and as a generalisation this notion does not appear to be particularly contentious. It is nevertheless unclear that this mechanism consistently applies to all paranormal beliefs. It is possible, for example, that parents' influence over their offspring's traditional religious beliefs is greater than that over their New Age beliefs, given the countercultural or 'rebellious' tenor of the latter, but even this elementary prediction lacks empirical documentation.

Peers

Once children start school the influence of their peers may become even more potent than that of their parents and particularly in adolescence peer pressure may have substantial consequences for a person's attitudes and behaviour. This is not to say that in adolescence peer influence on religiosity simply supersedes that of parental influence. The situation may well be much more complex than this; for example, it is possible that during adolescence parental influences are mediated through the choice of close friends (Martin *et al.*, 2003). Nevertheless, peers may have some influence on a person's paranormal beliefs, although again this relationship is empirically not well attested.

The influence of peers is best documented for the case of traditional religious beliefs. Peers' church attendance is one of the strongest predictors of the religiosity of adolescents and young adults (Gunnoe and Moore, 2002). Cavalli-Sforza *et al.*

(1982) also reported a correlation of about .2 between a person's religious beliefs and practices and those of his or her peers. While this relationship is substantially weaker than that for parental transmission, it is still a statistically significant one. It is possible, of course, that the correlation merely reflects a person's inclination to mix with people who have similar interests; that is, a concordance with peers' religiosity may be more a prerequisite than a product of the friendship. On the other hand, ratings of the perceived importance of peer influence on religiosity (Erickson, 1992; Hunsberger, 1985) do confirm the relationship. Particularly during adolescence, peers appear to be important in creating religious doubt and in instigating a change of faith (Altemeyer and Hunsberger, 1997; Ozorak, 1989; Smith *et al.*, 2003).

Erickson (1992) suggests that peers may affect a person's religious belief and practice in four ways. First, peers convey subcultural norms on the appropriateness of religious belief. Second, they provide models of how to engage in religious behaviour. Third, religious issues are one of the topics sometimes discussed and debated with adolescent peers. Fourth, peers may draw the person into social events (e.g., dances, excursions) offered by religious groups and thus encourage a greater involvement in formal religious activities.

Peers may also encourage superstitious beliefs. As Gill (1994) notes, superstitions are maintained through oral tradition: they are rarely written down. Peers might therefore be expected to serve as a major source of knowledge about superstitions. Given the frequency of superstitious behaviours in sport (Bleak and Frederick, 1998; Burger and Lynn, 2005; McClearn, 2004; Todd and Brown, 2003; Womack, 1992), peer interactions during sport may be a common context for the propagation of these beliefs. In terms of empirical evidence on the dissemination of superstitions more generally, some of the older studies support the contribution made by the peer group. Conklin (1919) asked college students to explain their practice of superstition: 38 per cent of women and 26 per cent of men indicated they did so 'because associates do'. Maller and Lundeen (1933) found that friends were the most commonly cited source of knowledge about superstitions and Emme (1940) found that the influence of peers rivalled that of parents in this regard.

Belief in extraterrestrial aliens may also be defended in terms of the alleged sighting of a UFO by a friend (Fox, 1979; Saunders and Van Arsdale, 1968). More generally, in her set of interviews Schriever (2000) found that friends are often cited as a source of diverse paranormal beliefs and disbelief. As far as I can ascertain, the contribution of peers to the formation of other nonreligious paranormal beliefs has not been documented more specifically, but presumably this contribution is substantial for New Age beliefs and possibly for some other categories of nonreligious paranormal belief.

Conjugal partner

One peer who may be especially influential in the formation or the modification of paranormal beliefs and practices is one's conjugal partner or spouse. Again, researchers have given little attention to this issue, but there are some studies of the influence of a conjugal partner on a person's religious belief.

O'Connor *et al.* (2002) reported that of various experiences of adolescence and adulthood, going to church with one's spouse is a significant predictor of the level of a person's religiosity. The causal interpretation of this association nevertheless is uncertain. One of the most common instances of spousal influence in this regard involves a person changing religious denomination in order to facilitate harmony in the conjugal relationship (Musick and Wilson, 1995). Some denominations and sects explicitly forbid 'mixed marriages' (Barker, 1989). There are cases of a person who wanted to marry a Catholic, for example, and who converted to Catholicism in order to ensure that the marriage ceremony could take place under the auspices of the Church. In some of these instances, of course, this change may have been only a token gesture and underlying religious beliefs may not have been modified in any way. Even where the conversion is more sincere, a denominational change may often entail a greater change to religious practice than to religious belief as such. In addition, it must be said that religious conversion is not an inevitable outcome in mixed marriages. According to data gathered by Lehrer and Chiswick (1993), a conflict between the partners' religious beliefs may just as often be a factor in the break-up of the relationship as it is a prompt to conversion.

In regard to nonreligious paranormal beliefs, it is feasible that after a conjugal relationship has been established, one may become interested in the paranormal beliefs of the partner and subsequently embrace these beliefs. In this respect the influence of a conjugal partner is comparable to that of any peer. In some conjugal relationships, however, the conversion of the partner to a belief system may be rather more coercive. Members of certain sects and cults, for example, may be strongly pressured to recruit their partner (Barker, 1989). Again, a correlation between partners' paranormal beliefs is not conclusive for the fact of conversion of one partner by the other. It is possible, for example, that paranormal beliefs were an element in the couple's initial attraction to one another. Cohn (1999) reported evidence she interprets as supporting an assortative mating preference in regard to belief in personal psychic ability: people tend to form a conjugal relationship with someone whose belief in this regard is similar to their own.

Educational institutions

Higher-level social units may also be significant for the development of paranormal beliefs and one such unit encompasses educational institutions. As will be established more comprehensively in Chapter 6 the intensity of most paranormal beliefs correlates with the type and the level of the person's education. Although data on the direction of these relationships are rather mixed, often it appears that the effect of education is to erode the level of paranormal belief. The causal interpretation of these correlations nevertheless is probably more complex than this simple inference admits. That is, the observed relationships might be due in part to some direct influence of an educational institution on the student's knowledge about paranormal beliefs but they may also implicate other processes such as the development of skills in critical thinking or the person's exposure to what beliefs it is culturally 'appropriate' to profess.

At the same time there are some situations in which an educational institution is actively involved in promoting a paranormal belief. By way of illustration, despite a series of famous court cases in the United States during the twentieth century, creationism continues to be taught in various guises in some schools and colleges (Goode, 2000a; Scott, 1996). Other belief systems (e.g., New Age therapies) may be propagated through privately run educational programs specific to the belief system, but the operators of these programs do not constitute an educational institution in the orthodox sense of this term.

The most common context for educational institutions' dissemination of paranormal beliefs is that of religious instruction. In a few countries religious instruction is mandatory at all levels of education. Certainly in most Western countries children can attend schools and colleges run by a church where religious instruction is typically a central part of the curriculum. In many other schools religious instruction is offered either as a compulsory or an elective subject. Researchers have documented the contribution of religious instruction in schools to the person's religiosity, even when other factors (e.g., parental transmission and peer influences) are taken into account (Barrett *et al.*, 2007; Erickson, 1992; Gunnoe and Moore, 2002), although in some studies the effect was found to be relatively weak (Francis, 1986).

Other paranormal beliefs (e.g., traditional superstitions) are not formally promoted by either mainstream or religious educational institutions. Indeed, as noted earlier, the curriculum of many such institutions may directly or indirectly serve to erode paranormal belief. On the other hand, one sceptical journalist has asserted that 'teachers form an occupational group peculiarly susceptible to the claims of the paranormal' (Saunders, 1983, p. 11) and, further, that in endeavouring to encourage a general attitude of open-mindedness schoolteachers actually foster paranormal beliefs in their pupils. Independent empirical support for these views nevertheless is lacking.

Social movements

Many paranormal beliefs are disseminated by subcultural groups or social movements dedicated to this purpose. Thus, in contemporary Western society diverse groups enthusiastically advocate the validity of belief in spiritism, New Age therapies, divinatory arts (e.g., astrology, palmistry), neo-pagan Wicca, Eastern mysticism and extraterrestrial aliens. The objectives of these social movements are not only advocacy and indoctrination but more fundamentally the recruitment of new members to the movement, with an associated emphasis on 'allegiance, loyalty and self sacrifice' (Zusne and Jones, 1982, p. 332). Thus, within this community of practice the recruit not only learns the concepts and the rituals expounded by the movement but also develops a fundamentally new sense of identity (Merriam *et al.*, 2003). The operation of such groups is most comprehensively documented for religious cults.

Although a distinction between cults and sects is not always rigorously respected, a sect is usually defined as a religious group that has broken away from an existing mainstream church, whereas a cult does not spring from an established church (Argyle, 2000; Cowan and Bromley, 2008; Nelson, 1968). The term 'cult' also tends to have negative connotations and in part for this reason some commentators (e.g., Barker, 1989) prefer to use the expression 'new religious movements' to encompass both cults and sects. In the present context, however, the focus is on the more destructive type of small religious group, so their description as a 'cult' is generally appropriate.

In terms of the broader perspective it may be noted that there are numerous cults and sects (Lewis, 2001). A review by Barker (1989) concluded there are probably about 2,000 of these social groups in North America, 600 in Britain, 10,000 in Africa and thousands more in other regions such as Japan, Korea, India, the Pacific Islands, South America and the West Indies. Better known movements include the Unification Church ('Moonies'), Ananda Marga, the People's Temple (of Jim Jones), the Church of Scientology, Hare Krishna, the Bhagwan Shree Rajneesh movement, the Divine Light Mission, the Branch Davidians, The Family and Falun Gong (Cowan and Bromley, 2008). Some religious cult movements, such as Heaven's Gate and the Raelians, also embrace UFO phenomena.

The belief systems of cults are diverse, but they can broadly be described as religious beliefs coupled with an emphasis on love, acceptance and the promise of personal transformation (Pavlos, 1982). That is, cults seek to inculcate not only beliefs (particularly paranormal beliefs) but also values. The belief system is under the pivotal control of the leader of the movement (Nelson, 1968); he or (less often) she is deemed by followers to possess special knowledge ('the truth') to which cult members may be granted access and is typically persuasive, charismatic and sometimes authoritarian. Few cults are organised around a committee; rather, the worldview of a venerated 'guru' or messianic figure completely dominates the movement's philosophical, social and political agenda.

People's involvement in a cult's belief system can usefully be addressed in terms of three developmental phases: recruitment to the group, participation in the group and departure from the group. Each of these phases is taken into account in the following analysis.

People who are attracted to a cult are often depicted as young, alienated and psychologically vulnerable (Pavlos, 1982).[1] Many scientific studies of cult recruitment practices have revealed the intentional use of psychological manipulation directed at the potential recruit's emotional needs and weaknesses (Barker, 1984; Cowan and Bromley, 2008; Singer and Lalich, 1995). By way of illustration, members of the Unification Church usually approach a potential convert in such public places as parks, bus stations and shopping malls, describe the movement's objectives in a rather innocuous fashion and invite the person to dinner and a lecture (Bromley and Shupe, 1979). When the person attends the function he or she is subjected to 'love bombing', that is, given effusive attention, empathy and acceptance. At the end of the function he or she is enthusiastically urged to return for a weekend workshop. With twenty-four-hour access to the person, group members conducting the workshop then use intensive persuasion techniques to build a sense of emotional and philosophical commitment to the cult's belief system; some recruits liken this process to brainwashing (Zusne and Jones, 1982). Further workshops may then ensue. Thus, the phase of recruitment focuses not only on the recruit's exposure to the broad principles (beliefs) of the movement but also on a sense of 'belonging'.

Once the person becomes a cult member the leader's control over his or her life becomes much more binding and comprehensive (Barker, 1989; Singer and Lalich, 1995). Often cults demand complete adherence to the group's practices relating to restrictions in speech and movement, disposal of finance and possessions, diet, sexual practices and marriage. There must be total obedience to and dependency upon the leader. Recruits may be required to live in a commune and be allowed very little access to 'outside' society, particularly to family members. Opportunities for thinking critically about the leader's worldview and for deviating from the cult's lifestyle may therefore be severely limited. The cult's coercive psychological and social influence on its members may exact a significant toll; indeed, there are reports that the physical and mental health of cult members can be compromised (Barker, 1989; Gasde and Block, 1998). On the other hand, many members find in the cult's belief system a strong sense of security that they previously had been unable to achieve (Kintlerová, 2000).

In time some people may become disaffected with life in a cult and wish to leave the group. The psychological bond with the group nevertheless may be very difficult to sever (Singer and Lalich, 1995). Attempted suicide, anxiety, panic attacks, feelings of guilt and emotional disorders are common among cult apostates (Swartling and Swartling, 1992) and specialised counselling interventions may be called for (Barker, 1989; Singer and Lalich, 1995). The unremitting techniques used to bond a recruit to the group therefore may impede the person's subsequent abandonment of the cult's belief system.

In summary, religious cults have been found to exert substantial effects on the development of paranormal beliefs for some people. This is not to claim that cult members had no paranormal beliefs before joining the group, but certainly the cult's methods of indoctrination serve to crystallise some of the paranormal beliefs embraced by the person and to intensify the level of adherence to them. Much the same may be said of other cults centred on the paranormal such as UFO cults (Klass, 2001; Tumminia, 2002). While other social movements involving paranormal beliefs may be less invasive and manipulative than a cult, such groups certainly play a role in disseminating these beliefs in society.

Social movements also are implicated in the advocacy of paranormal *disbelief* (Hess, 1993; Kurtz, 1996). One of the most influential groups of sceptics is the

Committee for the Scientific Investigation of Claims of the Paranormal or CSICOP (Frazier, 1996). CSICOP and other groups of sceptics employ showmanship and a range of rhetorical devices to 'debunk' paranormal beliefs in the eyes of the general public and thereby to discourage gullibility. More contentiously, sceptics also have ridiculed scientists who conduct research on the ontological reality and the nature of paranormal processes (Hansen, 1992). The extent of any influence of the sceptics' movement on people's paranormal belief and disbelief nevertheless does not appear to have been empirically assessed.

The media

Given the profound impact of modern information technology and the information media on so many other aspects of life, it would be very surprising if they did not influence also the formation of paranormal beliefs. Indeed, the sceptical commentator Randi (1992, p. 80) has vehemently blamed the prevalence of paranormal beliefs largely on 'the uncritical acceptance and promotion of these notions by the media'. This view has also been expressed, if less emotionally, by other commentators (e.g., Alcock, 1981; French, 2000; Gilovich, 1991; Grimmer and White, 1986; Humphrey, 1995; Kurtz, 1985b; Lett, 1992; Saunders, 1983).

Although it may be tempting to dismiss media representation of the paranormal simply in terms of 'entertainment' and artistic expression (Edwards, 2001), of all social institutions the media probably have the most profound role in disseminating the basic concepts associated with many paranormal beliefs. Religious broadcasts and both fictional and 'documentary' programs and articles expose a substantial portion of the population (Sanghera, 2002) to a very wide range of paranormal concepts (Clark, 2002, 2003; Hess, 1993), sometimes in rather subtle ways (Peterson, 2002). Even television commercials may contribute to this process (Maguire and Weatherby, 1998). Thus, in the absence of media influences, it is most unlikely that a person would encounter so many paranormal concepts solely through contacts with other people in the course of everyday life. Relatively few of us, for example, would be familiar with the notion of psychokinetic spoon-bending had it not been for the extensive publicity in the 1970s about Uri Geller's psychic performances.

The media may make a major contribution not only in exposing people to basic paranormal concepts but also in encouraging people to endorse a paranormal belief (Clark, 2002, 2003). For various reasons, media exposition of paranormal concepts seems to be remarkably persuasive both for the general level of paranormal belief and for the specific form taken by these beliefs. By way of illustration, only a very small number of people have claimed to have personally witnessed the Loch Ness monster; the prevalence of belief in cryptozoological life forms therefore seems to be largely a product of accounts of these creatures disseminated in the media. Children in particular will often appeal to a media presentation as the foundation of their beliefs: for many children, '...but I saw it on TV!' appears to constitute the ultimate proof of authenticity. Such an effect, of course, is not limited to children. Adult consumers are also prone to persuasion by media messages (why else would manufacturers spend such substantial sums on advertising their wares in the media?). The media, on the other hand, often are moved by the profit motive to provide consumers with entertainment in preference to accuracy and deceptive presentation of the paranormal therefore is not uncommon (Ejvegaard and Johnson, 1981; Emery, 1996; Jenkins, 2007; Klare, 1990; MacDougall, 1983; Meyer, 1986). In short, by presenting anomalous phenomena in a tantalising manner and with no apparent grounds for scepticism the media may be a relatively persuasive source of paranormal belief.

Randi's (1992) view that the media are largely responsible for people's 'paranormal gullibility' may nevertheless be overstated. Certainly, many young people are initially attracted to the vocation of parapsychology in part because of media coverage of the paranormal (McClenon, 1984, p. 171). On the other hand, Bartkowski (1998) has argued that the depiction of voodoo in the news media has created among the US population predominantly *negative* perceptions of this religious movement. A similar effect may have occurred in regard to the public perception of the Unification Church (Bromley and Shupe, 1979).

There is some empirical documentation of these various relationships. In a series of studies Sparks and his colleagues (Sparks and Miller, 2001; Sparks, Nelson and Campbell, 1997) observed a correlation between the strength of paranormal beliefs and the tendency to watch television programs (e.g., *The X-Files, Unsolved Mysteries*) that frequently depict paranormal phenomena. Otis (1979) reported a similar link between UFO belief and attendance at a screening of the movie *Close Encounters of the Third Kind,* and Fox (1979) found a correlation between UFO belief and reading of books and articles about UFOs. In this context it is of course uncertain if the media influenced the audience's paranormal belief or if people with strong paranormal beliefs are relatively more inclined to seek out entertainment consistent with their beliefs. Of some relevance to this interpretative dilemma are studies of paranormal believers' perception of the source of their beliefs. Preece and Baxter (2000) reported some qualitative evidence of children's appeal to the media to justify their paranormal beliefs. Quantitative data for this attribution are reported by Maller and Lundeen (1933) and Clarke (1995) for samples of college students and by Blackmore (1984) and Schriever (2000) for an adult sample. On the other hand, people's declared rationalisations for their beliefs may not necessarily reflect the actual sources of the beliefs.

Clearly what are required here are some laboratory studies in which media messages can be systematically manipulated by the researcher. Several such studies have been conducted by Sparks and colleagues. In one study Sparks *et al.* (1995) found that after viewers had been shown an episode of *Unsolved Mysteries* that depicted UFOs, belief in UFOs was greater than if viewers had watched an unrelated program. In a rather more sophisticated experiment, Sparks *et al.* (1994) presented to viewers a videotaped episode of a regular television program, *Beyond Reality,* in which reported paranormal events are re-enacted. For one group of viewers the opening segment of the program contained an assurance that the reconstruction was accurate; for a second group the assurance was that the depiction of paranormal activity was purely fictitious; for a third group, the segment added that the events portrayed were not only fictitious but in fact were scientifically impossible; and for a fourth (control) group, no such statements were presented. The control group showed a significant increase in paranormal belief following the video program, a result that was maintained in a re-assessment three weeks later. The group that had been warned of the scientific impossibility of the depicted events showed a significant decrease in paranormal belief. Differences between other conditions did not reach statistical significance. The authors concluded that televised depictions of the paranormal may exacerbate paranormal beliefs unless a very strong disclaimer accompanies the broadcast.

The possible impact on paranormal beliefs of non-television media deserves further scrutiny by researchers. Given recent technological advances which have enabled the creation of extraordinarily realistic special effects in movies, Flynn (1996) has argued these effects may compromise 'the popular capacity — or willingness — to distinguish the possible from the absurd' (p. 526). It is not known if this is the case or, on the other hand, if popular awareness of special effects in the electronic media makes people rather more sceptical about what they see in the media. The world wide web also has facilitated people's access to information and different points of view and thus the internet may now be another mediator of exposure both to paranormal concepts and to seemingly authoritative statements (both pro and con) about paranormal beliefs (Jenkins, 2007). Future studies presumably will better document these processes. Currently available data nevertheless support the view that the media can contribute to the level of paranormal belief and disbelief.

Culture

In addition to the specific social entities we have just examined, at an even more macroscopic level the dominant culture in which the person lives undoubtedly has an influence on the paranormal beliefs one is likely to endorse (McClenon, 2000). In some (e.g., Muslim) countries, for example, the dominant cultural belief system may be quite prescriptive for how its citizens will conduct their lives. Thus, traditional religious beliefs are an intrinsic part of the national sense of identity for many cultures. Traditional cultural beliefs may even impact upon people who are raised within subcultural groups that are not in full accord with the dominant cultural outlook. The fact that a person's society is predominantly Christian, for example, means that the person's social milieu will generally be marked by a Christian ethos and the cultural environment thereby will facilitate the development of Christian religious beliefs. That is, in a Christian culture one may well have an inclination to believe in a single deity and in an afterlife whether or not Christianity was explicitly promulgated in the childhood home or at school.

The impact of culture on paranormal belief is evidenced by cross-cultural variation in the endorsement of traditional religious beliefs and of more esoteric mystico-religious beliefs. This variation is well documented by anthropologists and other social scientists (e.g., Davies, 1988; Frazer, 1911; Reimer, 1995; Smith, 1992; Wilson, 1951). Cultural differences in other paranormal beliefs are not so well established; methodologically rigorous cross-cultural comparisons of nonreligious paranormal beliefs have rarely been conducted. Nonetheless, there are reports of some national differences in the prevalence of global paranormal belief (Torgler, 2007) and more specifically, of psi beliefs (de Barbenza and de Vila, 1989; Haraldsson, 1985b; McClenon, 1993; Tobacyk and Pirttilä-Backman, 1992; Tobacyk and Tobacyk, 1992), belief in cryptozoological life forms (de Barbenza and de Vila, 1989) and belief in reincarnation (Stevenson, 1977; TenDam, 1990). Sheils (1978) also has documented cultural variation in 'astral travel' or the spiritist view of out-of-body experiences. Further, some studies of the prevalence of paranormal beliefs in individual cultures tend to imply cross-cultural differences (e.g., Edge and Suryani, 2001; Haraldsson *et al.*, 1977; Kim, 2005; Walter and Waterhouse, 1999).

There is therefore some empirical testimony to the influence of culture on people's paranormal beliefs. On the other hand, the increasing globalisation of cultures may tend to reduce such cross-cultural variation in the future (Beyer, 1994; George and Sreedhar, 2006). Television and other media productions are already distributed multinationally and people's access to the world wide web cuts across cultural boundaries. In addition, increasing rates of immigration are enhancing the ethnic diversity of many countries. The associated growth in the exposure of people to the beliefs of other cultures may eventually serve to attenuate international differences in the population profile of paranormal beliefs. Indeed, Beyer (1994) and Shimazono (1999) have suggested that an effect of globalisation on religious belief is already evident.

In summary, diverse sociocultural structures evidently influence the form or type of the paranormal beliefs embraced by a person. Of rather more psychological interest, however, is why a person would be psychologically prone to endorse any given paranormal belief (or disbelief). A good deal of research effort has been directed at this question and the associated empirical literature is systematically surveyed in subsequent chapters. Predicating such research, however, is the issue of how paranormal belief can be quantitatively indexed. This topic is addressed in Chapter 3.

Notes

1.   This view perhaps is slightly simplistic in that many cults also seek to recruit elderly members (Barker, 1989).

Chapter 3: The psychometrics of paranormal belief

A definitive step in the scientific investigation of a phenomenon is to establish a means by which the phenomenon may be quantified. In the present context this means that progress in understanding the fundamental nature of paranormal belief depends in large part on the availability of a sound measure of such belief. Chapter 3 begins with a review of the development of measures of paranormal beliefs, then proceeds to examine whether these measures indicate paranormal belief to be a unitary variable or a multidimensional domain.

The evolution of measures of paranormal belief

The historical development of measures of paranormal belief is yet to be documented in a comprehensive fashion. Plug (1976) has compiled a helpful summary of the early efforts to operationalise superstitious belief and, among others, Gorsuch (1980, 1984) has critically addressed progress in resolving problems associated with the measurement of traditional religious belief. More generally, the emergence of factor-analytic procedures to determine the structure of paranormal belief scales was very briefly (and in some respects, inaccurately) summarised by Grimmer and White (1990). Otherwise, a thorough historical account of the development of such scales appears to be lacking. It is hoped that the current chapter will serve both to stimulate academic interest in this topic and to provide a psychometric context for the remainder of the monograph.

Contemporary researchers wishing to study paranormal belief have access to a variety of self-report questionnaires addressing paranormal belief in general or a specific facet of paranormal belief. A selection of these tests may be found in the Appendices. Although none of these questionnaire measures is immune from criticism, some of the more recent tests have been subjected to comprehensive psychometric evaluation in an endeavour to ensure that they yield both reliable and valid indices. As will be evident in the following review, however, the construction of relatively sophisticated tests for research purposes was a slow and intermittent process. To some degree the evolution of such scales was constrained by that of psychological test theory, the underlying conceptual and statistical framework essential to devising an effective measure of a psychological construct. Additionally, at some stages there may have been so few researchers devoted to the investigation of paranormal belief that the substantial time and labour necessary for the construction of a paranormal belief scale were not seen as a high priority within the discipline of psychology.

Scientific investigation of paranormal beliefs began with the study of superstitions. In the first few decades of the twentieth century the prevalence of superstitious belief was widely regarded in educational circles as a telling index of the level of ignorance within the general community. Thus, Dresslar (1907, p. 215) declared, 'for the good of the cause of education, we must not fail to recognise the fact that underneath what passes for average culture there lies undisturbed a great mass of irrational predisposition'. As a consequence of this outlook, particularly in the period between World Wars I and II, a remarkable amount of research effort by educationists and a few other social scientists was directed towards identifying factors that engendered superstitiousness and developing educational programs that might effectively be implemented to undermine such belief (Belanger, 1944; Blachowski, 1937; Caldwell and Lundeen, 1932; Conklin, 1919; Dresslar, 1907, 1910; Dudycha, 1933; Emme, 1940, 1941; Garrett and Fisher, 1926; Gilliland, 1930; Gould, 1921; Lehman and Fenton, 1929; Lundeen and Caldwell, 1930; Maller and Lundeen, 1933, 1934; Miller, 1929; Nixon, 1925; Peatman and Greenspan, 1936; Peters, 1916; Powers, 1931; Schuyler, 1939; Smith, 1930; Ter Keurst, 1939; Valentine, 1936; Vicklund, 1940; Wagner, 1928; Whitelaw and Laslett, 1932; Zapf, 1938, 1945a,b).

In the earliest of these studies (e.g., Conklin, 1919; Dresslar, 1907, 1910; Gould, 1921) participants typically were asked simply to recall as many superstitions as they could, then to indicate their endorsement of each belief either currently or at any time in the past. This research technique has several serious shortcomings. First, given that thousands of superstitions have been documented (Opie and Tatem, 1989; Radford and Radford, 1949), it would seem likely that this procedure would elicit only a small sample of prevailing superstitious beliefs (but see Dresslar, 1907). Second, the number of superstitions actually nominated by respondents may well be influenced by such factors as memory ability and level of motivation (Grimmer and White, 1990; Plug, 1976). Thus, this technique may yield a sample of beliefs that is of questionable representativeness. Third and perhaps most important, as Plug (1976) observes, it is difficult to elicit responses in this style of inquiry without using the word 'superstition', yet the very mention of this pejorative term would likely inhibit participants' willingness to acknowledge 'foolish' beliefs (see also Jueneman, 2001). For these reasons, it is doubtful that the index of superstitiousness generated in these early studies would be highly reliable or valid.

The questionnaire evaluation of paranormal belief appears to have been pioneered by parapsychologists or, as they were then known, psychical researchers; a very short scale was utilised in a study of superstitiousness conducted by Minot (1887) under the auspices of the American Society for Psychical Research. This study evidently had little impact on educational researchers in the early decades of the twentieth century.

A pivotal step in the evolution of measures of paranormal belief was taken in the study by Nixon (1925). Nixon proposed that superstitiousness could be indexed using a small but representative sample of such beliefs; statements of these beliefs could then conveniently be administered in the form of a self-report questionnaire. (A copy of Nixon's questionnaire is provided in Appendix 1.) Note that the items of this scale generally do not refer to beliefs about black cats, walking under a ladder and the like; people readily identify such statements as superstitions and may fear being considered ignorant if they endorse the statements. Rather, in compiling his questionnaire, Nixon chose items that might superficially appear to have some empirical legitimacy but which in fact were scientifically unsubstantiated. Examples of such items are, 'An expectant mother by fixing her mind on a subject can influence the character of her unborn child' and 'You can estimate an individual's intelligence pretty closely by just looking at his [*sic*] face'. Items in Nixon's scale ranged from pure superstitions ('It really is unlucky to have anything to do with the number 13') to 'statements that would occasion considerable discussion' among scientists (Nixon, 1925, p. 419). Thus, the questionnaire included items on telepathy, astrology, palmistry, phrenology and other purported phenomena which scientists of the time had not substantiated.

Nixon's (1925) questionnaire arguably marked the beginnings of a genuinely psychometric approach to the assessment of paranormal belief. The merit of this questionnaire certainly was recognised in the era of its development and some subsequent investigations of superstitiousness utilised Nixon's measure (e.g., Levitt, 1952; Whitelaw and Laslett, 1932). In addition, a few researchers sought to enhance the potential effectiveness of Nixon's questionnaire by including extra items. For example, Garrett and Fisher (1926) argued that Nixon's questionnaire might be improved by lengthening it, so they added ten new items to tap a slightly wider variety of superstitious beliefs. Gilliland (1930) endeavoured to discourage participants from routinely marking all items as 'false' by inserting ten 'buffer' items unrelated to superstitions, most of which would correctly be answered 'true' (see Appendix 2). Many other researchers were inspired by Nixon's measure to devise their own superstition questionnaires, either substantially expanding Nixon's set of items or compiling a completely new set (e.g., Dudycha, 1933; Emme, 1940; Lundeen and Caldwell, 1930; Maller and Lundeen, 1933; Miller, 1929; Powers, 1931; Ter Keurst, 1939; Zapf, 1938). A few researchers (e.g., Miller, 1929) also appear to have recognised that their measure's sensitivity could be improved by asking respondents to indicate the *degree* of their belief in each superstition (e.g., on a four-point scale) rather than simply to respond dichotomously (True/False).

Generally speaking, however, post-Nixon scale development was slow to incorporate methodological advances necessary to enhance the measures' psychometric quality. A notable exception in this respect was the work of Peatman and Greenspan (1935, 1936). These researchers compiled a seventy-item test, only half of which comprised statements related to superstitious beliefs; the other half entailed statements that all were true and which were included to camouflage the objective of the questionnaire. Additionally, Peatman and Greenspan (1935) took the innovative step of assessing the test-retest reliability of their questionnaire before using it to investigate the nature of superstitiousness. They reported a very high level of agreement (a correlation of .96) between participants' scores when the questionnaire was administered on two occasions one month apart. Although Peatman and Greenspan's report seems to have been the first to address the issue of the test-retest reliability of superstitiousness measures, earlier studies (Caldwell and Lundeen, 1934; Maller and Lundeen, 1934; Powers, 1931) had computed split-half reliability, that is, the correlation between one half of the test (e.g., the odd-numbered items) and the other half (the even-numbered items). In these analyses the split-half reliability was found to range from .81 to .93 (see also Zapf, 1938), suggesting there was a reasonable degree of internal consistency among the test items, although it is doubtful that coefficients of even this magnitude would justify the general presumption by researchers at the time that the set of items in these questionnaires represented a homogeneous domain. Not all superstitiousness tests showed adequate internal consistency; the split-half reliability of the test used by Belanger (1944), for example, was only .59.

Notwithstanding these isolated and relatively limited endeavours to document the reliability of a given measure, the fact remains that a substantial majority of the superstition questionnaires devised in the first half of the twentieth century lacked any psychometric backing. Indeed, Plug's (1976) review concluded that the principal criticism to be levelled at superstitiousness research during this period is that the reliability of the measurement of this construct was largely unknown.

The validity of the questionnaires in this era is likewise uncertain; that is, there is insufficient evidence that the superstition scales actually measured what they purported to measure. Prior to 1950 researchers generally appear to have been satisfied with mere face validity, the subjective impression that each item in the questionnaire did constitute an instance of an unsubstantiated belief. A more circumspect researcher, Rosalind Zapf (1938), nevertheless took the precaution of using more than one measure of superstitiousness, presumably assuming that if a given effect could be found with more than one questionnaire, the researcher might be rather more confident that the questionnaires were indeed tapping the same construct. The correlation between the two measures of superstitiousness in Zapf's study was .80, providing some support for the congruent validity of the scales. Subsequently, Zapf (1945a) also undertook what appears to have been the sole direct assessment of the predictive validity of a superstition questionnaire. From her own questionnaire Zapf selected twelve items that could readily be adapted for use as a performance test; these included such activities as breaking a mirror, opening an umbrella indoors and walking under a ladder. She then compared young teenagers' responses on these items to their actual behaviour in the corresponding performance tests and found a .79 correlation. On this ground Zapf concluded that her superstition questionnaire was 'reasonably valid' (p. 24).

In the first few decades of the twentieth century, therefore, there was considerable research into paranormal belief in the context of superstitiousness and this research effort was accompanied by the development of questionnaire measures of the construct of superstitious belief. By modern standards, however, the psychometric standing of most of these measures was not satisfactorily established. It is possible that continued vigorous investigation of superstitiousness would eventually have led to the construction of scales with sounder psychometric foundations, although even the more recent measures of superstitiousness such as Wildman's *Superstitiousness Questionnaire* (Killen *et al.*, 1974) and Zebb's *Superstitiousness Questionnaire* (Zebb and Moore, 2003), have not been subjected to extensive psychometric evaluation and have been devised largely on the basis of face validity. In any event, such speculation serves little purpose because in the three decades from 1940 the focus of research on paranormal belief moved predominantly from superstition to belief in extrasensory perception (ESP).

Although there were numerous studies of the ESP hypothesis before 1930 (for a brief review, see Richet, 1923), it is generally accepted that a coherent, sustained program of experimental ESP research was pioneered in the late 1920s by J. B. Rhine at Duke University in North Carolina (Mauskopf and McVaugh, 1980). Rhine's investigation of the existence of ESP had two noteworthy consequences for the study of paranormal belief. First, the publication of his book *Extra-Sensory Perception* in 1934 brought the academic debate over the ESP hypothesis into public prominence and thus ESP belief became a topical social issue. Second, Rhine's insistence on the need to identify the psychological characteristics of adept ESP performers led in the early 1940s to an interest in the so-called *sheep–goat effect*, namely, a tendency for people who believed in the possibility of success in an ESP experiment ('sheep') to score better on such tests than those who rejected this possibility ('goats') (Schmeidler and Murphy, 1946; for a review of the sheep–goat effect see Lawrence, 1993; Palmer, 1971).

The objective of preselecting people who potentially would perform well in an ESP experiment necessitated the development of an index of belief in ESP. Some experimental parapsychologists (e.g., Bevan, 1947; Eilbert and Schmeidler, 1950; Schmeidler and Murphy, 1946) categorised their participants as believers or disbelievers on the basis of an interview, but the use of simple questionnaires to ascertain ESP belief soon became more common. Following Schmeidler's original criterion (see Schmeidler and McConnell, 1958), many of these 'sheep–goat' questionnaires addressed belief in terms of the possibility of ESP occurring under the specific conditions of the experiment in which the respondent was to take part. An instance of this type of sheep–goat scale is that devised by Bhadra (1966; see Appendix 4); here respondents are gradually induced to declare if they believe their success in the forthcoming ESP test would be evidence of their psychic ability rather than simply a matter of luck. Other sheep–goat scales aimed to tap belief in ESP as more generally conceived, that is, without reference to a specific experimental context; one such measure was the *Sentence Completion Test of ESP Belief* (Van de Castle and White, 1955; see Appendix 3).

Although parapsychologists continue to be interested in the sheep–goat effect among experimental ESP test participants, there is now rather more interest in the dimension of belief in ESP in its own right. To this end sheep–goat scales have been further refined; for example, the technique of factor analysis has been utilised to assess the purity of the measure. The most extensively used questionnaire today, the *Australian Sheep–Goat Scale* (Thalbourne, 1995a; see Appendix 11), reportedly encompasses two factors, one tapping personal extrasensory experiences (accounting for 34 per cent of the variance) and the other, belief in post-mortem survival (15 per cent; Thalbourne, 1981). This scale also has been assessed for convergent validity (Thalbourne, 2001).

In the mid-twentieth century, however, research on paranormal belief proceeded on two or three relatively independent fronts. Parapsychologists investigated the nature of ESP belief, while a few researchers with a relatively sceptical orientation continued the traditional study of superstitious belief. In addition, a rash of UFO sightings in the 1950s and early 1960s (Sheaffer, 1996) prompted a very small number of social scientists (e.g., Saunders, 1968) to investigate belief in UFOs and extraterrestrial aliens, largely without reference to research on other paranormal beliefs. (For more recent work on the association between UFO belief and other paranormal beliefs see Basterfield and Thalbourne, 2002.)

The next major impetus to the study of paranormal belief came with the increased use of psychedelic drugs and the associated 'consciousness explosion' in the late 1960s. Public interest in the paranormal rose dramatically and as might be expected this social phenomenon spurred further empirical research into paranormal belief.

In this field of study the principal consequence of the 'consciousness explosion' was a substantial broadening of the defined scope of paranormal belief as reflected in the instruments designed to index this construct. Thus, in the early 1970s, research reports on *supernatural belief* began to appear (e.g., Jahoda, 1970; Kline, 1974; Pasachoff *et al.*, 1970; Salter and Routledge, 1971; Scheidt, 1973). In addition to items relating to traditional superstitions and ESP, the measures in these studies canvassed belief in such phenomena as ghosts, witchcraft, flying saucers, astrology, fortune-telling, a supreme being and a personal God. This change in the field's perspective has endured to the present day; most of the measures of paranormal belief since the mid-1970s (Caird and Law, 1982; Granqvist and Hagekull, 2001; Jones *et al.*, 1977; Kumar and Pekala, 2001; Otis and Alcock, 1982; Randall, 1997; Randall and Desrosiers, 1980; Sobal and Emmons, 1982; Tobacyk, 1988; Tobacyk and Milford, 1983) have not been confined to belief in a single narrow phenomenon such as superstitions or ESP but have instead surveyed belief in a rather wide range of phenomena. The term 'supernatural belief', however, has not endured, possibly because researchers felt that it implied belief in the involvement of some (e.g., demonic) agency, whereas many of the phenomena being addressed did not have this connotation even for ardent believers. For a brief time a few researchers (Alcock, 1975; Otis and Alcock, 1982; Windholz and

Diamant, 1974), perhaps seeking to emulate the Scottish philosopher David Hume (1777/1955), sought to resolve the dilemma by using the more atheoretical expression 'extraordinary belief', but this term is insufficiently specific and was never widely adopted. Researchers' use of the term *paranormal belief* became increasingly more standard from the late 1970s (e.g., Alcock and Otis, 1980; Greeley, 1975; Jones *et al.*, 1977).

The broadening of the defined scope of paranormal belief posed an additional and very fundamental question for the measurement of this construct. Is paranormal belief a single, homogeneous domain or do some of the specific beliefs constituting this domain represent discrete, relatively independent facets of paranormal belief? This issue concerns the dimensionality of paranormal belief and is addressed in the next section. I discuss the continued evolution of measures of paranormal belief in that context.

The dimensionality of paranormal belief

When in the 1970s paranormal belief came to be appreciated as much more extensive than either superstitiousness or belief in ESP alone, researchers at first continued as if specific types of paranormal belief were simply different expressions of a unitary construct. Just as Christianity, Judaism, Islam, Buddhism and Taoism may be deemed different forms of the single domain of faith termed 'religion', beliefs in superstitions, ESP, divination, astrology, palmistry, ghosts, spirit communication, God, witchcraft, flying saucers and the like were all assumed to be expressions of a common aspect of human psychology, namely, paranormal belief. Thus, responses to each of the items in Jahoda's (1970) *Index of Supernatural Beliefs* were made on a four-point scale, then simply summed to yield a 'global score' for paranormal belief. The tacit assumption of such a computation is that the constituent items of Jahoda's measure contribute to a homogeneous entity; in statistical terms, the items are assumed to load on a single factor. As more comprehensive measures of paranormal belief (as now more broadly conceived) were constructed, this common assumption came under challenge.

The first measure of paranormal belief to be developed with some cognizance of the issue of dimensionality appears to have been the *Belief in the Paranormal Scale*, or BPS (Jones *et al.*, 1977; see Appendix 5). After critical scrutiny and statistical analyses helped to eliminate redundant and otherwise unsatisfactory items from an initial pool of 108 items, the final version of the BPS contains twenty-five statements relating to psychic phenomena, the supernatural, the occult, divination and prophecy, legendary creatures and civilisations and other scientifically unattested phenomena. A few items were negatively worded in order to discourage the development of response sets (e.g., people who are inclined to disagree with every statement). Responses to each item are made on a five-point scale (1 = strongly disagree with statement to 5 = strongly agree with statement). Empirical assessments of the test's internal consistency, one-month test-retest reliability, predictive validity, concurrent validity and construct validity supported the psychometric adequacy of the BPS (Jones *et al.*, 1977). Jones *et al.* then examined the dimensionality of the BPS by performing a statistical analysis known as a rotated principal components analysis. This technique serves to identify factors or coherent, relatively independent subsets of variables being measured by an instrument.

The initial principal components analysis of the BPS revealed eight factors and after oblique rotation of these factors, three main factors emerged. The first factor, accounting for 42 per cent of the variance of responses to the BPS, tapped rather general paranormal belief; loading on this factor were items relating to the supernatural (e.g., ghosts, spirit communication, reincarnation), the occult (witches, spells), civilisations and creatures (Abominable Snowman, UFOs) and the notion that psychic phenomena are real and should be studied scientifically. The second factor, with 21 per cent of the variance, was termed the 'psychic phenomena' factor because all of the items loading on it addressed the reality of ESP or psychic phenomena. The third factor, accounting for 10 per cent of the variance, was not readily interpretable; items loading on it concerned such things as the Loch Ness monster and palmistry.

This analysis of the BPS therefore suggests that the domain of paranormal belief is not homogeneous but multidimensional. Somewhat surprisingly, this was not the inference drawn by Jones *et al.* (1977). The authors of the BPS had assumed that 'a general paranormal belief system existed' and they were almost apologetic that their efforts had not produced 'a "pure" measure' (p. 6). They concluded that the major (first) factor of the BPS did in fact tap the hypothesised 'general' dimension of paranormal belief and that there were 'perhaps more specified belief systems associated with individual manifestations such as ESP', adding that this was 'not surprising, given the wide range of content... contained in the items' (pp. 5–6). A presumption of the homogeneity of paranormal belief evidently was deeply entrenched among researchers; further factor-analytic studies had to be conducted before this conceptual edifice would begin to crumble.

Randall and Desrosiers (1980) developed the *Supernaturalism Scale* (see Appendix 6) with items surveying belief in astrology, faith healing, ESP, the notion that plants have some sense of consciousness, UFO visitations, magic and witchcraft. As a control for response set, half of the statements were worded in support of supernatural belief and the remainder were formulated from a sceptical perspective. Additional statements on traditional religious faith were included as 'buffer' items to obscure the purpose of the questionnaire; note that these items were not considered by Randall and Desrosiers as part of the 'supernaturalism' construct. A principal components analysis with orthogonal rotation was applied and four factors were identified. As will be argued below, however, the researchers' interpretation of some of the factors is contentious.

Factor 1 was reported to account for 70 per cent of the variance; most of the items loading strongly on this factor address belief in fortune-telling, but Randall and Desrosiers (1980) interpreted Factor 1 as a general supernaturalism factor. Factor 2, with 13 per cent of the variance, appears to index belief in anomalous or psi influence other than human telepathy; items loading most strongly on this factor concern psychic healing and plant communication. The authors of the test nevertheless depicted this factor merely as an acquiescence factor, that is, a tendency to agree with any statement. Contrary to this interpretation, half of the items for Factor 2 had a negative loading, that is, they were sceptically-oriented statements with which high scorers on this factor would have to *disagree*. Factor 3 accounted for 10 per cent of the variance; items loading on the factor relate to astrology and Randall and Desrosiers justifiably identified it as an astrology factor. The researchers nevertheless interpret this finding to indicate that there is a separate group of people who accept astrology but who do not rate highly on 'supernaturalism as a generalized trait' (p. 497). The portion of the variance for which Factor 4 accounted was not specified, but items loading on this factor concern belief in UFOs and extraterrestrial beings. Again, Randall and Desrosiers inferred from this outcome that there is a group of rational people who believe there is sound scientific evidence for the existence of UFOs but who should not be considered as having supernatural beliefs. Thus, as with the conclusions reached previously by Jones *et al.* (1977), the interpretation of factor-analytic outcomes by Randall and Desrosiers incorporated several contortions of logic in order to sustain the view that paranormal belief (or 'supernaturalism') is unidimensional. A more parsimonious interpretation of the data would be that paranormal belief is, in fact, multidimensional.

Otis and Alcock's (1982) *Extraordinary Beliefs Inventory* (see Appendix 7) consists of thirty items in six descriptive categories, namely luck, spirits, religion, psychic phenomena, creatures (e.g., the Loch Ness monster) and fortune-telling. The internal consistency of each category was satisfactory, ranging from .68 (for the two-item Creatures set) to .92 (for the seven-item Religion set). The formulation of six separate categories and the computation of a separate score for each category might be taken to imply Otis and Alcock's sensitivity to the multidimensionality issue, but it is regrettable that any such sensitivity did not extend to an application of a principal components or factor analysis to validate the nominated categories. Otis and Alcock did not publish their questionnaire in full, which is perhaps why it was not used extensively by later researchers.

Brief mention also may be made of a study by Caird and Law (1982) of religious beliefs the researchers term 'non-conventional'. A set of sixty items on Eastern religions, occultism, spiritualism, psychic development and tenets of alternative lifestyles was subjected to principal axis factor analysis followed by oblique rotation. Five factors in aggregate accounted for 51 per cent of the variance and were labelled General Eastern Beliefs (e.g., Buddhist or Hindu beliefs about reincarnation), Theosophic Beliefs (universal metaphysical beliefs such as those about God and a divine plan), Spiritualist Beliefs (spirits, mediumistic communication), Alternate Lifestyles (e.g., use of psychedelic drugs, tolerance of unconventional ideas) and Interest in Psychic Development (development of psychic powers as spiritual advancement).

Many commentators would not regard Caird and Law's *Non-Conventional Beliefs* scale as an index of paranormal belief and certainly the questionnaire does contain a relatively atypical and unrepresentative selection of items on paranormal belief. On the other hand, the items of the scale do meet the criteria for paranormal beliefs set down in our working definition. For the purposes of the present survey Caird and Law's project serves to reinforce two elementary points. First, the construction of a measure of paranormal belief should begin with the specification of a clear definition of the construct to be indexed (Hartman, 1999); somewhat surprisingly, this seems to have rarely been the case. Second, the number and the identity of factors arising from any factor-analytic investigation of the dimensionality of paranormal belief depends fundamentally on the range of items that are included in the analysis. By way of a simple illustration, Caird and Law failed to observe, for example, an 'astrology' factor of paranormal belief for no other reason than that they did not include items about astrology in their item pool; the findings of Caird and Law's study therefore cannot properly be taken to cast doubt on the status of astrological belief as a discrete factor of the domain of paranormal belief. The number and the nature of factors of paranormal belief must be assessed with items that cover the broadest possible range of beliefs in the paranormal.

To this end, much of the recent debate over the factorial structure of paranormal belief has centred on the set of items that comprise the *Paranormal Belief Scale* (PBS; see Appendix 8), a measure originally developed by Tobacyk and Milford (1983). Tobacyk selected sixty-one items deemed to sample 'as wide a range of paranormal beliefs as possible' (p. 1030). Responses to the items were made on a five-point scale. Principal axis factor analysis was applied; as oblique rotation reportedly revealed little evidence of dependence between the resultant factors, Tobacyk and Milford elected to use orthogonal rotations for the final factorial solution. Although thirteen factors were generated, only seven were considered meaningful; most of the remaining factors were based on only one or two items and reportedly were unstable. The authors therefore opted for a seven-factor solution.

Tobacyk and Milford (1983) labelled these seven PBS factors Traditional Religious Belief (accounting for 17 per cent of the variance), Psi Belief (12 per cent, but loading principally on items that address psychokinesis or direct effects of mind over matter), Witchcraft (7 per cent), Superstition (4 per cent), Spiritualism (3 per cent), Extraordinary Life Forms (3 per cent) and Precognition (2 per cent). The clearest marker items for each factor or subscale then were selected, resulting in a twenty-five-item measure of paranormal belief with seven subscales. The four-week test-retest reliability was .89 for the total PBS score and from .60 to .87 for the individual scales. Tobacyk and Milford cited additional studies to support the construct validity of the PBS.

Tobacyk (1988) later slightly amended the PBS by adding one item to the Precognition scale, changing items in three of the scales and replacing the five-point response scale with a seven-point scale. These modifications were reported to have improved the reliability and the validity of the measure. The *Revised Paranormal Belief Scale* is included as Appendix 9.

One or other of the two versions of the PBS have been utilised in the majority of studies of paranormal belief conducted since the mid-1980s (Goulding and Parker, 2001). The principal advantage of the PBS is that it covers a broad range of the phenomena that many researchers want to canvass in any study of paranormal belief. This is not to say that the instrument has no shortcomings. Some of its items now are becoming a little dated; for example, 'There is life on other planets' is probably taken as scientific fact by most people today, given that 'life' includes primitive forms such as algae. Further, apart from this reference to 'life on other planets' the PBS does not survey belief in UFOs and related phenomena, despite the fact that the global score on the PBS has been reported to correlate substantially ($r = .67$) with UFO-related beliefs (Patry and Pelletier, 2001; L. G. Pelletier, personal communication, 31 July 2001; *cf.* Thalbourne and French, 1997). Some researchers are frustrated by the questionnaire's omission of items for religious concepts outside the Judeo-Christian tradition and yet others dispute the classification of religion as a paranormal belief (Fitzpatrick and Shook, 1994; Hergovich *et al.*, 2008; Kristensen, 1999; Lawrence, 1995; Sullivan, 1982; Williams *et al.*, 1989). Additionally, a few items in the PBS are not well expressed. It is difficult to understand, for example, how anybody could disagree with the statement, 'witches do exist', as there clearly are people who perform Wiccan rituals and describe themselves as a witch (Moody, 1971/1974). Belief in the *magical powers of witches* therefore should be solicited through a more carefully worded item. Finally, as Lawrence (1995) has noted, twenty-five or twenty-six items are not likely to be sufficient to sample in a reliable fashion seven independent facets of paranormal belief.

Notwithstanding these concerns, it must be reiterated that the PBS has made an unparalleled contribution to empirical research into paranormal belief. Arguably the most significant contribution of Tobacyk and Milford's (1983) report is that it appeared to have established the multidimensionality of paranormal belief. None of the individual factors accounted for a sufficiently large portion of the variance and at the same time loaded on a sufficiently broad sample of paranormal beliefs to be justifiably construed as the 'general paranormal belief' factor. This outcome effectively proscribed the tactic used by Jones *et al.* (1977) and by Randall and Desrosiers (1980), namely, to claim that the factor accounting for the largest portion of the variance is an index of the homogeneous domain of paranormal belief and the remaining factors are not truly paranormal beliefs at all. Thus, it seemed that paranormal belief now had to be accepted as a multidimensional domain.

Again, there are grounds for caution in regarding Tobacyk and Milford's (1983) evidence for multidimensionality to be conclusive. The precise number of dimensions of paranormal belief clearly remains a matter of contention. As we have seen, while Tobacyk and Milford (1983) argued for seven factors, Jones *et al.* (1977) opted for three factors, Randall and Desrosiers (1980) claimed four and Caird and Law (1982) reported five. To a limited extent this disparity can be attributed to differences in the scope of the items subjected to the factor analysis. The issue nevertheless is rather more complex than this account would admit. Although Haraldsson and Houtkooper (1996) administered the PBS to an Icelandic sample and observed seven factors similar to those reported by Tobacyk and Milford (1983), some other researchers have been unable to replicate this factor structure with the PBS. Davies (1988) replicated all of Tobacyk and Milford's factors except traditional religious belief; Thalbourne (1995a) found evidence of two factors; Persinger and Richards (1991) observed two factors for female respondents and one factor for males; and Thalbourne *et al.* (1995) extracted only a single factor. Using the PBS and additional items to provide a larger item pool, Johnston *et al.* (1995) found only four factors.

The specific technique employed to identify factors may influence the outcome, so this issue has been the focus of some debate. Tobacyk and Milford's (1983) reliance on orthogonal rotation of factors has also been criticised by Lawrence (1995) and Thalbourne (1995a) on the grounds that a third of the intercorrelations among the subscales are over .30; that is, the factors are not uncorrelated as is strictly required for the application of this technique. When oblique rotation has been used, the number of extracted factors appears to be less than seven. A re-analysis of Tobacyk and Milford's (1983) original correlation matrix using oblique rotation suggested to Lawrence (1995) that there may be only four factors in the PBS. Subsequent research with independent samples revealed five oblique factors (Lawrence and De Cicco, 1997; Lawrence *et al.*, 1997). After spirited exchanges between Lawrence and Tobacyk (e.g., see Lawrence, 1995; Tobacyk, 1995), Tobacyk and Thomas (1997) declared the PBS may still consist of seven factors but with a mix of oblique and orthogonal factors; they did not offer any additional data to support this view.

More recently, Hartman (1999) criticised Tobacyk and Milford's (1983) technique for reducing their original thirteen factors to seven. Using the data gathered by Lawrence and De Cicco (1997), Hartman applied what he considered to be a more appropriate method of factor extraction and concluded that four factors were the most the data could reasonably support. Finally, Hartman reiterated Lawrence's (1995) view that the twenty-five or twenty-six items of the PBS cannot adequately sample a multidimensional paranormal belief domain.

In short, despite the evident utility of the PBS for other research issues, this instrument has not provided a definitive assessment of the precise number of factors that comprise paranormal belief. Two further impediments to realising this objective — and ones that may well apply to other measures of paranormal belief — have been identified by Lange *et al.* (2000). First, these authors noted that statistical techniques for investigating the dimensionality of a domain assume at least an interval-level measure. Lange *et al.* recommended that in order to meet this criterion the scoring of paranormal-belief instruments would best be reformulated under a measurement model known as a Rasch model of scaling. Second, they argued that analysis of the dimensionality of paranormal belief is futile unless the instrument being used is known to be free from differential item functioning (see also Irwin, 2001a). Differential item functioning occurs when questionnaire items are interpreted differently depending on such extraneous characteristics of the respondent as age or gender. For example, the PBS item, 'Black cats can bring bad luck' might have different connotations for young people than for old people or for women than for men. This phenomenon has serious ramifications for the validity of measurement because it violates the assumption of local independence under which items' measurement properties should not be affected by extraneous factors.

On these grounds Lange *et al.* (2000) analyzed a large sample of data on the PBS and converted scores to a Rasch model, progressively removing items that showed differential item functioning for age and gender and then applied a principal component analysis. From the sixteen remaining items of the PBS two factors were extracted, one labelled New Age Philosophy (psi and psychic powers generally, astrology, astral projection) and the other, Traditional Paranormal Beliefs (witchcraft and the devil and perhaps better termed 'belief in black magic'; see Appendix 9, Scoring details).

This is not to claim that the domain of paranormal belief is composed of only two factors but, rather, that there is evidence for only two factors when the potential confound of differential item functioning is duly taken into account. The fact that Lange *et al.* did not obtain a factor for belief in superstitions, for example, cannot properly be taken to imply that superstitions are not paranormal beliefs. Tobacyk and Milford (1983) simply did not devise items that indexed these beliefs in a way that was free from differential item functioning and thus it remains to be determined whether superstitions are a discrete factor of paranormal belief (as concluded by Tobacyk and Milford) or are merely part of Lange *et al.*'s Traditional Paranormal Beliefs. Additionally, it is possible that the sixteen PBS items analyzed by Lange *et al.* still are marked by differential item functioning in relation to some variable other than age and gender. Ethnicity and nationality, for example, might be possible extraneous factors in this regard (see Haraldsson and Houtkooper, 1996).

The two-factor solution extracted by Lange *et al.* (2000) nevertheless does support the view that paranormal belief should be considered a multidimensional domain. Further research into the dimensionality issue unfortunately must await the development of a psychometrically satisfactory measure of paranormal beliefs. In this regard it is regrettable that many recently developed instruments such as the Anomalous/Paranormal Belief subscale of the *Anomalous Experiences Inventory* (Kumar and Pekala, 2001; Appendix 10), the *Paranormal Short Inventory* (Randall, 1997; Appendix 12), the *Exeter Superstitions Questionnaire* (Preece and Baxter, 2000; Appendix 13), the *New Age Orientation Scale* (Granqvist and Hagekull, 2001;

Appendix 14) and the *Psi Inventory* (Sebastian and Mathew, 2001) continue to index paranormal belief by a global score, implying the existence of a unifactorial domain. For research purposes other than the dimensionality of paranormal belief, perhaps the most defensible measure currently available is Tobacyk's (1988) *Revised Paranormal Belief Scale* (Appendix 9) scored under a Rasch model for the two factors specified by Lange *et al.* (2000).

More recently there has been a preliminary report on the construction of the *Smith Idiosyncratic Reality Claims Inventory* (Smith and Karmin, 2002). An initial list of twenty-nine paranormal beliefs was reduced through factor analysis to twenty-three items rated on a four-point scale (1 = definitely not true to 4 = definitely true) and generating scores on five factors, named Literal Christianity (e.g., 'the virgin birth account of Jesus is literally true'); Magic ('supernatural voodoo rituals can have a magical effect that cannot be explained by today's science'); Space aliens ('flying saucers from other worlds have visited Earth'); After death ('reincarnation is a fact'); and Miraculous powers of meditation, prayer and belief ('through belief or faith alone, one can achieve miraculous superhuman feats that can't be explained by today's science'). The inventory is still in the formative stage and has yet to be assessed, for example, for differential item functioning. Although this measure surveys a broad range of beliefs and does appear to confirm the multidimensional nature of paranormal belief, the sufficiency of twenty-three items to index five factors in a valid manner must be open to question. Further development of the questionnaire is eagerly awaited.

By way of a conclusion to this analysis, the evidence presently available does point to the likelihood of paranormal belief being a multidimensional domain, but a more confident conclusion to this effect must await the results of further research and test development. Again, it must be emphasised that if paranormal belief is multidimensional, the number and identity of the component dimensions are yet to be determined. This fact has some significance for the subsequent chapters of this monograph, where the empirical literature on paranormal belief is reviewed. These chapters cite empirically established correlates of global indices of paranormal belief and correlates of various facets of paranormal belief as indexed, for example, by the original seven subscales of Tobacyk and Milford's (1983) PBS. Such data should ideally be considered in terms of the patterns they exhibit across the diverse indicators of paranormal belief and the implications of these patterns may then be examined in relation to theories of the psychology of paranormal belief. Henceforth, in reporting a correlate of global paranormal belief there is no presumption that paranormal belief is indeed unifactorial and in reporting a correlate of superstitiousness, for example, the assumption is that superstitions are an instance of paranormal belief but are not necessarily a discrete psychometric factor of this domain.

For the sake of completeness I mention briefly a few other psychometric cautions. Before drawing generalisations about paranormal beliefs from research findings the reader should take into account the era in which the research was undertaken. For example, as noted above, a good deal of research into superstitious beliefs was conducted in the period between World Wars I and II. But the level and pattern of adherence to paranormal beliefs in a given society may change over time (Kennedy, 1939; Levitt, 1952; Randall, 1990; Tupper and Williams, 1986), so correlates of superstitiousness identified in the early research might not necessarily still be applicable. For the sake of comprehensiveness the historical findings are cited in the subsequent chapters, but the reader is advised to check if these findings have been replicated in more recent studies.

A further psychometric difficulty is that the data may depend to some degree on the context of their measurement. Various contextual effects may be relevant here. For example, there are indications that the format of the survey questionnaire can influence respondents' acknowledgment of some of their paranormal beliefs. According to Gray (1990b), respondents give lower estimates of the extent of their paranormal belief when they simply have to check on a list the anomalous phenomena in which they believe rather than to indicate their *degree* of belief in each phenomenon in turn. Schmeidler (1985, p. 2) and Grey (1988) similarly remark that including or excluding a 'don't know' or 'uncertain' response option can substantially affect the level of paranormal belief evidenced by a questionnaire. That is, if respondents are prevented from checking an agnostic option, they have to declare either a belief or a disbelief and thus the evident level of belief or disbelief can be inflated.

A further contextual characteristic that can influence responses is where test scores may depend in part on the position of the paranormal belief measure in relation to other tests in the inventory being administered. These order effects in studies of paranormal belief have occasionally been reported (e.g., Dudley, 2002). Such effects are best minimised by counterbalancing across participants the order in which individual tests are administered. When the primary concern is the potential effect of questions about the paranormal upon the validity of the other concurrently administered measures the researcher may choose to have the paranormal belief index as the final test, thereby ensuring that its items cannot confound responses to preceding measures.

Attitudes of the investigator or test administrator are another pertinent contextual factor. In two studies Layton and Turnbull (1975) found that participants' ESP belief scores varied with the experimenter's expressed attitude toward the evidence for ESP. Much the same effect was obtained by Crandall (1985), Watt and Baker (2002) and Wiseman and Schlitz (1997). Further, Fishbein and Raven (1967) noted that their measure of belief in ESP could be manipulated by prior presentation to subjects of either an article promoting the existence of ESP or one advocating the methodological inadequacy of ESP experiments. These studies suggest that the measurement of paranormal belief can be subject to the demand characteristics of the test situation. It is important to appreciate that such manipulations by the experimenter might not be explicit or even intentional; even subtle nonverbal acts (e.g., facial expressions) may convey to participants the attitudes of the test administrator. This is not to say that the experimenter's behaviour necessarily changes participants' paranormal beliefs but rather it may influence the participants' willingness to admit to these beliefs (Irwin, 1985b). The possibility that participants may be somewhat sensitive about fully disclosing their paranormal beliefs is consistent with recent research by Subbotsky (2001) showing there can be a degree of disparity between explicit (i.e., verbal) and implicit (e.g., performance) indices of paranormal belief. Potential reticence is attested also by reports that in conversational contexts believers commonly preface their claims by stressing they had previously been sceptical about paranormal phenomena, whereas disbelievers tend to assert their former openness to the existence of the paranormal (Alcock, 1981, p. 48; Lamont, 2007). Situational factors that potentially could compromise the open acknowledgment of paranormal beliefs should therefore be given close attention by researchers.

A related factor is the conscientiousness of the participant. Irwin (2003b) found small but significant correlations between paranormal belief scores and a tendency to give inconsistent responses to items in a separate questionnaire. That is, a (possibly small) number of respondents may show slightly higher paranormal belief scores because they completed questionnaires in a rather lax or frivolous manner. In the development of new measures of paranormal belief some thought should be given to the inclusion of a 'lie scale' or some such index of conscientiousness of responding.

With the above cautions kept in mind we may now proceed to a critical discussion of the major theoretical depictions of paranormal belief and the extent of their empirical support.

Chapter 4: The social marginality hypothesis

In this and the following three chapters some relatively broad and influential theories of paranormal belief are described and critically evaluated in terms of the available empirical literature. Throughout these chapters the evidence is cited in a reasonably comprehensive fashion to serve as a resource for researchers and, more fundamentally, to document the extensiveness of the support for a given relationship; null results, however, are typically cited only where they constitute a substantial proportion of the relevant literature. The first theory of paranormal belief to be considered is the social marginality hypothesis.

According to some sociological commentators (Bainbridge, 1978; Glock, 1964; Glock and Stark, 1965; Greeley, 1975; Lanternari, 1963; Stark and Bainbridge, 1980; Warren, 1970; Wuthnow, 1976) the people most susceptible to paranormal belief are members of socially marginal or disadvantaged groups, for example, the poorly educated or the unemployed who have characteristics or roles that rank low among dominant social values. This view is generally known as the *social marginality hypothesis*. It is held that the privation, loss of control over life and alienation associated with marginal social status encourage such people to appeal to magical and religious beliefs, presumably because these beliefs bring some emotional compensation to their lives. Belief in mystical processes, for example, may bring some sense of empowerment to the socially disempowered. Similarly, a belief in the rewards of an afterlife may seem to justify passive acceptance of a current life of privation (e.g., Jang and Johnson, 2003). When socially marginalised people search for some sense of meaning in the events and circumstances of their life, therefore, many may be drawn to a paranormal explanation, even if that explanation is unverified or, indeed, intrinsically unverifiable. In Lett's (1992, p. 383) view, 'it matters not, apparently, whether their explanations are true or false; it only matters that they are emotionally satisfying'.

A putative historical example of the marginality hypothesis has been formulated by two feminist commentators, Owen (1990) and Zingrone (1994). These authors propose that the marginal status of women in the Victorian era goes some way towards an explanation of the involvement in spiritualist mediumship by many British women in the period between 1860 and the early 1890s. While women in Victorian England were by no means without influence, they certainly lacked the social, political and economic power of a fully autonomous individual. Middle-class women in particular could not achieve financial independence: work as domestic servants was considered too demeaning but few other vocations were accessible to them. The gender stereotype of the 'Victorian lady' emphasised submissiveness, humility, self-sacrifice and maternal obligations. By the middle of the nineteenth century some middle-class women were beginning to show signs of restlessness over their social marginalisation (Owen, 1990), but there were few effective avenues for redressing the power imbalance between men and women and progressive reforms were very slow in coming.

Victorian women were expected to stand as models of virtue and to facilitate the propagation of religious values in the family and in English society at large. One of the few domains in which women were conceded to have any authoritative role therefore was in regard to their supposed spiritual sensitivities. It is not surprising, then, that many women were attracted to the spiritualist movement which emerged in the 1860s. Although there certainly were some notable male mediums in Victorian England, the substantial majority were women and some of them were able to achieve at least moderate financial gains from their service as a link to the spirit world.

But the personal benefits for female spiritualist mediums evidently went far beyond any increase in financial independence. According to Owen (1990) and Zingrone (1994), spiritualism also served as an important outlet for women's expression of their thwarted need for power. In effect, 'spiritualist culture held possibilities for attention, opportunity and status denied elsewhere' (Owen, 1990, p. 4). This feature is clearly illustrated by the activities of female mediums during the spiritualist séances that became extremely popular in this era. In the context of a séance the medium could engage in behaviour that simply would not have been tolerated in everyday life but which was nevertheless socially acceptable to those attending the séance (the 'sitters') as a manifestation of the spiritual realm. While seemingly possessed by the spirit of a deceased personality, the medium could therefore be remarkably unconventional. During the medium's spirit communications her language might become highly profane and include not only obscenities but blasphemies, none of which could ever have been condoned from women in polite circles of English society. In some instances she even became lewd: the 'materialised spirit' could appear in flimsy, even erotic, clothing and might encourage sitters to touch her body in order to confirm the spirit's materialised state; caresses and kisses might be bestowed on male sitters; and on occasion more explicit sexual acts were reported to have taken place in the subdued lighting of the séance room (Owen, 1990; Moore, 1977).

Within the confines of the séance room, therefore, female mediums were temporarily freed from some of the constraints of their gender-based marginal social status. Paradoxically, this increased power for personal expression was achieved by a declared renunciation of power. Under the theory of spiritualism the medium was thought to be a mere passive vessel for spirit possession, totally surrendering the self or conscious personality to become a conduit to the spirit world. At the same time it should be acknowledged that the medium's behaviour in her séances need not have been a consciously driven challenge to the Victorian stereotype of womanhood; certainly from a spiritualist point of view, she was simply fulfilling her socially prescribed spiritual obligations in an appropriately passive fashion. The practice of spiritualism nonetheless may have served in some degree to sublimate problems arising from the marginalised status of women in English society. Thus, Owen (1990, p. 234) observes that in the 1890s and the early twentieth century, substantial advances in women's social and political power were paralleled by a decline in materialisation séances and, indeed, in the popularity of the whole spiritualist movement. In short, this historical episode illustrates how social marginalisation may have a fundamental (although not necessarily conscious) motivational role in a person's attraction to paranormal beliefs.

Although the foregoing example is potentially instructive in several respects it cannot, of course, be regarded as evidential support for the social marginality hypothesis. At best one could say that the hypothesis appears to throw some light on specific aspects of spiritualist practice in Victorian England. An adequate assessment of the social marginality hypothesis, on the other hand, must rely more fundamentally on the empirical evidence for a relationship between indices of social marginality and paranormal belief.

As defined by sociologists, the primary indices of social marginality include (old) age, (female) gender, (low) socioeconomic status, (minority) ethnicity and (homosexual) sexual orientation. Researchers have sought to relate the endorsement of paranormal belief to each of these factors. Thus, in this context the demographic correlates of paranormal belief are pivotal: under the social marginality hypothesis the demographic characteristics of paranormal believers should be those that signify social marginality. It is to a review of demographic correlates that we now turn.

Demographic correlates of paranormal belief

Demographic variables investigated as potential correlates of paranormal belief include age, gender, socioeconomic status, ethnicity and culture, sexual orientation and other minor factors. Each of these variables will be addressed in turn.

Age

With the major exception of traditional religious beliefs, most paranormal beliefs appear to be stronger in young adults than in elderly people. Indeed, Emmons and Sobal (1981b, p. 52) concluded that age is the strongest of all demographic correlates of paranormal belief.

Global paranormal belief has been found to be negatively correlated with age (Boy, 2002; Hartman, 1976). Similarly, Heintz and Baruss (2001) reported that global paranormal belief was lower in a group of elderly people (over sixty years of age) than for a normative sample of undergraduate students. A similar trend is evident for specific facets of paranormal belief. A negative relationship between

ESP belief and age has been found in American (Emmons and Sobal, 1981b; Randall, 1990; Sobal and Emmons, 1982; Tobacyk, Pritchett and Mitchell, 1988), New Zealand (Clarke, 1991a) and English (Blackmore, 1984) samples, although it was not significant in Haraldsson's (1981) Icelandic survey. Emmons and Sobal (1981b), Newport and Strausberg (2001), Randall (1990), Sobal and Emmons (1982) and Tobacyk, Pritchett and Mitchell (1988) all reported that belief in witchcraft falls across progressively older age groups and the same trend is noted for belief in spiritualism (Newport and Strausberg, 2001; Tobacyk, Pritchett and Mitchell, 1988), ghosts (Clarke, 1991a; Emmons and Sobal, 1981b; Newport and Strausberg, 2001; Rice, 2003; Sobal and Emmons, 1982), extraordinary life forms (Emmons and Sobal,1981b; Sobal and Emmons, 1982; Tobacyk, Pritchett and Mitchell, 1988) and astrology (Emmons and Sobal, 1981b; Randall, 1990). A negative relationship between age and endorsement of superstitious beliefs has been reported by Blachowski (1937), Dudchya (1933), Jahoda (1970), Tobacyk, Pritchett and Mitchell (1988), Torgler (2007), Wagner (1928) and Wiseman (2003). Finally, Rice (2003), Westrum (1979) and a recent Gallup poll (Newport and Strausberg, 2001) suggested that belief in visitations to Earth by extraterrestrial aliens may also be highest in young people. On the other hand, there seems to be no relationship between age and beliefs in faith healing and plant consciousness (Randall, 1990), although the incidence of these paranormal beliefs evidently is low in all age groups.

As noted above, traditional religious belief seems to be a major exception to the general trend of a decline in the incidence of paranormal beliefs across groups of increasing age. Tobacyk, Pritchett and Mitchell (1988) and Emmons and Sobal (1981b) found no significant age-related differences in religious belief, other studies (e.g., Christopher *et al.*, 1971; Heintz and Baruss, 2001; Jupp, 2008; McAllister, 1988; Moberg, 1972; Verdoux *et al.*, 1998) have actually observed an *increase* in religiosity among the elderly and one analysis by Argue *et al.*, (1999) identified more complex patterns of age-related increases in religiosity.

In seeking to understand the negative correlation between age and most paranormal beliefs we should note that all of the research cited above was cross-sectional rather than longitudinal in design. This makes the interpretation of the correlational data somewhat uncertain: although the data might well testify to the effects of aging or developmental processes on adherence to paranormal beliefs, they could also reflect generational differences (see Crockett and Voas, 2006; Martin, 1998; Tilley, 2003). The goal of a truly developmental perspective on paranormal beliefs is further compromised by the dearth of studies of such belief in children (for a possible investigative model see Fry, 2000; Hatton, 2001). In addition, one of the few available studies with children has indicated the importance of taking account of both explicit and implicit expressions of belief: Subbotsky (2001) found that while children's explicit (verbal) endorsement of paranormal beliefs did decline with age, behaviour consistent with these beliefs did not show such a marked decline. Perhaps this disparity extends into adulthood.

Another complication is possible differential item functioning across age groups; that is, some items of the belief questionnaire may be interpreted differently depending on the respondent's age. By way of illustration, people in one age group may be inclined to interpret a question about the existence of heaven in a very literal way whereas those of another age group may interpret the term 'heaven' in a metaphorical sense and people in yet another age group may take the item to signify 'I act as if heaven exists, whether or not it really does'. Lange *et al.* (2000) have demonstrated the occurrence of age-related differential item functioning in the case of the most widely used measure of paranormal belief, Tobacyk's (1988) *Revised Paranormal Belief Scale*. In the present context it is important to appreciate that indices of paranormal belief marked by age-related differential item functioning cannot demonstrate conclusively that a correlation of belief scores with age testifies to the variation in the *intensity* of belief with age; rather, people of different ages may simply vary in the meanings they draw from the test items and thereby tend to achieve different scores. For details of the debate over this potential confound, see Irwin (2000a), Lange *et al.* (2001) and Vitulli (2000). Fortunately, Lange *et al.* (2000) have developed a two-factor procedure for scoring the *Revised Paranormal Belief Scale* that is free from age-related differential item functioning. My own research with this measure (Irwin, 2001a) found scores on the two factors Traditional Paranormal Beliefs and New Age Philosophy still to decline with age, but the effect sizes were small. Callaghan (2000) confirmed the age-related decline in New Age Philosophy, but the decline in Traditional Paranormal Beliefs did not reach statistical significance. Similar results were reported by Houran and Lange (2001), except that the correlation between New Age Philosophy and age was anomalously positive in a university student sample.

In any event, the predominant negative relationship between age and paranormal belief is at odds with the social marginality hypothesis (Emmons and Sobal, 1981b), at least for Western society. Youthfulness is highly valued in Western society. Some middle-aged and older adults make substantial efforts to mask visible signs of aging: dyeing their greying hair, using cosmetic preparations to minimise facial wrinkles and even resorting to cosmetic surgery in an endeavour to maintain a youthful appearance. The aged themselves constitute a socially marginal group, often derided by other people as stupid, obsolete, economically unproductive and an unwelcome drain on society's resources. To a lesser extent, even middle-aged people are socially marginalised in that they are commonly deemed to be unable to keep pace with technological changes or to appreciate significant shifts in social mores. Age, or more precisely, agedness, signifies social marginality and disempowerment in Western society (Mirowsky, 1995). Under the social marginality hypothesis, therefore, older people should be relatively prone to paranormal belief but for most facets of this domain the reverse is the case. Even for religious belief, where a positive relationship with age has sometimes been reported, it is doubtful that the data confirm the social marginality hypothesis:

increased religiosity in old age is likely to be a reflection of factors other than feelings of privation and disempowerment. A generational characteristic, for example, might partly underlie this relationship: elderly people may be more likely to have been raised as regular church-goers than are younger generations (McAllister, 1988). Similarly, the aged may be relatively likely to reflect on the prospect of their life coming to an end and in this context religious beliefs may take on increasing cogency (Fishman, 1992), prompting more frequent religious observance (Francis and Kaldor, 2002).

In summary, to the extent that age is a marker of social marginality the available empirical findings are not encouraging for the social marginality hypothesis of paranormal belief. Contrary to the hypothesis, most paranormal beliefs are negatively related to age and the effect sizes are small. Additionally, even the reported positive correlations between religious belief and age are inconclusive for the theory in that they could also be attributable to factors other than social marginality.

Gender

The endorsement of most, but certainly not all, paranormal beliefs is slightly stronger among women than among men. Higher scores by women on global measures of paranormal belief have been reported by Bhushan and Bhushan (1987), Boy (2002), Bressan (2002), Canetti and Pedahzur (2002), Göritz and Schumacher (2000), Irwin (1985b), McGarry and Newberry (1981), Randall (1990), Randall and Desrosiers (1980), Schulter and Papousek (2008) and Tobacyk and Milford (1983), although no difference between the sexes was found by Donovan (1998), Fox and Williams (2000), Hartman (1976), Houran, Kumar *et al.* (2002), Houran and Williams (1998), Jones *et al.* (1977) and Sjöberg and Wåhlberg (2002). Women also are more inclined to report they believe they have had parapsychological (psychic) experiences (e.g., Fox, 1992).

With regard to specific dimensions of paranormal belief, women generally show stronger endorsement of the following.

Astrology	Clarke, 1991a; Emmons and Sobal, 1981b; Fichten and Sunerton, 1983; Gray, 1990a; Grey, 1988; Kim, 2005; National Science Foundation, 2002; Newport and Strausberg, 2001; Plug, 1975; Rice, 2003; Salter and Routledge, 1971; Wuthnow, 1976; Za'vour, 1972
ESP, especially telepathy and precognition	Blackmore, 1997; Clarke, 1991a, 1993; Emmons and Sobal, 1981b; Gray, 1990a; Haraldsson, 1981, 1985b; Heard and Vyse, 1998; Irwin, 1985b; Kennedy, 1939; National Science Foundation, 2002; Persinger and Richards, 1991; Rice, 2003; Thalbourne, 1981; Thalbourne *et al.*, 1995; Tobacyk and Milford, 1983

Hauntings	Haraldsson, 1985b; Newport and Strausberg, 2001; Rice, 2003
New Age spirituality	Farias *et al.*, 2005; Levin *et al.*, 1994
Other forms of divination	Kim, 2005; Lehman and Witty, 1928
Psychic healing and other alternative health practices	Gray, 1990a; Ni *et al.*, 2002; Rice, 2003
Reincarnation	Gray, 1990a; Rice, 2003
Spiritualism	Heard and Vyse, 1998; Newport and Strausberg, 2001; Persinger and Richards, 1991
Superstitions	Blum, 1976; Blum and Blum, 1974; Clarke, 1993; Conklin, 1919; Emme, 1940; Gregory, 1975; Lewis and Gallagher, 2001; Plug, 1975; Scheidt, 1973; Torgler, 2007; Wagner, 1928; Wiseman, 2003; Zebb and Moore, 2003; Zeidner and Beit-Hallahmi, 1988
Traditional religious concepts	Black, 1990; Clarke, 1993; Emmons and Sobal, 1981b; Flere, 2007; Hay and Morisy, 1978; Heard and Vyse, 1998; Jupp, 2008; Lewis, 2002; Mohammadi and Honarmand, 2007; Newport and Strausberg, 2001; Smith *et al.*, 2003; Tobacyk and Milford, 1983; Verdoux *et al.*, 1998

Note, however, that the trend for traditional religious concepts may be culture specific (Loewenthal *et al.*, 2002).

This general pattern nevertheless is reversed for some other dimensions of paranormal belief. Thus, on average men are the stronger believers in UFOs and extraterrestrial aliens (Bainbridge, 1983; Clarke, 1991a, 1993; Gray, 1990a; Lewis, 2002; Newport and Strausberg, 2001; Patry and Pelletier, 2001; Pekala *et al.*, 1992; Preece and Baxter, 2000; Rice, 2003; Sparks, Pellechia and Irvine, 1997; Vitulli and Luper, 1998; Westrum, 1979), although women predominate among people who claim to have been actually abducted by aliens (Bader, 2003). Men also are the stronger believers in extraordinary life forms such as Bigfoot (Lewis, 2002; Persinger and Richards, 1991; Thalbourne *et al.*, 1995; Tobacyk and Milford, 1983; Tobacyk and Pirttilä-Backman, 1992; Tobacyk, Pritchett and Mitchell, 1988). These specific gender differences evidently emerge in adolescence, if not earlier (Preece and Baxter, 2000).

Findings in relation to belief in witchcraft are rather mixed. Several investigators have reported that this belief does not vary with gender (Emmons and Sobal, 1981b; Haraldsson, 1985b; Tobacyk and Milford, 1983). Among the few statistically significant findings, Salter and Routledge (1971) and Tobacyk and Pirttilä-Backman (1992) reported belief in witchcraft to be higher among men, whereas Heard and Vyse (1998) and Persinger and Richards (1991) found that women embrace this belief more strongly. It is possible that gender differences in a belief in witchcraft are moderated by various other (e.g., cultural) factors; this issue calls for future empirical clarification. Cultural factors might also underlie the occasional set of atypical findings; for example, in a sample of college students in a southern state of the US Vitulli and Luper (1998) found beliefs in ESP and 'life after death' were stronger among men than among women, contrary to the general trend.

All of the above trends for gender were identified using measures of paranormal belief that either are known to be marked by gender-related differential item functioning (Lange *et al.*, 2000) or have unproven status in this respect. Using Lange *et al.*'s (2000) indices of paranormal belief that have been shown to be free from this psychometric flaw, Irwin (2001a) found women to have slightly stronger belief than men in both traditional paranormal concepts and New Age tenets but the effect sizes were small. These findings were confirmed by Houran, Wiseman and Thalbourne (2002), but similar studies by Callaghan (2000), Houran and Lange (2001) and Houran and Thalbourne (2001) yielded nonsignificant results for gender.

Finally, it may be mentioned that one study (Vitulli *et al.*, 1999) reported an interaction between gender and age for global paranormal belief, but in an attempted replication using a measure of paranormal belief free from gender- and age-related differential item functioning no such interaction effect was found (Irwin, 2001a). In addition, one study (Westrum, 1979) found an interaction effect between gender and ethnicity for UFO belief, with black males having the strongest belief and black females the weakest. This observation warrants contemporary replicatory investigation in relation to the full range of paranormal beliefs.

To the extent that being a woman continues to be socially devalued, the social marginality hypothesis predicts that women should present with stronger paranormal beliefs than do men. Taking account of findings over the full range of paranormal beliefs it is evident that this prediction is confirmed for some types of belief but disconfirmed for others. The available empirical literature offers at best only partial support for the social marginality hypothesis and even this level of support is compromised by weak effect sizes. In any event, clearly the hypothesis would have to be modified in order to accommodate the evidence that some paranormal beliefs are actually stronger among men than among women.

Additionally, it must be stressed that the observed gender differences may reflect factors other than social marginality. Thompson and Remmes (2002) attributed the disparities in paranormal beliefs between genders to differences in 'gender ideology' or social prescriptions of what it is to be male or female (see also Flere, 2007). More specifically, Scheidt (1973) has speculated that the different level of paranormal belief between genders is essentially a product of more basic differences in attitudes to science and religion; specifically, males typically have been socialised to take more interest in and to be better informed about scientific matters than about religious issues, whereas the reverse may tend to be the case for females (Zusne and Jones, 1982, p. 186). Although still rather simplistic, this perspective would appear to have greater scope than the social marginality hypothesis for accommodating reports of stronger belief in UFOs and extraordinary life forms among men.

Other gender-linked factors such as the structural location of women in society (de Vaus and McAllister, 1987) are worthy of consideration in this context. That is, gender differences in the pattern of paranormal beliefs may reflect not so much the social marginality of women as the *different* social roles of men and women. Some feminist parapsychologists, for example, have pursued this option by construing the different social roles in terms of power relations. Thus, Schlitz (1994) has discussed the link between gender differences in paranormal belief and power relations within contemporary Western society. In Schlitz's analysis a belief in traditional religious concepts is seen to serve the socially designated feminine role of sustaining loving and supportive relationships, even in the face of death. At the same time other paranormal beliefs may seemingly be used by women to subvert the power structure, as mentioned earlier for English women's involvement in spiritualist mediumship during the nineteenth century (Owen, 1990; Zingrone, 1994). Similar constructions have been made of the practice of witchcraft in early modern Europe and North America (e.g., Bever, 2002).

Whether or not these analyses are thought persuasive, the actual role of power relations in the development of paranormal beliefs nevertheless requires empirical substantiation and at present there is a dearth of such data. One study, that by Simmonds and Roe (2000), examined the relationship between global paranormal belief and gender role (as indexed by a sex-role inventory), but the correlation was not significant. In any event, both this approach to gender differences and the more general social marginality hypothesis have difficulty in accounting for the facts that the observed effect sizes for gender are small and that some paranormal beliefs are stronger in men. As a demographic correlate of paranormal belief, gender exposes as many insufficiencies in the social marginality hypothesis as it provides instances of support. In no sense is this intended to deny the role played by paranormal beliefs in the lives of women (see Bennett, 1987); rather, at this point we simply leave open the possibility that paranormal beliefs may serve more complex psychological functions in the lives of *both* sexes than is encapsulated by the social marginality hypothesis.

Socioeconomic status

Socioeconomic status is a key element of social marginality. Under the social marginality hypothesis it would be predicted that people with low socioeconomic status would tend to compensate for their marginality by endorsing paranormal beliefs. Few investigations nevertheless have been made of socioeconomic status in relation to paranormal belief, possibly because of the difficulty of its measurement and the perceived intrusiveness of some of the questions in the indices.

In one early study Sheils and Berg (1977) found socioeconomic status to be unrelated to global paranormal belief in a sample of American university students, but a similar study in Argentinean universities by de Barbenza and de Vila (1989) found a significant negative relationship for global paranormal belief and for belief in traditional religious tenets, witchcraft and precognition. Zeidner and Beit-Hallahmi (1988) also found a negative relationship between socioeconomic status and superstitious beliefs in young Israeli adolescents. In each of these studies, however, socioeconomic status was assessed in terms of the income, education, or occupation of the participant's *father*. In many instances this may have been an inaccurate index of the student's socioeconomic status. Additionally, the ranges of both paranormal beliefs in young adolescents and parental socioeconomic status in a student sample may be unrepresentative of that in society as a whole; the extent to which the above findings can be generalised is therefore uncertain. A recent survey of the relationship between paranormal beliefs and income in an adult sample yielded mixed results (Rice, 2003): most beliefs were uncorrelated with income, but whereas belief in astrology showed a negative correlation, the relationship for belief in psychic healing was positive.

In an analysis undertaken by Emmons and Sobal (1981b) unemployment was used as one indicator of social marginality. Unemployment, of course, is also an important aspect of socioeconomic status. Paranormal beliefs found by Emmons and Sobal to correlate with unemployment included those relating to ESP and its individual forms, extraordinary life forms, ghosts and angels, but only for the last of these was the relationship positive. Indeed, in most types of paranormal belief surveyed by Emmons and Sobal unemployed people tended to show comparatively low paranormal belief. This trend is contrary to the social marginality hypothesis.

Warren (1970) used as an index of social marginality the degree of inconsistency among the person's income, education and occupation. This index was found to correlate with extraterrestrial belief, with people high in status inconsistency relatively inclined to claim they had seen UFOs. In a subsequent analysis of the same data, however, Warren (1975, cited by Westrum, 1977) found that status inconsistency had a smaller effect than general socioeconomic status and, indeed, Warren (cited by Westrum, 1979) reported UFO experients to have relatively high socioeconomic status. In part on this basis Fox (1979) and Zimmer (1984) concluded that no significance should be assigned to Warren's initial results for status inconsistency. In any event, Warren's findings for socioeconomic status itself do contradict the social marginality hypothesis and they are supported by a more recent study of UFO abductees conducted by Bader (2003).

Few other studies have examined individual dimensions of paranormal belief in this context. Some of the older surveys (Lundeen and Caldwell, 1930; Ter Keurst, 1939) found superstitious beliefs to be stronger in geographical regions of low socioeconomic status, although there is some doubt that this trend has survived in more recent times (Jones *et al.*, 1977). Wuthnow (1976) also reported belief in astrology is stronger in people who are unable to work or who are looking for a job, but in the study by Emmons and Sobal (1981b) the correlation between astrological belief and unemployment was not significant.

There are some claims of a relationship between lower socioeconomic status and traditional religious belief, at least in the US (Zusne and Jones, 1982). Several qualifications nevertheless need to be made on this point. First, the relationship might not be evident in every country; indeed, the reverse may be the case in Britain (Stark, 1964). Second, the observed direction of the relationship seems to be crucially dependent on the index of religiosity being used. Devotionalism may be comparatively strong among lower socioeconomic groups, but church attendance and participation in church programs is reported to be more frequent among middle and high socioeconomic groups (Hoge and Roozen, 1979). Third, the direction of the relationship might also depend on the index of socioeconomic status used. While high income may well be associated with relatively low religiosity, the rate of unemployment tends to be highest among those who do not endorse religious beliefs (Mol, 1985). Finally, the magnitude of the relationship between socioeconomic status and traditional religiosity tends to be too small to have much explanatory value (Mueller and Johnson, 1975).

These few reports of an inverse relationship between socioeconomic status and beliefs in religion, superstitions and astrology nevertheless are at least consistent with the social marginality hypothesis. Again, the causal interpretation of these correlative associations is a matter for speculation. The social marginality hypothesis proposes that low socioeconomic status inspires a need for a compensatory paranormal belief. But it might be equally as plausible to argue that people who embrace some types of paranormal belief may be just as 'irrational' or injudicious in other aspects of their behaviour and thereby less likely to achieve social and economic success. Thus, for the reported associations between low socioeconomic status and paranormal belief, there are no clear indications as to which factor should rightly be considered the 'cause' and which the 'effect'.

In summary, it may be said that only a small number of empirical findings on the association of socioeconomic status to paranormal belief are consistent with the social marginality hypothesis, that these arguably are inconclusive for the hypothesis and that many of the findings of Emmons and Sobal (1981b) were outright contrary to the social marginality hypothesis.

Ethnicity and culture

Ethnicity may affect the narrative construction of ostensibly paranormal events (e.g., Saethre, 2007), but this observation does not bear directly on the social marginality hypothesis. Ethnic background has nevertheless been included in some investigations of paranormal belief because of the socially marginal status accorded to some ethnic groups within a given society. In surveys of American samples this variable usually has been operationalised in terms of whether or not the respondent is black.

Emmons and Sobal (1981b; Sobal and Emmons, 1982) found belief in ESP and in all its individual forms to be *lower* among black Americans than among other ethnic groups in the general population. Similar findings for belief in psychic healing and in UFOs have been reported (Bader, 2003; Rice, 2003). These data are of course contrary to the social marginality hypothesis. On the other hand, in a survey of university students by Tobacyk, Miller, Murphy and Mitchell (1988) blacks showed a higher belief in precognition than did whites. Murphy and Lester (1976) reported no dependence of ESP belief upon the ethnic background of college students.

Results in relation to other paranormal beliefs are just as confused. Tobacyk, Miller, Murphy and Mitchell (1988) noted further that in their sample of university students, blacks showed stronger belief than whites in spiritualism, superstitions and witchcraft, whereas white students had the higher level of traditional religious belief. Emmons and Sobal (1981b) and Tobacyk, Miller, Murphy and Mitchell (1988) each reported belief in extraordinary life forms to be stronger among whites than among blacks and Lewis and Gallagher (2001) reported a similar trend for superstitious beliefs concerning Friday the 13th. Therefore, in terms of ethnicity within the US the social marginality hypothesis evidently does not apply uniformly across the different dimensions of paranormal belief.

One study has examined ethnic differences in paranormal belief outside the American context. Otis and Kuo (1984) surveyed Singapore university students and found Chinese, Indian and Malay students to differ mainly in regard to religious beliefs, with the Chinese students generally showing greater scepticism. Given the relative standing of these ethnic groups in Singaporean society, these findings are not fully consonant with the social marginality hypothesis.

As with other demographic correlates of paranormal belief ethnicity provides mixed testimony to the validity of the social marginality theory. Some types of paranormal belief such as spiritualism, superstitions and witchcraft are indeed found to be higher in some socially marginal ethnic groups. But there are also instances in which other types of paranormal belief, such as traditional religious belief, ESP and belief in extraordinary life forms, are comparatively weak in a marginal ethnic group. Further, other paranormal beliefs do not seem to vary with ethnicity within a given culture. Complex interactions may be operating here between ethnicity, geographical region and educational level. Although these relationships warrant further study, when taken in isolation the factor of ethnicity does not look to be particularly promising for the validation of a social marginality account.

Ethnicity within a given nation may be an index of social marginality but clearly it also taps into cultural differences. The possible role of these differences might be identified through comparisons of paranormal belief *between* cultures or national groups. Several studies of this type have used Tobacyk's (1988) *Revised Paranormal Belief Scale* as the measure and Louisiana university students as the standard referent group. In comparison to the latter group, university students in

Finland are reported to show lower belief scores for traditional religious concepts, witchcraft and superstitions, but they had higher scores for belief in extraordinary life forms (Tobacyk and Pirttilä-Backman, 1992). A sample of Polish university students had relatively low scores for traditional religious belief, witchcraft and superstition and high scores for psi belief (Tobacyk and Tobacyk, 1992). Students at a British liberal arts college scored lower in traditional religious belief, superstitions, extraordinary life forms and precognition and higher in spiritualist belief (Davies, 1988). Australian university students had lower traditional religious belief and stronger belief in spiritualism and precognition (Irwin, 1991a). Icelandic students were found to be more sceptical on all scales except spiritualism (Haraldsson and Houtkooper, 1996).

In a study using another questionnaire, Otis and Kuo (1984) compared paranormal beliefs among university students in Singapore to those of Canadian students. The Singapore sample showed a substantially higher level of global paranormal belief. This cross-cultural difference was most marked for scales indexing religious concepts and spiritualist phenomena, although differences were also evident for individual items concerning extraordinary life forms and precognition. McClenon (1990) also reported college students in the Republic of China to have a higher level of belief in ESP than their American counterparts. Finally, on the basis of separate national surveys, Torgler (2007) identified higher superstitiousness in formerly Communist countries and Haraldsson (1985b) reported the level of belief in telepathy to be 73 per cent in both Britain and Iceland and that in Sweden to be slightly lower, at 66 per cent.

These cross-cultural studies at least offer testimony to the fact that the level of paranormal belief in an individual is in part a function of the person's broader cultural environment. For example, there may be some variation in the extent to which a given paranormal belief is integrated into the mainstream culture and this in turn may influence the likelihood of the individual's endorsement of that belief. As the above cross-cultural data suggest, religious belief may be much more an integral part of mainstream culture in the US than it is in many other countries. Alternatively, there may be cultural characteristics that prompt people to embrace paranormal beliefs with a marginal rather than mainstream standing. For example, in seeking to account for paranormal beliefs among Polish students in the early 1990s, Tobacyk and Tobacyk (1992) pointed to the high level of social control and the constant conflict between worldviews (e.g., atheistic and materialistic Communist policies *versus* the principles of the Church) that existed at the time in Poland (see also Torgler, 2007). The causes of cross-cultural differences in paranormal belief are likely to be extremely complex and often subtle.

If the social marginality hypothesis is deemed by its advocates to provide a general account of the intensity of paranormal belief, does this hypothesis accommodate evidence of cross-cultural differences in paranormal belief? At a fundamental level it is not clear how the social marginality hypothesis would directly apply *between* cultures. Are the feelings of disempowerment and alienation felt by a marginalised group towards the larger society felt also by the residents of one nation towards those of another? Evidence of relative privation should surely be far more salient to a group within a society than between one nation and another. Although people may know that another country is more privileged than their own, they are not confronted with the consequences of this fact to anywhere near the extent that they are aware of the inequalities within their own country. It is therefore unlikely that cross-cultural differences in paranormal beliefs are substantially and directly motivated by cross-cultural perceptions of relative privation of the sort advocated in the social marginality hypothesis.

On the other hand, perhaps the effects of social marginality within a culture can have indirect consequences for cross-cultural variations in paranormal belief. Under the social marginality hypothesis a country characterised by equality of opportunity and strong egalitarianism would have little need for paranormal beliefs, because no discriminable group of the country's citizens should be marginalised. A country within which there are marked inequalities, however, would be predicted to provide fertile ground for the development of paranormal beliefs. In this way cross-cultural differences in paranormal beliefs might arise not because of one nation's perception of the privileged position of another nation but because of different degrees of marginalisation operating independently within each nation. It is doubtful, however, that this account could accommodate the cross-cultural data reviewed above. First, the cross-cultural differences in level of belief do not seem to relate in a simple linear fashion to my (admittedly subjective) estimates of the extent of marginalisation of groups within the respective nations. Second, a basic and recurrently evident weakness in the social marginality hypothesis is that it does not differentiate among paranormal beliefs. The social marginality hypothesis therefore does not address the common finding that in a comparison between two nations, some paranormal beliefs are stronger in one country and yet different paranormal beliefs are stronger in the other country. If the prevalence of social marginalisation within a given culture is a fundamental cause of the level of paranormal belief, then other things being equal all types of paranormal belief should be affected by this factor to much the same degree. The available cross-cultural data certainly suggest that this is not the case. Again, the social marginality hypothesis is exposed as too simplistic, if it has claim to any validity at all.

Sexual orientation (homosexuality)

While homosexuality might now be socially acceptable to a far greater extent than in the past, homosexuals remain a relatively marginalised group in most societies. Indeed, homosexual behaviour is still illegal in some countries. Even in areas where homosexual acts between consenting adults are not legislatively prohibited, widespread social disapproval of homosexuals may persist. McBeath (1985) has speculated that homosexual people tend to be open to parapsychological experiences. If so, they may well have comparatively strong paranormal beliefs. To the extent that homosexuality is marginalised, this speculation is consistent with the social marginality hypothesis.

There appears to have been only one study directly addressing an association between homosexuality and intensity of paranormal belief. Thalbourne (1997) found no differences between groups of predominantly homosexual and predominantly heterosexual men in scores on his *Australian Sheep–Goat Scale* (Thalbourne and Delin, 1993), a global index of belief in ESP, psychokinesis and life after death. This study therefore failed to support the social marginality hypothesis. There is nevertheless a need for more extensive investigation of the issue, canvassing both homosexual men and women as well as a wider range of specific paranormal beliefs.

Other demographic variables

Mainstream political orientation seems unrelated to belief in ESP, psi phenomena in general and other basic parapsychological concepts (Alcock, 1975; Haraldsson, 1981; Sheils and Berg, 1977). Randall (1997) reported, however, that a group of politically alienated conservative voters had a relatively strong global belief in a set of notions including fortune-telling, astrology and UFOs. Randall speculates that these 'protest voters' may have a more general propensity to endorse 'extreme views', a trend that might be interpretable in terms of the social marginality hypothesis. More incisive research is warranted into possible interrelationships among political radicalism, social marginality and specific paranormal beliefs.

To the extent that divorced and separated people are seen by others to have marginal status in society, marital status may be a pertinent demographic variable for the social marginality hypothesis. Emmons and Sobal (1981b; Sobal and Emmons, 1982) found married people to have relatively strong religious beliefs but also comparatively low levels of belief in ESP and its different forms, astrology, witchcraft and extraordinary life forms. Wuthnow (1976) similarly found divorced and separated people to have substantially higher belief in astrology than did married, widowed or 'never married' respondents. Although the data base still is very small, marital status is one characteristic of social marginality that does provide reasonably consistent evidence for the social marginality hypothesis of paranormal belief, always assuming, of course, that sociologists confirm that divorced or separated people are considered socially marginal. But even here religious belief appears to be an exception to the general trend.

Other factors such as education and religiosity usually are regarded as demographic variables but they are addressed in later chapters.

An assessment of the social marginality hypothesis

The identified demographic correlates of paranormal beliefs necessarily constitute data to be taken into account in the formulation of an effective theory of paranormal belief. I do not advocate this as a major priority; after all, the relationships established in this chapter typically are of small magnitude and thus of limited explanatory value. We nevertheless must still assess the standing of the social marginality hypothesis in relation to the empirical evidence.

Following the lead of sociologists, researchers have considered the variables of age, gender, socioeconomic status, ethnicity, sexual orientation and other demographic characteristics as an index of social marginality. The review of the empirical literature nevertheless has failed to find a single dimension of paranormal belief showing at least moderate correlation with these indices that is *uniformly* consistent with the social marginality hypothesis. Perhaps a complex combination of the indices could provide a basis for future research into the issue (for an initial step in this direction see Rice, 2003). At present it is fair to say the social marginality hypothesis of paranormal belief, when taken in isolation, does not satisfactorily accommodate the available evidence.

One of the apparent shortcomings of the social marginality hypothesis is that it addresses paranormal belief in an indiscriminate or global fashion; that is, it does not permit researchers to anticipate differential effects of group marginalisation on the individual types of paranormal belief. Such differential effects, while small, clearly exist. The review of the empirical literature attests to the fact that in some instances a given demographic factor correlates positively with some paranormal beliefs but negatively with other beliefs. This observation suggests that if social marginality does have a substantial bearing on the strength of paranormal beliefs, it cannot be the sole factor that needs to be encompassed by a viable theory of paranormal belief. Indeed, the very fact that many paranormal beliefs are embraced by a majority of the population (see Chapter 1) appears to disqualify the social marginality hypothesis *a priori*, given it would require that a majority of the population be socially marginalised. The most positive assessment we can make of the social marginality hypothesis is to conclude that it is too simplistic. At the very least it needs to be amended to allow the incorporation of additional explanatory processes.

Finally, it may be argued that the social marginality hypothesis does not give due attention to mediating variables. That is, if social marginalisation does facilitate the endorsement of paranormal beliefs, why and how does it do so? In this context it seems important to go beyond the bald sociological link between marginalisation and paranormal belief by asking what psychological functions in a marginalised person are served by a paranormal belief. A few proponents of the social marginality hypothesis (e.g., Glock, 1964; Stark and Bainbridge, 1980) make passing references to such concepts as empowerment and restoring a sense of control over life, but psychological processes are generally not accorded centrality in these expositions. At the risk of indulging my bias as a professional psychologist I would argue that greater attention should be given to psychological mediators of paranormal belief. In so doing it could become apparent that social marginalisation may be only one element — perhaps even a relatively minor element — in instigating the fundamental processes that foster the formation of paranormal beliefs. This view is elaborated in the next three chapters.

Chapter 5: The worldview hypothesis

This chapter surveys the principal attitudes, beliefs and behaviours associated with the endorsement of paranormal beliefs. In addition to being of interest in their own right, these correlates have a bearing on the so-called *worldview hypothesis*.

According to Zusne and Jones (1982, 1989), paranormal belief is simply one facet of a broader worldview, a view that is primarily characterised by a highly subjective and esoteric perspective on humanity, life and the world at large. For example, under this worldview events may be interpreted more in terms of intangible mental and metaphysical processes than in relation to observable or physical factors. Truth is held to be revealed wholly by the exercise of contemplation and reflection and it is evident by its consistency both internally and with other endorsed truths. By contrast, people with an extremely objective, materialist worldview are inclined either to deny or to take no interest in the existence of things that are not physically observable; further, they will seek to discern truth through systematic, unsentimental observation of external events. The *worldview hypothesis* therefore interprets paranormal belief as a product of a broad subjectivism, a common human approach to 'making sense of the world' (Zusne and Jones, 1982, p. 192).

A putative example of the perspectives posited under the worldview hypothesis is provided by the two poles of popular conceptions of the nature of death (Shneidman, 1973; Spilka *et al.*, 1977). People with a highly subjectivist outlook tend to see death as a transition to another state of existence; for example, death might be regarded as a passage to an afterlife or heaven, or as a preface to rebirth in another body, or as the joining of one's spirit with a universal cosmic consciousness. These views of death are judged by their adherents as coherent and internally consistent because they engender a sense of understanding of the meaning or purpose of existence. Such views, of course, are anathema to people with a strongly objectivist perspective. For the latter group there is in death no observable evidence of any transition from one form of life to another and thus these notions of post-mortem survival are either dismissed out of hand or ignored as an essentially unproductive, irresolvable conundrum. In the objectivist view, death is purely a biological process, the natural end of the life cycle, the irrevocable functional cessation of an organism. The worldview hypothesis therefore construes polar views about death as merely one instance of the expression of a broader dimension of worldviews ranging from idealistic subjectivism to tough-minded rationalist objectivism.

A fundamental implication of the worldview hypothesis is that paranormal belief should tend to be found in conjunction with other beliefs and practices that share the subjective and esoteric orientation. The evidence on this point is surveyed in the following sections.

Involvement in the paranormal

Under the worldview hypothesis the esoteric orientation inherent in paranormal belief should be reflected also in the believer's behaviour. In particular, one type of behaviour expected to have an association with paranormal belief is an involvement in psychic activities of various sorts. Rather surprisingly, this issue has received relatively superficial attention from researchers, possibly because the association may seem so predictable as to be trivial. There is nevertheless a substantial conceptual issue here, namely: are paranormal beliefs purely intellectual concepts or do these beliefs have implications for a person's behaviour? If paranormal beliefs are nothing more than abstractions activated only in response to social scientists' questionnaires, there is little merit in seeking to interpret them as a component of a 'worldview' that underlies the believer's fundamental approach to the world at large.

Several associations between global paranormal belief and involvement in the paranormal have been identified. A high (or a moderate to high) level of global paranormal belief is associated with a tendency for the individual to seek entertainment (e.g., a movie) that has a paranormal theme (Otis, 1979; Sparks and Miller, 2001; Sparks, Nelson and Campbell, 1997); to read about paranormal or psychic phenomena (Irwin, 1985b; Sheils and Berg, 1977); to participate in courses on parapsychology or on psychic development (McGarry and Newberry, 1981; Neppe, 1981; Roney-Dougal, 1984); to visit professional psychics for a psychic reading (Roe, 1998); to read published horoscopes (Presson, 1997); and to dabble in satanic practices (Leeds, 1995). In addition, paranormal believers are probably more ready to participate in tourist activities with a paranormal theme (e.g., 'ghost walks' or visits to haunted sites) (D. Inglis, personal communication, 24 March 2003; Inglis and Holmes, 2003; see also Houran, Wiseman and Thalbourne, 2002). Some paranormal believers might also be inclined to practice as a medium or psychic (Gallagher *et al.*, 1994), although there is evidence that people who give psychic readings form a distinct subgroup of paranormal believers (McGarry and Newberry, 1981). More tangentially, global paranormal belief is reported to be related to a tendency to interpret anomalous experiences as paranormal (Ayeroff and Abelson, 1976; Benassi *et al.*, 1979; Bressan, 2002; French *et al.*, 2001; French *et al.*, 2002; Hergovich, 2004; Hodgson and Davey, 1887; Jones and Russell, 1980; Singer and Benassi, 1981; Tobacyk, Wells and Miller, 1998; Wiseman and Morris, 1995; Wiseman *et al.*, 2003; Wiseman *et al.*, 1997; Wiseman and Smith, 2002); to the selective discounting of information not compatible with a paranormal interpretation (Russell and Jones, 1980; Subbotsky, 2004; Singer and Benassi, 1981; Wiseman and Smith, 2002); to the claim of having had psychic experiences (Clarke, 1995; Donovan, 1998; Fox and Williams, 2000; French *et al.*, 2008; Gallagher *et al.*, 1994; Glicksohn, 1990; Haight, 1979; Houran, 2001; Houran, Kumar, Thalbourne and Lavertue, 2002; Houran and Thalbourne, 2001; Houran and Williams, 1998; Irwin, 1985b; Lewis, 2002; McClenon, 1982; Murphy and Lester, 1976; Polzella *et al.*, 1975; Rattet and Bursik, 2001; Royalty, 1995; Sheils and Berg, 1977; Thalbourne and Houran, 2000) or mystical experiences (Thalbourne, 1998–99); and to the use of mind-expanding drugs or other techniques to induce an altered state of consciousness (Gallagher *et al.*, 1994; Houran and Williams, 1998; Kumar, Pekala and Cummings, 1993; Pizzagalli *et al.*, 2000; Roney-Dougal, 1984; Simmonds and Roe, 2000; Thalbourne and Houran, 2000).

Researchers have given little attention to the behavioural correlates of specific paranormal beliefs. One exception to this generalisation is in regard to traditional religious belief. There are reports that the self-reported strength of religious conviction is related to the frequency of church attendance and participation in other religious activities such as prayer and bible reading (Haraldsson, 1981; Hoge and Roozen, 1979; Mol, 1985), but the effect sizes here were not as high as one might at first expect. Additionally, drug use was reported by Houran and Lange (2001) to be unrelated to the intensity of traditional paranormal beliefs but, as might be expected, this variable did correlate with New Age beliefs.

When considered collectively the above findings clearly suggest that paranormal belief is attitudinal. That is, paranormal belief evidently does have some influence on behaviour and thus is something more than a mere cognitive abstraction. This connection is essential to the viability of the worldview hypothesis: as noted above, paranormal belief cannot validly be regarded as an element of a broader influential worldview if such belief has no observable consequences for behaviour.

More systematic research of the issue nevertheless is warranted. To date the research has focused largely on the behavioural correlates of global paranormal belief. Specific paranormal beliefs, particularly those other than traditional religious belief, warrant further study in this context. Additionally, the correlational nature of the available data leaves open the question of causality. Indeed, causal processes here might actually be quite complex. For example, the association between paranormal belief and paranormal involvement could well be bi-directional or circular, with beliefs encouraging involvement and involvement serving to reinforce beliefs. Further research effort is necessary to clarify causal issues.

If paranormal belief can have implications for a person's behaviour in relation to psychical matters, it is legitimate to consider whether it might also impact on other domains of behaviour.

Religious beliefs and practices

To the extent that some researchers have defined belief in traditional religious concepts as a paranormal belief, it may seem somewhat redundant to ask whether paranormal beliefs are associated with religious beliefs. On the other hand, it must be remembered that some commentators have disputed the status of traditional religious belief as a paranormal belief (Fitzpatrick and Shook, 1994; Hergovich *et al.*, 2008; Kristensen, 1999; Lawrence, 1995; Sullivan, 1982; Williams *et al.*, 1989). More fundamentally, the association between religious and nonreligious paranormal beliefs certainly is pertinent to the worldview hypothesis and therefore it needs to be addressed here.

Some studies have sought to relate paranormal belief to religiosity, that is, the strength of religious attitudes or spirituality in a nonsectarian sense. The trends to date generally are positive but by no means uniformly so. Goode (2000b) found that belief in fundamental religious concepts was positively associated with belief in ESP, UFOs, astrology and numerology. According to Haraldsson (1981) and Thalbourne (1995b; 2003; Thalbourne *et al.*, 1995; Thalbourne and Hensley, 2001; Thalbourne and Houtkooper, 2002; Thalbourne and O'Brien, 1999), there is a positive statistical dependence between ESP belief and self-reported religiosity, although this relationship was not confirmed in some other studies (Clarke, 1991a; Irwin, 1985b; Svensen *et al.*, 1992). Tobacyk and Milford (1983) nevertheless found a significant positive relationship between belief in precognition and religiosity (as indexed by their Traditional Religious Belief subscale). Irwin (1985b) reported global belief in a broader range of parapsychological phenomena (including telepathy, precognition, psychokinesis, astral projection and psychic healing) to correlate positively with religiosity; this relationship was confirmed by Hergovich *et al.* (2005) and by Williams *et al.* (2006) but was not statistically significant in the survey by Alcock (1975). Rudski (2003b) found religiosity correlated positively with superstitiousness and supernatural belief (e.g., ghosts) and Torgler (2007) reports a positive correlation between religiosity and superstitiousness.

Other findings are even less uniform. Tobacyk and Milford (1983) observed religiosity to correlate positively with belief in witchcraft and negatively with spiritualism and to be uncorrelated with superstitiousness and belief in extraordinary life forms. According to Clarke (1991a), religiosity correlates positively with belief in psychic healing and negatively with UFO belief. In Grimmer and White's (1990) survey religiosity correlated positively with belief in divinatory arts but negatively with psi belief. Several additional negative relationships with religiosity have been reported in the literature. In a survey by Duncan *et al.* (1992) college students to whom religion was important were relatively *less* likely to believe in ESP, reincarnation, astrology, the devil and possession by the devil. Beck and Miller (2001) also found a negative correlation between religiosity and global paranormal belief (predominantly psi belief and spiritism). Similar findings are reported by Hillstrom and Strachan (2000) in regard to beliefs in telepathy, precognition, psychokinesis, psychic healing, UFOs, reincarnation and communication with spirits. Finally, Emmons and Sobal (1981a) found people with no religious preference were relatively likely to endorse nonreligious paranormal beliefs (e.g., telepathy) but less likely to favour religious ones (e.g., angels). Occasionally researchers have found no relationship between paranormal beliefs and religiosity (e.g., Sparks, 2001).

By way of a summary to this point of the analysis, the associations between religious and nonreligious paranormal beliefs are often positive, but several observations are inconsistent with this trend. National and regional cultural differences may help to explain the discrepancies, but this factor certainly does not accommodate all the findings (Goode, 2000b). Some recent research (e.g., Bainbridge, 2004; Lewis and Gallagher, 2001; MacDonald, 2000; McKinnon, 2003; Orenstein, 2002) suggests the associations may even be nonlinear. For example, among people who do not attend formal church services, religiosity and other paranormal beliefs may correlate positively; that is, within this segment of the population endorsement of diverse nonreligious paranormal beliefs may often be associated with a nonsectarian belief in a God and an afterlife. On the other hand, many regular churchgoers (at least for some denominations) may be explicitly instructed that nonreligious paranormal beliefs are unacceptable in the eyes of the church and thus for high levels of religiosity there may be a *negative* correlation between religiosity and the acknowledgment of nonreligious paranormal beliefs. A study by Bainbridge (2004) broadly supports the nonlinear association by citing evidence for two competing processes in the relationship between religious and nonreligious paranormal beliefs. Under one process, involvement in traditional religion may discourage nonreligious belief because the religion's belief system is sufficient for an adequate understanding of life and the universe, so there is simply no need for further paranormal concepts; indeed, to this end the religious group may explicitly proscribe or belittle such beliefs. At the same time, conventional religion may implicitly facilitate nonreligious paranormal belief by appearing to endorse the general validity of supernatural explanations of human and physical phenomena. Bainbridge's data suggest that both of these processes occur (see also Torgler, 2007); indeed, the two opposing processes may operate even within the same person and serve to cancel each other out. In any event, such moderating factors as church attendance or other active involvement in an organised religion could undermine the application of simple linear correlational methods for probing the association between religious and nonreligious paranormal belief.

Another variable in the religious domain to have been investigated in this context is religious affiliation, that is, the specific religion or religious denomination with which the individual identifies. At least within the range of religions and denominations so far canvassed, nominal religious affiliation appears to have only weak links with the intensity of paranormal belief. Religious affiliation has been reported to have no significant correlation with either global paranormal belief (Jones *et al.*, 1977) or ESP belief (Murphy and Lester, 1976). In one survey of American college students, however, Duncan *et al.* (1992) found that Protestants had stronger beliefs than had Catholics in the devil, possession by the devil and witches, but weaker beliefs in reincarnation and haunted houses. Similarly, Donahue (1993) reported slight variation across six Protestant denominations in the endorsement of New Age beliefs such as astrology and reincarnation, although even this variation may have been confounded by regional factors. Sheils and Berg

(1977) claimed a relationship between belief in a broad range of parapsychological phenomena and religious orthodoxy, but Thalbourne's (1981) reanalysis of their data indicated the result was not statistically significant.

The association of paranormal belief with religion can be explored not only in relation to beliefs but also to behaviours. Indeed, studies of the role of religious affiliation may erroneously assume that such affiliation means involvement in religious activity. The danger of this assumption is suggested by MacDonald's (2000) study of Canadian college students with a declared religious affiliation; MacDonald found that students who were actively involved in religious observance had a *lower* level of nonreligious paranormal belief than those who were not active in their religious expression.

Looking now specifically to research on religious practices, we note that Haraldsson (1981) found ESP belief among Icelanders to correlate positively with praying, attendance at religious gatherings and reading about religious matters. Similar results were obtained for an American sample by Thalbourne (1984). Church attendance, the most common religious practice to be surveyed in this context, is reported to have no relationship with global paranormal belief (Jones *et al.*, 1977) nor with belief in various parapsychological phenomena (Alcock, 1975; Sheils and Berg, 1977), but Plug (1975) and Wuthnow (1976) found a negative relationship between church attendance and belief in astrology.

In summary, some data do suggest a positive relationship between paranormal belief and aspects of religious belief and practice and to this extent there is a degree of empirical support for the worldview hypothesis. That is, some traditional religious beliefs and some specific nonreligious paranormal beliefs might well reflect, at least in part, a broad subjectivist approach to the world at large. On the other hand, there are also reports of *negative* relationships between religious variables and a few specific paranormal beliefs, as well as several failures to find any association. These suggest the worldview hypothesis is by no means universally applicable.

Other beliefs and attitudes

There are additional indications that paranormal belief is concomitant with (other) rather subjective notions of the ways in which the world functions. One respect in which this may be the case is in regard to the psychological world. The very nature of paranormal belief suggests that paranormal believers see humans as more than mere physical or biological structures. This impression is borne out by some empirical work. Stanovich (1989) reported ESP belief to correlate positively with a dualist (mind/body) philosophy of human nature; this finding has been replicated by Svensen *et al.* (1992) and Thalbourne (1999) in Australian samples and indeed some writers (Humphrey, 1995; Schumaker, 1990) deem dualism to characterise the fundamental predisposition to paranormal belief. Paranormal believers' conviction in nonphysical dimensions of human existence is reflected also in their beliefs about their post-mortem fate; ESP belief (Andrews and Lester,

1998; Haraldsson, 1981; Thalbourne, 1996) and global paranormal belief (Irwin, 1985b) are positively correlated with belief in life after death. That believers immerse themselves in subjective aspects of life is supported further by reported associations between the level of belief in ESP or broader parapsychological phenomena and both an inclination to interpret dreams (Haraldsson, 1981; Irwin, 1985b; Thalbourne, 1984, 1998) and an inclination to be self-reflective or to devote attention to subjective experience more generally (Davies, 1985; Glicksohn, 1990).

The subjective worldview may be evident in other domains, too. One such domain may entail the belief in a just world, that is, the fanciful notion that good people will tend to fare well in life and bad people one day will inevitably get their just desserts. Some unpublished data of my own suggest a (weak) relationship between belief in a just world and paranormal belief, at least for New Age beliefs, although the data of Thalbourne (1995a) failed to confirm this. Believers also may be readier than sceptics to amend their notions of the world's operation purely on the basis of their subjective interpretations of events (Delpech, 1957). Similarly, in one of my own studies (Irwin, 2003a) using the *World Assumptions Scale* (Janoff-Bulman, 1989) both New Age and traditional paranormal beliefs were found to correlate with the tendency to infer a sense of the world's meaningfulness from life events. Parker (2000) also has documented this relationship in the context of psi belief.

Paranormal believers' general tendency to adopt a subjective worldview does not necessarily mean that they reject the value of contributions made by those who promote an objective worldview. People who believe in the paranormal neither distrust nor reject science (Otis and Alcock, 1982), nor do they have idiosyncratic attitudes to the scientific investigation of ESP (Johnson and Jones, 1984; but *cf.* McClenon, 1982) or to modern technological society (Schouten, 1983).

More direct investigations of the worldview hypothesis

In an endeavour to test the worldview hypothesis in a more direct way Zusne and Jones (1982, pp. 192–4) developed the *World View Scale*. This questionnaire contains items reflecting either a subjective or an objective view of the universe and human behaviour. In a preliminary study (Zusne and Jones, 1982) global paranormal belief was reported to be greatest for people scoring high in subjectivism on this scale. Subsequently, however, Zusne and Jones (1989) dismissed the statistical significance of their findings as unimpressive. Their factor analysis of the scale also suggested that the questionnaire was not a sufficiently pure index of subjectivism/objectivism, being confounded with another dimension involving a need to understand the world.

An experimental study by Sappington (1990) can be interpreted as another relatively direct test of a link between subjectivism and paranormal belief. Sappington sought to manipulate the level of endorsement of paranormal belief by groups of experimental participants. One technique was to provide objective information about paranormal phenomena in the form of a videotape about parapsychologists' research efforts to authenticate these phenomena. Emotional information about the phenomena was manipulated through a videotape in which the presentation of parapsychological research was supplemented with a commentator's enthusiastic descriptions of personal accounts of the paranormal. Sappington found that the endorsement of paranormal beliefs could be changed by increasing the participants' emotional arousal but not by varying the amount of objective information provided to participants. To the extent that emotional arousal serves to heighten subjectivism in reasoning processes, Sappington's finding could be interpreted as consistent with the role of a subjective worldview in paranormal beliefs.

Other interpretations of Sappington's (1990) experimental results nevertheless are possible. It is feasible, for example, that the presentation of personal anecdotes made participants more willing to be frank about their personal paranormal beliefs as distinct from merely expressing a view on the perceived persuasiveness of research being conducted in parapsychological laboratories. It could be instructive to undertake a similar experiment that utilises a videotape of self-described 'parapsychologists' speaking enthusiastically or sceptically or neutrally about their experimental findings and then to assess separately the participants' paranormal beliefs and their opinions of the persuasiveness of parapsychological experiments.

An assessment of the worldview hypothesis

Notwithstanding the shortcomings of past attempts to test the worldview hypothesis in a relatively direct manner and despite a few contrary empirical findings, it is fair to say there is diverse correlational evidence in general support of the hypothesis. Although most of the available data bear upon global paranormal belief rather than on specific dimensions, they are certainly informative and should be taken into account by any comprehensive theory of paranormal belief.

The worldview hypothesis nevertheless does not seem sufficient in itself. Granted some tendency of paranormal believers toward subjectivism, there remains a need for more fundamental determinants of paranormal belief to be ascertained. That is, what styles of cognitive processes and of personality underlie paranormal beliefs and this broader subjectivist belief system alike?

The 'worldview' associated with paranormal belief also goes beyond being merely 'subjective' to encompass such aspects as the extent to which the person regards life as subject to his or her control. Three principal lines of research are pertinent to this issue.

The first explores the notion that paranormal believers may have unwarranted beliefs about the extent to which they are unable to influence their own feelings and perceptions of life events. Study of this notion has relied on the *Irrational Belief Scale*, a measure of respondents' inclination to hold beliefs identified by Ellis (1962) as common but nonetheless irrational assumptions about the unavoidability of external influences upon their feelings and behaviour. Scores on this scale have been found to correlate positively with beliefs in traditional religious concepts, spiritualism, precognition and superstitions (Roig *et al.*, 1998; Tobacyk and Milford, 1983). Again, this finding certainly is consistent with the subjectivist worldview hypothesis but it also signals the potential significance of the person's specific beliefs about control.

The second approach to the assessment of self-perceived control in the worldview of the paranormal believer studies self-efficacy. Self-efficacy pertains to the expectation that one can successfully take steps to achieve desired outcomes in various domains of life. Tobacyk and Shrader (1991) reported that both general self-efficacy and social self-efficacy correlated negatively with the superstition component of the *Revised Paranormal Belief Scale* (RPBS; Tobacyk, 1988); correlations with other factors of the RPBS were not reported. Although further research of this kind is warranted, Tobacyk and Shrader's finding is consistent with the notion that paranormal believers generally see themselves as lacking the ability to exercise control over facets of their life.

The third line of research concerns the more fundamental dimension of locus of control. This construct refers to people's disposition to believe their fate either to be in their own hands or to be the consequence of external factors beyond their control. Those who believe personal outcomes are contingent largely on their own behaviour and attributes are said to have an *internal* locus of control. People with an *external* locus of control, on the other hand, believe personal outcomes are governed predominantly by other powerful individuals and institutions, luck, chance and so on.

Although there may be some variation across cultures (Davies and Kirkby, 1985; Groth-Marnat and Pegden, 1998; Peltzer, 2002; Tobacyk and Tobacyk, 1992) and for people who perform as mediums or psychics (McGarry and Newberry, 1981), the general trend is that paranormal belief is associated with an external locus of control. This relationship has been documented for global paranormal belief (Allen and Lester, 1994; Dag, 1999, 2002; Göritz and Schumacher, 2000; Groth-Marnat and Pegden, 1998; Irwin, 1986; Jones *et al.*, 1977; Peltzer, 2002; Randall and Desrosiers, 1980; Thalbourne *et al.*, 1995; Tobacyk and Milford, 1983) and for specific beliefs in ESP (Allen and Lester, 1994; Dag, 1999; Irwin, 1986; Polzella *et al.*, 1975; Thalbourne *et al.*, 1995), precognition (Dag, 1999; Groth-Marnat and Pegden, 1998; Irwin, 1986; Thalbourne *et al.*, 1995; Tobacyk and Tobacyk, 1992), witchcraft (Dag, 1999; Groth-Marnat and Pegden, 1998; Peltzer, 2002; Tobacyk, Nagot and Miller, 1988; Tobacyk and Tobacyk, 1992), superstitions (Allen and Lester, 1994; Dag, 1999; Davies and Kirkby, 1985; Irwin, 1986; Jahoda, 1970; Peltzer, 2002; Peterson, 1978; Scheidt, 1973; Thalbourne *et al.*, 1995; Tobacyk, Nagot and Miller, 1988; Tobacyk and Tobacyk, 1992; Todd and Brown, 2003), spiritualism (Allen and Lester, 1994; Dag, 1999; Davies and Kirkby, 1985; Groth-Marnat and Pegden, 1998; Thalbourne *et al.*, 1995; Tobacyk and Tobacyk, 1992), reincarnation (Alprin and Lester, 1995) and extraordinary life forms (Allen and Lester, 1994; Dag, 1999; Tobacyk and Milford, 1983). The two fundamental dimensions of Traditional Paranormal Beliefs and New Age Beliefs have also been reported to correlate with an external locus of control (Newby and Davis, 2004). On the other hand, belief in traditional religious tenets may be related to an *internal* locus of control, particularly in women (Mohammadi and Honarmand, 2007).

In a similar vein paranormal belief is also related to the extent to which a person views his or her life as being governed by luck. Irwin (2000c) identified two relationships in this context. First, endorsement of nonreligious paranormal beliefs, particularly precognition, was associated with a global belief in luck. Second, people who believe in both extraordinary life forms and superstitions were inclined to believe they were often the victims of bad luck. In this context it may be instructive to note McGarry and Newberry's (1981) finding that students who endorse paranormal beliefs perceive the world as unpredictable, difficult or problem-laden and unjust.

Paranormal believers of various sorts therefore are inclined to maintain that they are vulnerable to external forces beyond their control. Thus, paranormal believers are relatively likely to see the world in which they live as rather threatening (Sica *et al.*, 2002). I will readdress this theme in the next two chapters when I survey styles of thinking and personality factors in paranormal belief.

In summary, the worldview hypothesis has been valuable in drawing broad attention to the idea that paranormal beliefs are part and parcel of a fundamentally subjective perspective on life. At the same time there are empirical findings that point to the additional presence in the believer's worldview of a sense of vulnerability to uncontrollable events in life. This factor would seem to have explanatory potential beyond the immediate context of correlations between paranormal belief and locus of control. First, it is possible that perceived vulnerability to uncontrollable events and a concomitant need for a sense of control could underpin many of the research findings offered in support of the worldview hypothesis. That is, observed correlations of paranormal belief with religious beliefs and practices, a dualist philosophy, belief in post-mortem survival and perception of the world as unpredictable and problem-laden might readily be reframed in terms of an underlying need for control over life (and death). Second, the limited evidence consistent with the social marginality hypothesis (see Chapter 4) might equally be reinterpreted in terms of a need for control experienced by socially marginalised groups. These considerations indicate the importance of proceeding to an examination of the personality dynamics that might be served by both paranormal and associated belief systems.

Chapter 6: The cognitive deficits hypothesis

There is no rigid distinction between cognitive variables and personality variables and certainly the status of either in any given person has implications for the other. But the intended emphasis of this chapter is on thought processes that may be differentially characteristic of paranormal believers; broader aspects of believers' personality profiles are addressed in Chapter 7.

Many sceptical researchers have had a particular interest in the nature of cognitive processes associated with paranormal belief. The hypothesis underlying this interest is usually not formalised, but for convenience of exposition it will here be referred to as the *cognitive deficits hypothesis*. Under this view the believer in the paranormal is held variously to be illogical, irrational, credulous, uncritical and foolish. Alcock (1981, pp. 48–53), for example, depicts paranormal believers as credulous, dogmatic and generally inept in basic intellectual skills.

Admittedly, some of the sceptical commentary on parapsychological issues is purely rhetorical, designed in part to discredit parapsychological research as a legitimate scientific enterprise (Irwin, 1999a). Thus, even parapsychologists themselves are targets for sceptical derision: the discipline of parapsychology is debunked as a 'pseudoscience' (Alcock, 1981) and 'a prime example of magical thinking' (Bunge, 1991, p. 136), its researchers are ridiculed as 'closet occultists' (Romm, 1977) and its explanatory concepts are dismissed as 'a reversion to a pre-scientific religio-mystical tradition' (Moss and Butler, 1978, p. 1077).

At the same time there is rather more to the sceptical position than mere belligerent rhetoric. A substantial body of sceptical research has been devoted to the empirical specification of the supposed cognitive deficits associated with paranormal belief. Regardless of its original inspiration, the data base generated by this research effort is an important contribution to the study of paranormal belief in that it testifies to the cognitive processes of paranormal believers, whether or not these processes are deemed deficient in some respect. The aim of the present chapter is to provide a systematic survey and critique of research bearing on the cognitive deficits hypothesis.

Cognitive correlates of paranormal belief

Cognitive correlates of paranormal belief examined by researchers include general educational attainment; level of scientific and other specialist education; intelligence, reasoning skills and memory abilities; attributional processes; and creativity and imagination. Each of these topics is addressed in turn.

Educational attainment

One potential index of cognitive functioning is general educational attainment. A few studies therefore have examined the relationship between paranormal belief and marks achieved in academic work. Consistent with the cognitive deficits hypothesis the grades of college students were found by Belanger (1944) to correlate negatively (but weakly) with superstitiousness and similar findings have been reported for global paranormal belief (Messer and Griggs, 1989; Musch and Ehrenberg, 2002) and for belief in ESP, precognition and psi generally (Messer and Griggs, 1989). Also using a college student population, Tobacyk (1984) reported a negative correlation between grade point average and both superstitiousness and belief in spiritualism. In a sample of high school students, on the other hand, grade point average was found to correlate *positively* with both belief in psi and traditional religious belief (Tobacyk *et al.*, 1984).

It is difficult here to disentangle the effects of educational achievement from those of social indoctrination. That is, in high school students a belief in psi might well be indicative of an inquiring mind, but in the course of further education students may become increasingly aware of the derision of paranormal beliefs by many academics. Further research might usefully be undertaken into interactions between paranormal beliefs, grades, age (or educational stage) and awareness of instructors' attitudes.

A more convenient index of educational attainment is the familiar demographic variable, 'highest level of education'. The level of paranormal belief among university and college students is deemed by some researchers to be unacceptably high in some absolute sense (Wilson and Frank, 1990), but comparative studies of the relationship between level of education and the intensity of paranormal belief have proved to be rather inconsistent. Tobacyk *et al.* (1984) unexpectedly found that global paranormal belief was related positively to highest educational attainment, a finding replicated by Farha and Steward (2006), but in other studies the reverse was found (Lord, 1958; Schulter and Papousek, 2008); nonsignificant findings have also been reported (e.g., Sjöberg and Wåhlberg, 2002). The relationship for ESP or psi belief is positive in some studies (Emmons and Sobal, 1981b; Haraldsson, 1985b, p. 149; Newport and Strausberg, 2001; Rice, 2003; Tobacyk *et al.*, 1984) and negative in others (Gray, 1987; Haraldsson, 1985b, p. 149; Otis and Alcock, 1982; Pasachoff *et al.*, 1970). Educational attainment seems to correlate positively with belief in witchcraft (Emmons and Sobal, 1981b; Tobacyk *et al.*, 1984) and alternative health practices (Ni *et al.*, 2002) and to correlate negatively with belief in spiritualism (Newport and Strausberg, 2001; Otis and Alcock, 1982), superstitions (Blum and Blum, 1974; National Science Foundation, 2002; Schuyler, 1939; Torgler, 2007; Wuthnow, 1976), astrology and UFOs (Donahue, 1993; National Science Foundation, 2002; Newport and Strausberg, 2001; Rice, 2003; Salter and Routledge, 1971). Results for traditional religious belief (Christopher *et al.*, 1971; Emmons and Sobal, 1981b; Johnson, 1997; Jupp, 2008; Newport and Strausberg, 2001; Otis and Alcock, 1982; Sobal and Emmons, 1982) and for extraordinary life forms (Emmons and Sobal, 1981b; Otis and Alcock, 1982; Sobal and Emmons, 1982; Tobacyk *et al.*, 1984) are mixed.

The variability of these findings might be due in part to methodological differences across studies. Some investigators have surveyed members of the general adult population, some have surveyed groups of students at different stages of their education and others have compared across samples of the general public, students and academics. In any event, educational attainment is surely a very crude measure of cognitive functioning and depending on the context could be confounded with socioeconomic status, chronological age, generational differences, developmental level, social roles associated with particular vocations and exposure to forms of social indoctrination other than education. Additionally, the direction of causation is equivocal: for example, an observed association between religiosity and low educational achievement may be due to adolescents' heavy engrossment in religious matters to the neglect or even the abandonment of their studies (Barker, 1989). Unless these potential confounds are statistically or procedurally controlled, educational attainment will not provide a viable variable for an incisive assessment of the cognitive deficits hypothesis.

Scientific and other specialist education

A few researchers have endeavoured to relate paranormal belief more specifically to the amount of scientific education the individual has had. Singer and Benassi (1981) even went so far as to suggest that the population level of paranormal belief can be used as an index of the inadequacy of science education in the US.

In these studies the typical experimental design has been to examine paranormal belief in university and college students across various academic majors. Two studies (Otis and Alcock, 1982; Padgett *et al.*, 1981), however, surveyed paranormal beliefs of professors in different disciplines.

Salter and Routledge's (1971) study of global paranormal belief yielded the unanticipated result that students enrolled in the natural or biological sciences had stronger paranormal belief than did students of the humanities. In other investigations of specific paranormal beliefs, this finding nevertheless is reversed. In comparison to students in the humanities, science students have weaker paranormal belief (Aarnio and Lindeman, 2005; Bhushan and Bhushan, 1987; Morier and Keeports, 1994; but see Walker *et al.*, 2002) and, more specifically, lower belief in ESP (Happs, 1987; Padgett *et al.*, 1981), parapsychological phenomena (Otis and Alcock, 1982), psychic healing (Gray and Mill, 1990), New Age therapies (Grimmer and White, 1992), UFOs (Happs, 1987), superstitions (Gilliland, 1930; Lehman and Fenton, 1929; Preece and Baxter, 2000; Smith, 1930; Vicklund, 1940; Za'rour, 1972), astrology (Gray and Mill, 1990; Preece and Baxter, 2000), spiritualism and traditional religious belief (Otis and Alcock, 1982).

One interpretation of this trend is that exposure to the principles of scientific thinking will reduce the level of paranormal belief (e.g., Valentine, 1936).

Commentators such as Dudycha (1933) and Lilienfeld *et al.* (2001), however, caution against any expectation that a general program of scientific education will generalise substantially to paranormal belief. Indeed, Matthews (1996, p. 97) has lamented, 'years of science instruction just washed over students'. For education to have a major impact on the level of paranormal belief the educational program may have to be specific to the paranormal.

The empirical literature offers a good deal of support for this case. Various sceptically oriented courses explicitly debunking the paranormal are reported to have had the effect of reducing the strength of all manner of paranormal beliefs (Banziger, 1983; Caldwell and Lundeen, 1932; Emme, 1940, 1941; Gray, 1984, 1985, 1987; McBurney, 1976; Tobacyk, 1983c; Wesp and Montgomery, 1998; Zapf, 1938). A course more sympathetic to the scientific scrutiny of parapsychological claims, on the other hand, was found by Irwin (1990b) to influence paranormal beliefs differentially, there being a slight enhancement of belief in PK but a fall in belief in superstitions, extraordinary life forms, witchcraft and one traditional religious concept (the devil). Similar courses in experimental parapsychology were found by Vitulli (1997) to have no effect on the level of ESP belief and by Clarke (1991b) to have no effect on any of a range of paranormal beliefs.

On balance, therefore, it remains unclear if observed associations between education and paranormal belief may be ascribed to a cognitive aptitude for 'critical thinking' or, on the other hand, to the individual's exposure to information (in the guise of 'real facts') and academically desirable views, or indeed to some combination of both. Once again, in the context of evaluating the cognitive deficits hypothesis it seems educational variables are simply too ambiguous to serve as reliable indices of cognitive functioning.

Intelligence and memory abilities

An immediately obvious means of testing the cognitive deficits hypothesis is to assess the relationship between paranormal belief and intelligence (IQ). For reasons that remain opaque there is, however, a dearth of research into this relationship. Several early studies of superstitiousness (e.g., Belanger, 1944; Emme, 1940, 1941; Ter Keurst, 1939; Zapf, 1945b) found this paranormal belief to correlate negatively (but weakly) with IQ; many years later Killen *et al.* (1974) and Thalbourne and Nofi (1997) confirmed those results. The only study to have comprehensively examined specific types of paranormal belief in this context appears to be that by Smith *et al.* (1998). In this investigation IQ correlated negatively with belief in psi, precognition and spiritualism, as well as with global paranormal belief. These findings are consistent with the cognitive deficits hypothesis, although it would seem that not all types of paranormal belief are related to intelligence. Null results, however, have also been reported (e.g., Stuart-Hamilton *et al.*, 2006). Additionally, one contrary finding has been reported by Jones *et al.* (1977). To their expressed surprise, these researchers found a *positive* correlation between intelligence and global paranormal belief. Although it is at odds with the data of Smith *et al.* (1998), this finding would appear to stand as a challenge to the cognitive deficits hypothesis, perhaps all the more so because of the investigators' sceptical orientation. Nonetheless, it should be noted that although the findings on IQ and paranormal belief are mixed, the data base is still very small. This issue will have to be clarified by further research.

Another possibility is that paranormal believers are deficient not in general intelligence but in a particular type of intelligence. Specifically, paranormal belief might be related to poor skills in dealing with quantitative concepts. A few researchers have explored this possibility in the context of the person's comprehension of mathematical probability. French (1992) has argued that if some people have an inaccurate notion of the likelihood of a given event occurring by chance alone, they may be inclined to dismiss too readily an explanation of that event as chance and to accept instead a paranormal account. For example, if the chances of a dream 'coming true' purely by chance are assumed to be very low, the dreamer may be relatively likely to construe the dream as extrasensory or precognitive. A similar position is taken by Sutherland (1992) and by Esgate and Groome (2001).

Consistent with this view, Blackmore and Troscianko (1985) and Brugger *et al.* (1991) reported evidence that ESP believers sometimes are poorer than nonbelievers in estimating the probability of events. On the basis of such data, Brugger *et al.* (1995, p. 1306) concluded that 'belief in ESP might thus arise from an overestimation of the meaningfulness of naturally occurring coincidences'. O'Keeffe and Villejoubert (2002) have cautioned, however, that the index of paranormal belief used in the above studies was psychometrically inadequate. Further, it should be noted that in these studies the probability estimation task typically related to the outcomes of rolling dice or dealing a hand of cards. When Blackmore (1997) conducted a study using items more closely representative of real-life situations, there was no differential tendency for ESP believers to underestimate the probability of events. It should be added that there seems little reason to expect the probability misjudgment view of ESP belief to generalise to other paranormal beliefs. Indeed, Roberts and Seager (1999) and Stuart-Hamilton *et al.* (2006) were unable to replicate the finding of Blackmore and Troscianko (1985) when the index of paranormal belief was global rather than confined to ESP. Musch and Ehrenberg (2002) also reported that when differences in general cognitive ability are statistically controlled, the apparent relationship between paranormal belief and poor understanding of probability is eliminated. Again, Dagnall *et al.* (2007a) and Rogers *et al.* (in press) found that paranormal believers did not show a generalised misunderstanding of the various principles of probability theory, but rather, they had different standards when judging if an outcome would be likely to arise by chance. A comprehensive study by Bressan (2002) found that rather than misunderstanding probability as such, paranormal believers were simply more likely to ascribe meaning to ambiguous situations. For example, paranormal believers were more ready to perceive patterns in essentially random sequences (see also Blackmore and Moore, 1994; Bressan *et al.*, 2008; Brugger, Regard, *et al.*, 1993). Perhaps for this reason paranormal believers are more inclined than nonbelievers to see correspondences between horoscopes and their lives, even when the horoscopes are not generated on the basis of their own birth sign (Munro and Munro, 2000; Wiseman and Smith, 2002). Similarly, paranormal believers may be relatively inclined to ascribe validity to an assessment of their personality divined from their handwriting (so-called graphology), even when the assessment is a 'one size fits all' description generated without any reference to themselves (Boyce and Geller, 2002).

At present, there is insufficient evidence to support a conclusion that paranormal believers in general are deficient in quantitative intelligence. The findings cited in support of this view might be better explained in terms of a difference between believers and nonbelievers in the style with which they approach a quantitative reasoning task (see also Matthews and Blackmore, 1995). This issue is examined more specifically below in relation to the contrast between intuitive-experiential and analytical-rational reasoning styles.

The possible association between paranormal belief and memory, another facet of human intelligence, has been all but ignored by researchers. A study of tangential relevance here was undertaken by Dudley (1999a). Students were asked to complete the *Revised Paranormal Belief Scale* (Tobacyk, 1988), a task construed by Dudley to engage participants in a 'critical evaluation of paranormal phenomena' (p. 313). The experimental group of participants was asked to rehearse a five-digit number while completing the belief questionnaire, whereas the control group was not. The experimental group showed a slightly higher average global paranormal belief than did the control group. This finding is interpreted by Dudley as demonstrating the importance of devoting sufficient working-memory capacity to the task of making a critical decision as to whether or not a phenomenon is truly paranormal. For some readers the implicit corollary of this interpretation may be that people subscribe to a paranormal belief because they have insufficient working-memory capacity to critically evaluate the underlying proposition about an anomalous phenomenon. Both Dudley's interpretation and the corollary are moot, for the following reasons. First, there is the slightly pedantic point that completing the paranormal belief questionnaire does not entail a judgment about the 'paranormality' of phenomena but rather a judgment of how strongly one agrees (or disagrees) that the phenomena occur. Second and more fundamental in the present context, is that Dudley's experimental task is not an index of the total capacity of a person's working memory but rather a means of demonstrating that completion of the belief questionnaire makes demands on working memory or requires 'mental effort'. The results of the study therefore may attest to the necessity of 'mental effort' in making a critical decision to endorse or not to endorse a paranormal belief, but they cannot properly be taken to show that people believe in the paranormal because they are actually *incapable* of allocating or *disinclined* to allocate due mental effort when they assess the validity of a paranormal claim. In particular, Dudley's study does not establish the differential memory abilities of paranormal believers and it thereby has no strong implications for the cognitive deficits hypothesis.

More recently, Wilson and French (2006) found an association between global paranormal belief and the tendency to create 'false memories' or to surmise one has had a specific encounter when in fact this is not the case. It remains unclear if this finding attests to poorer memory skills of paranormal believers or to some other more fundamental cognitive characteristic such as suggestibility.

On balance, it seems reasonable to conclude that research into paranormal believers' intelligence and memory skills has yet to yield unequivocal support for the cognitive deficits hypothesis.

Reasoning skills and reasoning styles

Not surprisingly, sceptical commentators have been especially focused on the role of flawed reasoning processes in the formation of paranormal beliefs. Thus, Shermer (1997) has proposed that most paranormal believers are 'normal people whose normal thinking has gone wrong in some way' (p. 45). A similar view was propounded by Gilovich (1991). On these grounds some researchers have investigated the relationship between paranormal belief and reasoning skills.

A variety of procedures has been utilised to index reasoning skills in such studies. By use of a *Critical Thinking Appraisal Scale*, Alcock and Otis (1980) observed believers in psi phenomena to have poorer critical thinking ability than did a group of nonbelievers, although Hergovich and Arendasy (2005) failed to replicate this finding. Gray and Mill (1990) devised fictitious abstracts of flawed scientific studies to assess critical abilities, finding a negative correlation between performance on this measure and the level of paranormal belief. Polzella *et al.* (1975) reported ESP believers to be less successful than nonbelievers in assessing the validity of three-term syllogisms. Under a similar experimental procedure, Wierzbicki (1985) found a relationship between global paranormal belief and errors in syllogistic reasoning. This finding is further supported by Roberts and Seager (1999), who reported that the intensity of paranormal belief is related to performance on a conditional (syllogistic) reasoning task but not to that on a probabilistic reasoning task.

Tobacyk and Milford (1983) nevertheless caution that uncritical thinking might not be characteristic of all dimensions of paranormal belief. Only two of the seven dimensions of their *Paranormal Belief Scale* — traditional religious beliefs and spiritualism — correlated significantly with a measure of uncritical inference; the former was associated with critical inference and the latter, uncritical inference. Using a nonverbal measure of reasoning ability, Hergovich and Arendasy (2005) found statistically significant negative correlations with the dimensions of traditional paranormal beliefs, traditional religious belief and superstition, but the correlations for all other dimensions were not significant. Notwithstanding the discrepant findings for traditional religious belief reported in these two studies, at best the available data may be taken to suggest that uncritical thinking is related to only some facets of paranormal belief.

A further potential limitation of the above studies of paranormal believers' reasoning skills is that in every instance the research was conducted by publicly professed sceptics. It is feasible that the relatively critical thinkers in these samples were aware of the investigators' sceptical attitude toward the paranormal and took this as a cue to be reticent about their own paranormal beliefs. That is, the observed relationships between paranormal belief and reasoning skills may have been generated as an unintentional experimenter effect, the suppression of the acknowledgment of paranormal beliefs among socially insightful participants.

Providing some support for this interpretation is a study by Irwin (1991a). The study was conducted in a setting in which the investigator is generally recognised as one who adopts an even-handed approach to parapsychological claims and who is not intent on debunking the paranormal. In this setting, all but one dimension of paranormal belief was found to be unrelated to reasoning skills: only strong religious beliefs were associated with relatively poor reasoning skills. However, even the latter correlation may have been an artefact of reticence. Within the Australian population from which Irwin's sample was drawn, there is a common attitude that 'clever' people are not religiously inclined. The sole significant relationship in Irwin's study therefore could still have been due to some critical thinkers' reluctance to acknowledge their religious beliefs rather than to cognitive deficits among believers. In another study by a parapsychologist, Roe (1999) similarly found that psi believers and nonbelievers did not differ in their capacity to identify logical flaws in accounts of fictitious experiments. This equivalence was reported also by Cook (2002), a parapsychology student, although she did establish a correlation between paranormal belief and the level of confidence expressed in the findings of the psi-supportive experiment. A recent constructive replication of Irwin's (1991a) study by Watt and Wiseman (2002; Wiseman and Watt, 2002) generally confirmed Irwin's findings, but their data suggested further that with a sceptical researcher paranormal believers evidently are more strongly motivated to perform well on the reasoning task than are nonbelievers. Thus, the differential findings of parapsychologists and sceptics may be due more to motivational effects on subjects' performance in the reasoning task than to effects on performance with the paranormal belief measure.

In addition to the context of the study the content of the reasoning task may impact on the results. Merla-Ramos (2000) reported that believers in witchcraft, extraordinary life forms and superstition solved relatively fewer syllogisms when the content of the syllogism concerned the paranormal rather than neutral topics and religious believers performed relatively poorly on syllogisms with religious content. Thus, it may be difficult for people to reason objectively when the context of the problem-solving task touches on deeply held beliefs, whatever those beliefs may be. Other studies confirm this effect (Evans *et al.*, 1983), although null findings have also been reported (e.g., Lawrence and Peters, 2004).

It is feasible that paranormal belief is fundamentally related not so much to reasoning *skill* as to reasoning *style*. Epstein and his co-workers (Denes-Raj and Epstein, 1994; Epstein, 1994; Epstein *et al.*, 1996; Pacini and Epstein, 1999) have shown that people vary in their relative reliance on two styles of reasoning or systems of information processing. The *analytical–rational* style is a rather slow, deliberative, effortful, conscious and primarily verbal process of conventionally logical or objective analysis of information, whereas the *intuitive–experiential* style is a rapid, automatic, subconscious, holistic and primarily nonverbal ('intuitive') process of subjectively driven analysis of information. Although people will use each of these reasoning styles depending on prevailing circumstances, a person may have a habitual preference for one or the other. Lindeman (1998) proposed that paranormal and other 'pseudoscientific' beliefs are associated with a tendency to prefer the intuitive–experiential style of reasoning. A report by Wolfradt *et al.* (1999) indicated that global paranormal belief is associated more strongly with reliance on the intuitive–experiential style than on the analytical–rational style, although both reasoning styles did seem to be implicated, at least in their sample of university students. Additionally, in a constructive replication (Uwe Wolfradt, personal communication, 7 April 2001) using the subscales of the *Revised Paranormal Belief Scale* (RPBS), the intuitive–experiential style was reported to have small but statistically significant correlations with belief in psi, precognition, spiritualism, witchcraft and superstition but not with traditional religious belief nor belief in extraordinary life forms. None of the belief subscales correlated significantly with the analytical–rational style, although most of the coefficients were negative. In a replication with a general community sample Irwin and Young (2002) found the intuitive–experiential style to correlate positively with all seven subscales of the RPBS (.32 to .45) and with both the New Age Philosophy factor (.50) and the Traditional Paranormal Beliefs factor (.42) of Lange *et al.*'s (2000) rescaling of the RPBS; conversely, the analytical–rational style correlated negatively with all seven subscales of the RPBS (-.17 to -.31), New Age Philosophy (-.29) and Traditional Paranormal Beliefs (-.23). Irwin and Young's data are slightly stronger and more clear-cut than those reported by Wolfradt and his colleagues, in part perhaps because they come from a community sample rather than university students. This basic finding has been replicated by Aarnio and Lindeman (2005), Genovese (2005) and Marks *et al.* (2008).

Styles of reasoning therefore seem to have some bearing on paranormal belief. Additionally, reliance on an intuitive–experiential style of reasoning may be a factor in intolerance of ambiguity, that is, a tendency to make precipitate interpretations of ambiguous situations. This is of interest in light of a reported relationship between intolerance of ambiguity and both traditional religious belief (Thalbourne *et al.*, 1995) and UFO belief (Houran, 1997), although the relationship with one index of global paranormal belief may be negative (Houran and Williams, 1998; Thalbourne and Houran, 2000). Incidentally, Keinan (1994) reported a similar link between low tolerance of ambiguity and magical belief (see Ch. 7).

Possibly consistent with the above pattern is the finding in some studies of a tendency for believers often to rely on the right cerebral hemisphere for semantic processing of information (Brugger, Gamma, *et al.*, 1993; Brugger, Regard *et al.*, 1993; Leonhard and Brugger, 1998; Pizzagalli *et al.*, 2001; Pizzagalli *et al.*, 2000). Such processing is coarse and poorly focused by comparison to left-hemisphere semantic processing and it can evoke a relatively high number of loose or uncommon semantic associations. The latter is characteristic of creative thought and of schizotypal thought patterns (Weinstein and Graves, 2002); these topics are addressed in a subsequent section of the present chapter and in Chapter 7.

Another cognitive style that may affect reasoning by the paranormal believer is field dependence, the tendency for environmental cues (the 'field') to influence perception of a focal object; for example, in judging the horizontality of a rod the field dependent person will be heavily influenced by the orientation of a frame surrounding the rod. Field dependence has been found to be a correlate of global paranormal belief, superstitiousness and psi belief (Hergovich, 2003; Roney-Dougal, 1987; Snel *et al.*, 1995). Field dependence is also an index of suggestibility, of which more will be said later in this chapter.

Finally, in the context of cognitive style mention may be made of the recent work of Lindeman (Lindeman and Aarnio, 2006, 2007; Lindeman and Saher, 2007; Lindeman *et al.*, 2008). She begins by differentiating three fundamental ontological categories termed physical, psychological and biological. Some people make confusions about the key characteristics of these categories; specifically, they attribute to a phenomenon in one category a core characteristic of another category. The walls of a house, for example, may be said to hold memories of past events at that site; in this instance a physical object (a wall) is construed to have an essentially psychological characteristic (memory). Research confirmed that paranormal believers are inclined to commit these ontological confusions (e.g., Lindeman and Aarnio, 2007; Lindeman *et al.*, 2008). The data reported by Lindeman and her colleagues can be interpreted in terms of the thinking styles of paranormal believers and thus warrant acknowledgment in this section of the review. Lindeman herself, however, uses the findings to argue for the validity of *defining* paranormal beliefs to entail such ontological confusions. That is, under Broad's (1949) definition of paranormality (see Chapter 1), the 'limiting principles' of science that are violated by paranormal phenomena entail the tenet that the core characteristics of each ontological category are specific to that category. Lindeman's research has interesting implications for differentiating paranormal beliefs from other scientifically disputed constructs (e.g., UFOs and cryptids cannot properly be regarded as paranormal under Lindeman's proposal), but this is an issue I defer for consideration in Chapter 8.

In summary, although study of the relationship between intelligence and paranormal belief seems to offer limited support for the cognitive deficits hypothesis, research on the reasoning styles of paranormal believers may be rather more illuminating for the bases of paranormal belief. Indeed, the role of an intuitive–experiential style of reasoning in this context is consonant with the account in Chapter 1 of the formation of what Sperber (1990) has termed *intuitive beliefs*. Further discussion of this view is undertaken in Chapter 8.

Attributional processes

In the previous chapter I noted that most facets of paranormal belief are related to an *external* locus of control, that is, a tendency to construe personal life events as being governed predominantly by other powerful individuals and institutions or by chance rather than by one's own behaviour and attributes. A relatively consistent pattern in how a person explains causally the things that happen to him or her is called by psychologists an *attributional style*. Attribution theory has been extended beyond the construct of locus of control (e.g., see Weiner, 1980, 1986), so that a person's causal attribution of an event is now typically classified in terms of at least three dimensions (Peterson *et al.*, 1982): its locus or controllability (internal or external causation), stability (whether the perceived causal process is depicted as stable and likely to persist into the future or as unstable and subject to change) and globalness (whether the perceived causal process is thought to influence just the specific event under consideration or a range of other events, too).

Documenting paranormal believers' attributional style is clearly of importance, as such research would potentially illuminate the cognitive processes through which a person constructs a given personal experience or reported phenomenon as 'paranormal' (see also Wiseman and Watt, 2006). It is regrettable therefore that apparently only one study has investigated the relationship between paranormal belief and attributional style beyond the dimension of locus of control. Dudley and Whisnand (2000) administered the *Revised Paranormal Belief Questionnaire* (Tobacyk, 1988) and the *Attributional Style Questionnaire* (Peterson *et al.*, 1982) to a small group of college students. The findings are reported in a very cursory manner, with the researchers observing that global paranormal belief was associated with 'a depressive attributional style' (p. 864). On the basis of earlier research on attributional style in depressed students (Seligman *et al.*, 1979), I take this to mean that global paranormal belief correlated positively with a tendency to make external, unstable and specific attributions about the causes of desirable events and internal, stable and global attributions about the causes of undesirable events. As Dudley and Whisnand combined into a 'composite positive score' the data on all three attributional dimensions and on both types of events (desirable and undesirable), it is a moot point as to whether the data do attest to each and every aspect of the pattern of a depressive attributional style described above. It is possible, for example, that the result reflected only the well-documented correlation with locus of control, with no contribution from the stability and globalness dimensions. In response to my query on this point Tom Dudley (personal communication, 10 April 2001) advised that none of the correlations between global paranormal belief and the individual attributional dimensions were significant; the predicted association was found only when the composite index was calculated. The possible relationship between paranormal belief and attributional style therefore remains inadequately studied. It could also be informative to know the attributional style associated with each separate type of paranormal belief, as there seems no necessity for these styles to be uniform (see Langdon and Coltheart, 2000).

To the extent that Dudley and Whisnand's (2000) findings do suggest a 'depressive attributional style' in paranormal believers and that this cognitive style is considered a psychological defect, some readers may infer that there is some support here for the cognitive deficits hypothesis. As argued above, however, this relationship is not well attested and further research on the issue is called for. The potential role of the affective state of depression in paranormal belief is addressed further in Chapter 7.

Creativity

Unlike the theme of deficits, correlates that are potentially complimentary to paranormal believers have received scant empirical consideration, particularly from sceptical investigators. There have nevertheless been suggestions (e.g., Krippner, 1962; Murphy, 1963) that parapsychological phenomena are associated with the creative personality. Perhaps, then, the cognitive domain of creativity has some significance for paranormal belief.

The empirical literature provides some indications that characteristics associated with the creative personality correlate with paranormal belief. Moon (1975) reported ESP belief to be higher in artists than in nonartists, a result that might be attributable to creativity. Other investigators have made a more direct test of the association by relating paranormal belief to standardised measures of creativity. Thus, Joesting and Joesting (1969) established a positive correlation between belief in ESP and creativity and Davis *et al.* (1974), Thalbourne and Delin (1994) and Thalbourne (1998, 2000) reported a similar result for belief in psi. Gianotti *et al.* (2001) also found a difference between paranormal believers and nonbelievers on a test of verbal creativity (the novelty of verbal associations). The relationship is supported further by observed relationships between paranormal belief and a close correlate of creativity known as *sensation seeking:* the individual's need for stimulation and variety of experience. Sensation seeking has been found to correlate positively with belief in psi (Davis *et al.*, 1974; Kumar *et al.*, 1993; Tobacyk and Milford, 1983; Zuckerman *et al.*, 1972), spiritualism (Tobacyk and Milford, 1983) and astrology (Brown *et al.*, 1974). There is one report of a small negative correlation between sensation seeking and superstitiousness (Curtis and Wilson, 1997), but this was not observed in other studies (e.g., Tobacyk and Milford, 1983).

Possibly related to the association between paranormal belief and creativity are findings of electroencephalographic studies that indicate paranormal believers have higher right-hemisphere activity and reduced or 'atypical' hemispheric asymmetry (Brugger, Gamma *et al.*, 1993; Brugger, Regard *et al.*, 1993; Leonhard and Brugger, 1998; Pizzagalli *et al.*, 2000; Pizzagalli *et al.*, 2001; Schulter and

Papousek, 2008). The right hemisphere of the brain is generally believed to be implicated in creative thought.

In any event, at least for some dimensions of paranormal belief, creativity is a pertinent factor. Again, this finding does not sit well with the cognitive deficits hypothesis, although the implacable sceptic might seek to interpret it in terms of suggested associations between creativity and psychopathology. The possible link between paranormal belief and psychological disturbance is addressed in Chapter 7.

Imagination

The evidence for a relationship between paranormal belief and creativity raises the somewhat broader question of whether paranormal believers tend to have a relatively active imagination. Believers' inclination to devote attention to their subjective experience (Davies, 1985; Glicksohn, 1990) has already been noted and Bainbridge (1978, p. 43) reported that some paranormal believers concede 'it is good to live in a fantasy world every now and then'. One index of the tendency to fantasise is hypnotic susceptibility: people with a strong fantasy life are not only creative but are also highly susceptible to hypnosis (Lynn and Rhue, 1988; Wilson and Barber, 1983). In this light, it is interesting to note that hypnotic susceptibility has been found to correlate positively with global paranormal belief (Atkinson, 1994; French *et al.*, 2001; Haraldsson, 1985a; Hergovich, 2003; Nadon *et al.*, 1987; but see Groth-Marnat *et al.*, 1998–9; Saucer *et al.*, 1992) and with the individual dimensions of belief in psi (Pekala *et al.*, 1992; Thalbourne, 1995b; Wagner and Ratzeburg, 1987), precognition, witchcraft, spiritualism (Haraldsson, 1985a), superstition (Hergovich, 2003) and UFOs (Pekala *et al.*, 1992). Collectively these results suggest that paranormal belief is linked to a cognitive style that involves a good deal of fantasising.

More direct scrutiny of this view is provided by measures of a personality construct known as *fantasy proneness*. Fantasy proneness entails a propensity to fantasise a large part of the time and to be deeply absorbed in or fully experiencing what is being fantasised (Lynn and Rhue, 1988). Two studies (Irwin, 1990a, 1991b) established that fantasy proneness correlates positively with global paranormal belief and with belief in traditional religious concepts, psi, witchcraft, spiritualism, extraordinary life forms and precognition. This general relationship has been successfully replicated by Lawrence *et al.* (1995), Allison (1996), Thalbourne *et al.* (1997), Thalbourne (1998), Perkins (2001), Finch (2002) and Rogers *et al.* (2007), although Sherwood (1999) failed to find such a relationship with retrospectively assessed fantasy proneness in childhood. One study (Lack *et al.*, 2003) documented a correlation between fantasy proneness and superstitiousness in the context of creative work, although the relationship with superstitious belief as more generally conceived was not significant in any of the other studies cited above. Believers in extraterrestrial aliens may also be fantasy prone (Bartholomew *et al.*, 1991; French *et al.*, 2008; Newman and Baumeister, 1996); most of the available data are not supportive of this view (Ring and Rosing,

1990; Rodeghier *et al.*, 1991; Spanos *et al.*, 1993), but on various methodological grounds Appelle *et al.* (2000) concluded that the issue remains open. Finally, in an experimental study Woolley *et al.* (2004) found that belief in a witch could most easily be induced in children who were fantasy prone.

Fantasy proneness is one facet of the domain of dissociative tendencies, that is, a habitual proneness to fragment or structurally separate mental processes that ordinarily would be integrated (Spiegel and Cardeña, 1991). There is some evidence that the capacity for dissociation and particularly that of a more pathological ilk, is positively correlated with global paranormal belief and with specific beliefs in psi, precognition, traditional religious concepts, spiritualism, witchcraft, superstition and extraordinary life forms (French *et al.*, 2008; Irwin, 1994b; Makasovski and Irwin, 1999; Rattet and Bursik, 2001; Sharps *et al.* 2006; Wolfradt, 1997). In terms of Lange *et al.*'s (2000) two factors of paranormal belief, dissociation was found by Houran *et al.* (2001) to correlate positively with New Age Philosophy but not with Traditional Paranormal Beliefs (black magic). Tobacyk, Wells and Miller (1998) also found believers in psi, spiritualism and extraordinary life forms to exhibit a relatively high incidence of dissociative (specifically, out-of-body) experience. Thalbourne and Houran (2000) similarly reported an association between global paranormal belief and a tendency to be introspective; it is possible the latter tendency is in part a dissociative characteristic.

The association between paranormal belief and fantasy proneness or dissociation is of interest not only in its own right but also in relation to the issue of the origins and functions of paranormal belief. Fantasy proneness and dissociative tendencies more generally seem to emerge partly as a result of childhood trauma such as physical abuse (Irwin, 1994c, 1999b; Lynn and Rhue, 1988). It is possible, therefore, that childhood trauma is a factor in explaining the individual's fundamental openness to paranormal belief (see Chapter 7).

So what does the empirical literature have to say for the cognitive deficits hypothesis? In light of the above review it must be said that the cognitive deficits hypothesis appears to be rather more successful as a polemical device for sceptical commentators than as an empirically grounded theory of paranormal belief. Studies of intelligence and reasoning skills are not encouraging for the hypothesis. Indeed, the findings of some of these studies and of investigations of other cognitive processes potentially less deprecatory of paranormal believers (e.g., creativity and reasoning style) suggest that the cognitive deficits hypothesis does not adequately depict the thought processes underlying paranormal belief. A more incisive understanding of the latter might be achieved by taking greater account of psychodynamic issues. It is to this topic that I now turn.

Chapter 7: The psychodynamic functions hypothesis

It is virtually a psychological axiom that beliefs are held because they serve significant psychodynamic needs of the individual (Katz, 1960). According to Taylor (Taylor, 1983; Taylor and Brown, 1988), beliefs can perform this function whether they are grounded in objective reality or are intrinsically delusory and thus parapsychologists and sceptics alike are interested in the functions served by paranormal beliefs.

The general view that paranormal beliefs are needs-serving will be termed the *psychodynamic functions hypothesis*. Sceptics usually take this hypothesis to mean that paranormal believers are in some respects psychologically deviant or dysfunctional and although this is not a necessary implication of the hypothesis, the personality correlates of paranormal belief clearly are data to be taken into account in this regard. Research into these correlates is reasonably substantial. The empirical literature nonetheless is fragmented and in need of some systematisation. The following survey thus constitutes both an attempt towards systematisation of the literature and a context for the assessment of the psychodynamic functions hypothesis.

Personality correlates of paranormal belief

Personality variables that have been studied as potential correlates of paranormal belief fall into three broad categories: social dimensions of personality, aspects of psychological adjustment and specifically psychopathological characteristics. In the following sections each of these categories is surveyed in turn.

Social dimensions of personality

One major facet of personality concerns the quality of the individual's interpersonal or social behaviour. To the extent that some paranormal beliefs are socially deviant it might be expected that these beliefs would correlate with social dimensions of personality.

Although paranormal believers may seek out others with similar views they may well be, according to Northcote (2007, p. 19), 'very much alone' in these interests. Introversion nevertheless does not appear to be related either to global paranormal belief (Charumathy and Anantharaman, 1983; Gallagher *et al.*, 1994; MacDonald, 2000; Thalbourne *et al.*, 1995; Willging and Lester, 1997; Williams *et al.*, 2007; Windholz and Diamant, 1974) or to most of its component dimensions

(Lester and Monaghan, 1995; Lester *et al.*, 1987; Page, 1935; Peltzer, 2002; Sjöberg and Wåhlberg, 2002; Ter Keurst, 1939; Thalbourne *et al.*, 1995), although there may be a tendency for traditional religious believers (MacDonald, 2000; Maltby and Day, 2001; Thalbourne *et al.*, 1995) and ESP believers (Peltzer, 2002; Thalbourne,1981; Thalbourne *et al.*, 1983; Thalbourne and Haraldsson, 1980) to be slightly extraverted.

This might be taken to suggest that the paranormal believer certainly is not inclined to be more socially withdrawn than the nonbeliever. On the other hand, Tobacyk (1985c) and Tobacyk and Pirttilä-Backman (1992) reported global paranormal belief and belief in psi, witchcraft, superstitions, spiritualism, extraordinary life forms and precognition to be positively correlated with a measure of social alienation. Similarly, Plug (1975) found a weak negative association between belief in astrology and the inclination to respond in a socially desirable way, although Zimmer (1984) observed no relationship between social alienation and UFO belief.

The characterisation of the paranormal believer as a socially alienated person is supported by evidence concerning social interest, that is, the capacity to transcend the limits of the self and to relate to the needs of other people. Thus, Tobacyk (1983b; Tobacyk and Tobacyk, 1992) found negative correlations between social interest and belief in psi, witchcraft, superstition, spiritualism, extraordinary life forms and precognition; the only dimension to correlate positively with social interest was traditional religious belief. The tendency among believers toward social alienation does not seem to be founded on any lack of trust in other people (McBeath and Thalbourne, 1985; Tobacyk, 1983b) nor on rebellious tendencies (Heard and Vyse, 1998). Rather, it appears to testify to a greater devotion of interest to the self than to others. With the exception of traditionally religious people, paranormal believers generally have low social motivation (Davis *et al.*, 1974). The lack of social interest is allied with low social anxiety: although most paranormal beliefs do not correlate with the tendency to respond in socially desirable ways (Tobacyk, 1985a), they are related to a lack of fear of social ridicule (Davies, 1985).

Research on the social aspects of personality therefore has yielded a reasonably coherent psychological profile. People who endorse nonreligious paranormal beliefs may be as sociable as nonbelievers, but perhaps believers are inclined to be more interested in the world of their own subjective experience than in the needs of other people. If this characterisation seems somewhat exaggerated, at least it signals the importance of addressing more specifically the psychological adjustment of paranormal believers.

Psychological adjustment

The sceptical view that paranormal believers are dysfunctional is addressed most directly by studies of psychological adjustment. One facet of psychological adjustment is the individual's perception of the self. Tobacyk and Milford (1983) studied the discrepancy between perceptions of the actual self and the ideal self in relation to paranormal belief, but the only dimension of belief to correlate with this measure was traditional religious belief: specifically, religious people saw their actual and ideal selves to be more closely matched than did nonreligious people. Fitzpatrick and Shook (1994) found that belief in precognition and superstitiousness were *positively* correlated with an index of self-esteem. Based on these few studies it would seem, therefore, that none of the various forms of paranormal belief is associated with a lack of self-esteem and for a few paranormal beliefs the reverse might be the case. Similarly, paranormal beliefs are not found to correlate with a failure to achieve a sense of one's identity (Fitzpatrick and Shook, 1994; Tobacyk, 1985b). On the other hand, some paranormal believers may have a relatively grandiose sense of their own importance and uniqueness. Tobacyk and Mitchell (1987) reported positive correlations between a measure of narcissism and belief in psi, witchcraft, spiritualism and precognition and the same relationship for psi belief was observed by Roe and Morgan (2002). Far from lacking self-esteem and a sense of identity, these paranormal believers may well feel specially empowered and be preoccupied with fantasies of unlimited power and success (Tobacyk and Mitchell, 1987). The significance of a need for a sense of control once again is indicated.

As a group, paranormal believers do not present as anxious people. Neither global paranormal belief nor most of its individual dimensions correlate with trait anxiety (Irwin, 1995; Jones *et al.*, 1977; Perkins, 2001; Smith and Karmin, 2002; Tobacyk, 1982; *cf.* Roe and Bell, 2003, 2007). On the other hand, there is a large literature linking religiosity to a subjective sense of well-being (Hackney and Sanders, 2003), with some reports of an association between religious belief and lower anxiety in adolescents (Abdel-Khalek, 2002) and in college students (Harris *et al.*, 2002). One study has identified a weak association between paranormal belief and hypochondria (Houran, Kumar, Thalbourne and Lavertue, 2002), but hypochondria does not signify a generalised state of anxiety.

The individual's anxiety about death also has received some study in this context. Traditional religious believers appear to have a relatively clear view about death's place in their life, although this conceptual understanding evidently has no bearing on other dimensions of paranormal belief (Tobacyk, 1983a; Tobacyk and Milford, 1983; Tobacyk and Pirttilä-Backman, 1992). At an emotional level, however, attitudes to death are more significant. A measure of the extent to which death and its implications are disturbing correlates positively with virtually all nonreligious dimensions of paranormal belief: death concerns are relatively substantial among believers in psi, witchcraft, superstitions, extraordinary life forms and precognition (Tobacyk, 1983a; Tobacyk and Pirttilä-Backman, 1992). Perhaps the intrinsic uncontrollability of death looms large in the minds of nonreligious paranormal believers. On the other hand, Lange and Houran (1997) reported a negative correlation between global paranormal belief and death anxiety. Lange and Houran's paradoxical finding nevertheless does accord with those for religious belief. Thus, although a sudden surge in death anxiety may serve to activate a belief in an afterlife at least in the short term (Osarchuk and Tatz, 1973), death anxiety appears to be relatively *low* among traditional religious believers (Alvarado *et al.*, 1995; Roff *et al.*, 2002; Thalbourne, 1996; but see Power and Smith, 2008). With regard to death anxiety as a correlate of paranormal belief, differentiation between religious and nonreligious beliefs might therefore be essential; use of a measure of global paranormal belief (as by Lange and Houran) may obscure these relationships.

Paranormal belief may be related to depression and bipolar (manic) depression, but to date the findings are mixed (*cf.* Andrews and Lester, 1998; Beck and Miller, 2001; Francis and Kaldor, 2002; Irwin, 1995; Miller *et al.*, 2002; Nambi *et al.*, 2002; Sharps *et al.*, 2006; Thalbourne and Delin, 1994; Thalbourne and French, 1995; Zebb and Moore, 2003). It is possible that paranormal belief is related not so much to depression as a *trait* or enduring characteristic of the person but rather to the *state* of depression. That is, paranormal belief might be high in situations that evoke a transitory mood of depression. Dudley (1999b, 2000) has conducted two studies suggesting that when a state of depression is induced in experimental participants, their paranormal beliefs are temporarily increased or activated. In one study (Dudley, 1999b) students were tested on the superstition scale of the *Revised Paranormal Belief Scale* (RPBS), then given a very difficult word puzzle to solve and immediately retested for the prevailing level of superstitious belief. By comparison to participants in a control condition, this group's level of superstitious belief was found to be higher after the state of relative helplessness had been induced in the participants. This finding was replicated by Kahler (2001) for belief in superstitions and in witchcraft but not for the other factors of the RPBS. Given that helplessness is a key cognitive feature of depression (Abramson *et al.*, 1978), Dudley's (1999b) experiment might be taken to suggest that paranormal belief may be linked with state depression. On the other hand, the pivotal factor here might well be the person's perceived controllability of the situation rather than state depression as such. The topic of perceived control is raised again later in this chapter. Nonetheless, Dudley's research has made a substantial contribution in highlighting the fact that the intensity of paranormal beliefs may vary not only among people but also with the situation. Contextual aspects of paranormal belief clearly deserve closer scrutiny by researchers.

Neuroticism is another key personality variable that has been studied in relation to paranormal belief. A positive relationship has been found between neuroticism and global paranormal belief (Gallagher *et al.*, 1994; Jawanda, 1968; Thalbourne *et al.*, 1995; J. Waugh, cited by Marks, 1986; Williams *et al.*, 2007; Windholz and Diamant, 1974) and for specific paranormal beliefs in traditional religious concepts, psi, precognition, witchcraft, spiritualism and astrology (Fichten and Sunerton, 1983; Thalbourne *et al.*, 1995), although null results also have been reported (MacDonald, 2000; Peltzer, 2002; Sjöberg and Wåhlberg, 2002), especially for school children (Lester and Monaghan, 1995; Ter Keurst,

1939; Willging and Lester, 1997). On the other hand, in terms of the fundamental personality dimensions (Costa and Widiger, 1994) the principal personality correlate of global paranormal belief appears not to be neuroticism but, rather, openness to experience (Egan *et al.*, 1999; Eudell and Campbell, 2007; Gallagher *et al.*, 1994; MacDonald, 2000), a dimension which in itself is not maladjustive, although it may be linked with a readiness to experiment with drugs and to engage in diverse esoteric practices. Interestingly, the correlation between openness to experience and traditional religious belief appears to be negative (Roccas *et al.*, 2002; Taylor and MacDonald, 1999; but see Wink *et al.*, 2007), contrary to that for paranormal belief more generally.

Although paranormal believers may be open to new experiences, they appear to be relatively reluctant to change their established beliefs (Bader, 1999; J. Waugh, cited by Marks, 1986), a finding that might be taken as indicative of at least rigidity or dogmatism. A few dimensions of paranormal belief do correlate positively with dogmatism, particularly belief in witchcraft, traditional religious concepts, superstition and psi (Alcock and Otis, 1980; M. Davies, personal communication, 15 March 2002; Thalbourne *et al.*, 1995; Tobacyk and Milford, 1983; *cf.* Auton *et al.*, 2003). Some writers (e.g., Zusne and Jones, 1982) view such findings as consistent with the notion that some paranormal believers have poor psychological adjustment. On the other hand, findings in relation to conscientiousness and authoritarianism, two personality correlates of dogmatism, do not fit well with this conclusion. Although conscientiousness in adolescence may be positively related to later religiosity (Wink *et al.*, 2007), conscientiousness was found by Egan *et al.* (1999) to be *negatively* related to global paranormal belief and findings for authoritarianism are mixed (Canetti and Pedahzur, 2002; Heard and Vyse, 1998; Randall, 1991). The relationship between paranormal belief and dogmatism may have more to do with a style of belief formation and maintenance than with psychological adjustment as such.

Few other explicit assessments of paranormal believers' general psychological adjustment have been undertaken. Some of the early studies (e.g., Maller and Lundeen, 1934; Ter Keurst, 1939; Zapf, 1945b) found a negative relationship between adjustment and superstitiousness, but more recent data (Irwin, 1991b, 1995; Tobacyk and Milford, 1983) do not confirm this. Irwin (1991b) found global paranormal belief and belief in witchcraft correlated negatively with one index of psychological adjustment, but these findings were not replicated with other measures of adjustment (Irwin, 1995). Religious belief, on the other hand, typically shows a positive relationship with psychological adjustment (for a review see Dew *et al.*, 2008).

The basis of possible links between paranormal belief and adjustment also deserves closer scrutiny. Sceptical commentators (e.g., Alcock, 1981) seem to construe paranormal belief as a *symptom* of maladjustment, but other interpretations can be advocated. For example, paranormal beliefs might be activated when the person's adjustment is under strain; that is, paranormal beliefs may serve as a type of adaptive behaviour or *coping mechanism* (Irwin, 1992; Lillqvist and Lindeman, 1998). The following discussion of the role of these beliefs as a coping mechanism also brings us closer to the issue of the *functions* of paranormal belief.

The use of religious faith in the management of problems in life is a familiar strategy and is also the subject of some psychological research (e.g., Baldacchino and Draper, 2001; Fabricatore, 2002; Kay *et al.*, 2008; Maynard *et al.*, 2001; Pargament, 1997; Pargament *et al.*, 1988; Siegel *et al.*, 2001; Taylor, 2001; Wong-McDonald and Gorsuch, 2000), but little attention has been given to the possible role of other paranormal beliefs as a coping mechanism. In the broader context factor-analytic studies have differentiated three global types of coping style (Cook and Heppner, 1997; Endler and Parker, 1994; Lazarus and Folkman, 1984). *Task-oriented coping* entails an attempt to actively change or eliminate a problematic situation (e.g., attacking the source of stress directly or trying to negotiate a compromise). In *emotion-oriented coping* the overriding concern is for one's psychological integrity and thus this coping style focuses on the management of emotional distress (e.g., seeking sympathy from another person or projecting blame onto another person). Finally, in *avoidant coping* one simply tries to ignore the problem or distance oneself from it (e.g., distracting oneself with other activities or denying that the situation is of any personal consequence). Callaghan (2000; Callaghan and Irwin, 2003) investigated the association between these coping styles and the two factors of the *Revised Paranormal Belief Scale* extracted by Lange *et al.* (2000). She found Traditional Paranormal Beliefs correlated positively with emotion-oriented coping, (marginally) negatively with task-oriented coping and nonsignificantly with avoidance; New Age Philosophy correlated positively with an avoidant style, negatively with task-oriented coping and (marginally) positively with the emotion-oriented style. All statistically significant relationships nevertheless were very weak. A similar study by Rogers *et al.* (2006) suggested that these relationships may be moderated by facets of emotional intelligence.

Callaghan's (2000) findings are not encouraging for the view that paranormal beliefs are a type of coping mechanism. On the other hand, it might still be argued that such beliefs constitute a coping style that is different in kind from the above three styles, as Carver *et al.* (1989) have argued for religious belief (see also Pargament, 1997). Further, it is possible that paranormal beliefs are relatively specialised for use in defending against a specific type of perceived threat to the individual. There is certainly more scope for investigating the notion that rather than being a symptom of maladjustment, activation of paranormal belief is an adaptive response to a particular class of perceived threat to the person's psychological well-being. Further speculation on this issue is undertaken later in the chapter.

Psychopathology

The search for evidence of psychopathological tendencies in paranormal believers has not been pursued by sceptical researchers as enthusiastically as one might expect. There are, of course, frequent clinical observations of paranormal beliefs among psychologically disturbed patients (Fisman and Fisman, 1999; Greyson, 1977; Page, 1935; Persinger, 1987; Yip, 2003), but the issue demands rather more rigorous empirical investigation than isolated case studies permit. To date, the study of psychopathological tendencies as a correlate of paranormal belief has been undertaken for only a small number of dimensions.

As temporal lobe epileptics commonly report parapsychological experiences and paranormal beliefs, some researchers have investigated the possibility of a link between paranormal belief and complex temporal lobe symptoms among members of the general (i.e., nonclinical) population. A questionnaire index of complex temporal lobe signs is reported to correlate with global paranormal belief (MacDonald and Holland, 2002; Persinger and Makarec, 1991–2; Simmonds and Roe, 2000) and with beliefs in psi, precognition, spiritualism, witchcraft, superstition and extraordinary life forms (Morneau *et al.*, 1996; Persinger and Richards, 1991; Skirda and Persinger, 1993). This is not to imply that paranormal believers typically are prone to epileptic seizures; rather, believers and nonbelievers evidently tend to differ in temporal lobe lability, that is, the incidence, duration and intensity of transient electrical activity in the temporal lobe of the brain as purportedly measured by the questionnaire.

The validity of the questionnaire index of temporal lobe lability nevertheless has been subject to some criticism (Ross, 1994) and therefore electroencephalographic (EEG) investigation of the above relationship is called for. As noted earlier, EEG studies indicate that paranormal believers have higher right-hemisphere activity and reduced or otherwise 'atypical' hemispheric asymmetry (Brugger *et al.*, 1993; Gianotti *et al.*, 2002; Leonhard and Brugger, 1998; Pizzagalli *et al.*, 2000; Pizzagalli *et al.*, 2001; Schulter and Papousek, 2008), but data bearing specifically on temporal activity are lacking.

Of all possible psychopathological correlates of paranormal belief, greatest scrutiny has been given to magical ideation, an index of schizotypy, or proneness to schizophrenia. Schizotypy is a dimensional variable; that is, it indexes varying degrees of schizophrenic-like behaviours that occur in the general population (Claridge, 1997). Although Windholz and Diamant (1974) had observed that global paranormal belief was correlated with the Schizophrenia scale of the *Minnesota Multiphasic Personality Inventory* (MMPI), subsequent interest in this issue was instigated largely by Eckblad and Chapman's (1983) inclusion of items about parapsychological phenomena in the construction of their *Magical Ideation Scale*. The implication was that the interpretation of personal experience in terms of paranormal belief was symptomatic of schizotypy. In an investigation of this notion, Thalbourne (1985) found that an independent measure of ESP belief was correlated with magical ideation scores whether or not the parapsychological items were retained in Eckblad and Chapman's scale. Thalbourne and his colleagues have replicated this result in several different samples (Thalbourne, 1994, 1998; Thalbourne *et al.*, 1995; Thalbourne *et al.*, 1997; Thalbourne and Delin, 1994; Thalbourne and French, 1995).

More recent studies by Gallagher *et al.* (1994), Genovese (2005), Goulding (2004, 2005), Peltzer (2003), Pizzagalli *et al.* (2000), Simmonds (2001) and Simmonds and Roe (2000) have confirmed a positive relationship between global paranormal belief and schizotypy. In an extension of Thalbourne's (1985) initial study Anderson (1988) found ESP belief and global paranormal belief correlated positively with magical ideation (with or without the parapsychological items), as well as with a measure of schizotypy distinct from magical ideation. Anderson's results admittedly may have uncertain generality: Anderson used trance mediums to represent extreme paranormal believers and it is doubtful that this population would be typical of believers in general (see McGarry and Newberry, 1981). Again, Williams (1989) reported that magical ideation (with or without the parapsychological items) correlates positively with global paranormal belief and with belief in traditional religious concepts, psi, witchcraft, superstition, spiritualism, extraordinary life forms and precognition. With the exception of traditional religious belief, Williams also confirmed these results using a different index of schizotypy. Much the same pattern was found by Tobacyk and Wilkinson (1990), Thalbourne *et al.* (1995) and Peltzer (2003), except in regard to traditional religious belief: in Tobacyk and Wilkinson's (1990) sample the correlation for traditional religious belief was negative for men and nonsignificant for women and in Peltzer's (2003) sample this correlation was not statistically significant. This disparity might reflect differences in religious conservatism between the Louisiana population sampled by Tobacyk and Wilkinson, the Australian population sampled by Williams and by Thalbourne *et al.* (see also Irwin, 1991a) and the South African population sampled by Peltzer. Lester's (1993) American sample and Sjöberg and Wåhlberg's (2002) Swedish sample also showed a negative relationship between belief in religious concepts and psychoticism. The bases of the contradictory findings for traditional religious belief warrant further investigation, but at least there is a consistent trend in the relationship of nonreligious paranormal beliefs to schizotypy. In addition, there are reports of a positive correlation between schizotypy and both belief in UFOs (Chequers *et al.*, 1997; Parnell, 1988) and New Age beliefs (Farias *et al.*, 2005).

There is, therefore, a clear association between proneness to schizophrenia and a wide range of paranormal beliefs (with traditional religious belief a possible exception to this trend). Many sceptics presumably would rest their case at this point: people who endorse nonreligious paranormal beliefs are simply 'crazy'. But two major objections may be raised to a conclusion formulated in these extreme terms.

First, the data on the relationship between paranormal belief and schizotypy simply do not justify the baldness of the sceptical interpretation. With the strength of the correlation at about .6 or less (e.g., Thalbourne, 1985; Thalbourne and Delin, 1994), the majority of the variance in paranormal belief is *not* explained by schizotypy. Further, the schizotypy scores of paranormal believers are by no means at a grossly psychotic level. In a follow-up to her original survey Williams (Williams, 1995; Williams and Irwin, 1991) found that although members of an Australian psychical research group and a sample of schizotypes (close relatives of people with schizophrenia) had similar paranormal beliefs, the former group had lower schizotypy scores, almost as low as those of a control group from the general population. The research findings thus point at most to a partial role of a mildly dysfunctional tendency rather than to the pivotal involvement of severe, overt psychiatric disturbance. This is not to deny that some schizophrenic patients have paranormal beliefs but rather to assert that paranormal believers cannot be dismissed out of hand as suffering schizophrenic delusions. Indeed, one study (Irwin and Green, 1998–9) found that paranormal belief had no significant relationship with a proposed biological marker for schizophrenia (Frith and Done, 1989).

Second, there are some identifiable subgroups of paranormal believers to whom the sceptical conclusion does not apply. Compared to the schizotypes, the psychical research group in Williams' (1995) study had low schizotypy scores and they ascribed life events more to personal responsibility than to the role of chance. In other words, the psychical researchers' attraction to paranormal beliefs may reflect rather different psychodynamics from those of schizotypes. Psychical research group members and others actively involved in the paranormal, of course, are not representative of paranormal believers as a whole (McGarry and Newberry, 1981), but Williams' findings indicate the magical ideation research might best be interpreted to show that the characteristic of schizotypy may illuminate the attraction of paranormal beliefs for many *but not all* people. It should be remembered, too, that many schizotypes in the general population lead healthy, well-adjusted lives (Claridge, 1997; McCreery and Claridge, 2002). The sceptical conclusion that paranormal believers are psychologically dysfunctional is therefore at best an overgeneralisation and at worst a misrepresentation.

More recent research has elaborated the relationship between paranormal belief and schizotypy. The domain of schizotypal traits is in fact multifactorial (Mason *et al.*, 1997; Raine *et al.*, 1994), which raises the possibility that paranormal beliefs might be differentially related to the individual facets of schizotypy.

Goulding (2005) reported that paranormal believers in general had elevated scores on all components of schizotypy. At the same time the different types of paranormal belief could vary in their relationship to the dimensions of the schizotypy domain. Such was found to be the case by Irwin and Green (1998–9). The cognitive-perceptual factor of schizotypy, which in the general population parallels the schizophrenic symptom of delusions, was related to belief in spiritualism and precognition, especially for women. The results can be interpreted to suggest that this subset of paranormal beliefs might be endorsed primarily because such beliefs, like delusions, are derived through intuitive–experiential reasoning rather than being grounded on reliable and critically evaluated objective information. Follow-up analyses by Houran *et al.* (2001) similarly found the cognitive–perceptual factor to predict the New Age Philosophy component of paranormal belief (Lange *et al.*,

2000). A study by Hergovitch *et al.* (2008) also confirmed the predictive utility of this factor.

According to Irwin and Green (1998–99) the disorganised factor of schizotypy, indicative of a tendency toward a formal thought disorder, predicted belief in extraordinary life forms and witchcraft and disbelief in precognition and traditional religious concepts, especially among men. This finding cautions against the sceptical generalisation (e.g., Alcock, 1981) that all paranormal believers are necessarily irrational. Schofield and Claridge (2007) also found cognitive disorganisation to relate to people's evaluation of their paranormal experiences.

Finally, the facet of schizotypy concerning interpersonal deficits was found by Irwin and Green (1998–99) to predict belief in spiritualism and disbelief in psi and witchcraft. Perhaps some paranormal beliefs are more dependent than others on effective interpersonal relationships for their dissemination and nurturance. In any event, this result disconfirms the hypothesis that paranormal beliefs are uniformly a consequence of social maladjustment.

The foregoing studies at least indicate the complexity of the association between schizotypy and paranormal belief. Some recent attempts to clarify this relationship have utilised the statistical technique of cluster analysis, a procedure for objectively identifying subgroups of a population defined by their scores on a prespecified set of variables. Cluster analyses of scores on the three factors of schizotypy (e.g., Loughland and Williams, 1997) have revealed four discriminable subgroups. First, there is a cluster of 'low schizotypes' who are marked by low scores on all three factors. Second, 'high schizotypes' show high scores on all factors. Third, 'negative schizotypes' score highly on the factor relating to interpersonal deficits but not on the other two factors. Fourth, 'benign' or 'happy' schizotypes exhibit high scores only on the cognitive–perceptual factor. How do these four schizotypal subgroups rate on paranormal belief? Results of two studies to date (Goulding, 2004; Holt *et al.*, 2008) are mixed, due in part perhaps to the difficulty of replicating the four-cluster solution in small samples, but there are indications that while high schizotypes show relatively strong belief in psi (as expected), so too do benign or happy schizotypes. As benign schizotypes are otherwise well-adjusted (Claridge, 1997; Goulding, 2004; McCreery and Claridge, 2002), these findings further moderate the simplistic conclusion that paranormal believers are quintessentially prone to psychosis. Further investigation of the hypothesis with broader measures of paranormal belief would be welcome.

Collectively the research on this topic prompts a final cautionary comment. That paranormal believers as a group tend to have (some) schizotypal tendencies is more an observation to be explained than a sufficient explanation in itself. It is possible that some clinically oriented variables correlate with paranormal belief simply because they intrinsically entail reality testing deficits. Reality testing entails 'a set of perceptual, cognitive and sensorimotor acts that enables one to determine one's relationship with the external physical and social environments' (Reber, 1995, p. 640). Clinically oriented variables reflecting impaired reality testing may well include schizotypy, as well as dissociativity and fantasy proneness. Each of these dimensions might readily be reconstructed in terms of the concept of reality testing deficits (see Lenzenweger *et al.*, 2001). Further, these correlates of paranormal belief are themselves known to be intercorrelated (Irwin, 2001b; Lynn and Rhue, 1988; Merritt and Waldo, 2000). Thus, the variables' relationship with paranormal belief may point to a more fundamental involvement of reality testing deficits in the formation of such beliefs. Evidence that paranormal beliefs are indeed predicted by deficits in reality testing has been established by Irwin (2003b, 2004) and the role of such deficits is discussed further in the following chapter.

In any event, given that some schizotypal (and other) people may be attracted to specific types of paranormal belief, under the psychodynamic functions hypothesis the question still remains as to the *functions* served by paranormal beliefs for people who may have some mildly dysfunctional tendencies. It is in such terms that an effective theory of paranormal belief should be couched. We therefore now turn more explicitly to the topic of origins and functions.

Personality and the functions of paranormal belief

Although the role of culture and socialisation processes in the formation of paranormal beliefs is not to be denied, as argued in Chapter 2 it is probable that culture is responsible not for paranormal belief *per se* but rather for the specific *forms* that the beliefs might take. That is, membership in various cultural groups and subgroups will govern the characteristics of paranormal beliefs embraced by the individual. For this reason, some correlates of individual dimensions of paranormal belief presumably would reflect the operation of cultural and subcultural factors; for example, generational and gender differences in endorsement of paranormal beliefs may largely reflect socialisation processes. But as Krippner and Winkler (1996) and Schumaker (1990) cogently argued, for these cultural influences to be effective the individual must be intrinsically susceptible to them. The form of paranormal beliefs may have cultural origins but the origins of susceptibility to the beliefs — or the 'need to believe' (Krippner and Winkler, 1996) — must be sought in the psychodynamic domain.

A clue to the psychodynamic origins of paranormal beliefs might be found by examining the psychological functions they may serve. Speculation on these functions has been undertaken principally by sceptics. Alcock (1981, p. 40), Frank (1977, pp. 556–7), Grimmer (1992), Lillqvist and Lindeman (1998), Lindeman (1998), Marks and Kammann (1980, p. 156), Moody (1971/1974, p. 233), Schumaker (1990), Singer and Benassi (1981, p. 50) and Zusne and Jones (1982, p. 210) all advocate the significance in this context of a basic human psychological need for a sense of understanding of life events. An assurance of order and meaning in the physical and social world is thought to be essential for emotional security and psychological adjustment (Anderson and Deuser, 1993; Fisher and Fisher, 1993; Flammer, 1995; Heider, 1958; Hobfoll *et al.*, 2002; Lefcourt, 1973; Rozin and Nemeroff, 1999; Shapiro *et al.*, 1996; Taylor, 1983;

White, 1959). Traumatic events and anomalous experiences, however, pose a potential threat to that assurance, in essence because they imply that the world sometimes is uncertain, chaotic and beyond the individual's understanding and mastery. By incorporating a system of paranormal beliefs, the individual has a cognitive framework for effectively structuring such events so that they appear comprehensible and thereby able to be mastered, at least intellectually. Under this view paranormal belief constitutes a cognitive bias through which reality may be filtered without threatening the individual's sense of emotional security. In essence, paranormal beliefs achieve this effect by creating an 'illusion of control' (Langer, 1975; Presson and Benassi, 1996) over events that are anomalous or are in reality not controllable by the individual.

A few researchers have sought to investigate the hypothesis that paranormal belief represents the creation of an illusion of control as a psychological response to a strong underlying need for control. The first part of the hypothesis is addressed by studies of the illusion of control in paranormal believers. Survey data reported by Tobacyk and Wilkinson (1991) and Joukhador et al. (2004) establish a correlation between paranormal beliefs and the tendency to enjoy games of chance; this is consistent with the view that paranormal believers think they have some control over these games. More direct evidence is provided by an experiment conducted by Blackmore and Troscianko (1985). These researchers asked participants to estimate the degree of control they had over the outcome of a computer-generated coin-tossing task. In half the trials control over the outcome was possible through adept timing of the response to stop the coin spinning; in the remaining trials this strategy could not be exercised. Under both conditions, subjects who believed in ESP felt they were exercising greater control over the outcome than did nonbelievers, yet actual performance on the task did not differ. Similar results are reported by Ayeroff and Abelson (1976) and Benassi et al. (1979). In a questionnaire study Rudski (2003a) also found the illusion of control to correlate with global paranormal belief and with beliefs in superstition and precognition. Collectively these findings are consistent with the view that paranormal belief is associated with an illusion of control.

It must be stressed, however, that the illusion of control is a transitory and situation-specific phenomenon (Sweeney et al., 1980). Paranormal believers do not function under a habitual delusion that they are in control of all facets of their life; indeed, the previously cited data on a relationship between paranormal belief and an external locus of control (see Chapter 5) indicate that paranormal believers perceive much of their life to be governed by factors outside their control. Additionally, it is particularly noteworthy that the illusion of control is found only among people with a high desire for control (Burger, 1992; Burger and Cooper, 1979). It is likely, therefore, that a proneness to the illusion of control over fundamentally uncontrollable events is a simple consequence of paranormal belief and an antecedent need for control. That is, in people with a strong need for a sense of control, the activation of paranormal beliefs may bolster the transient impression that one can influence events that in fact are not contingent on one's behaviour, provided these events are perceived not to be subject to the control of other people and there is also no strong evidence that that one has failed to control the events (Matute, 1994, 1995; Rudski, 2001). In psychodynamic terms, however, the crucial feature of paranormal belief is not that such belief can induce an illusion of control over a limited range of events but rather that it springs from a need for a sense of control in a world that the believer sees as being largely under the control of other people or external factors. A transient illusion of control may in fact do little to redress this perception of the world nor to sate the underlying need for control.

A need for control therefore warrants closer examination as a potential motivational factor in the development of paranormal belief. A few studies have addressed this issue. Irwin (1992) proposed that paranormal believers' underlying need for control over their world might be expressed in the domain of interpersonal behaviour. Psychology students were each asked in a questionnaire (the *FIRO-B* scale; Schutz, 1978) to provide an independent estimate of a close friend's expression of control in behaviour toward other people. These estimates were found to correlate positively with the friends' global paranormal belief scores. When the students' friends completed the *FIRO-B* scale themselves, however, the correlation between controlling tendencies and paranormal belief was not significant. The latter result could have been due to a lack of openness in the individuals' representation of their own interpersonal behaviour but it might also suggest that the need for control may operate outside the individual's awareness. In any event, there are indications here that paranormal believers do have a need for a sense of control over their interpersonal world (or at least that they give that impression to others). In a subsequent study Irwin (2000b) identified two relationships that are instructive in this context. Belief in broadly spiritual tenets was endorsed by people, particularly women, who try to exert strict control over their physical environment but who publicly repudiate any desire for control over life events. In addition, belief in psi, especially among women, was found to be associated with a desire for control over life events and a feeling of control over events in the sociopolitical arena. An unpublished reanalysis of these data in terms of the two factors of paranormal belief identified by Lange *et al.* (2000) indicated that the predictors of New Age Philosophy were similar to those described above for belief in psi, with a weaker trend for the same pattern for Traditional Paranormal Beliefs. A need for control therefore appears to serve as a significant dynamic among paranormal believers.

This theme was further explored in a novel manner by Keinan (2002). In an experimental study Israeli university students were interviewed during either a low-stress condition or a high-stress condition and asked questions designed to elicit the superstitious behaviour of knocking on wood (e.g., 'Has anyone in your immediate family suffered from lung cancer?'). The frequency of this behaviour depended on an interaction between the level of stress and the participant's desire for control: the superstitious behaviour was most evident when people with a strong need for control were under a high level of stress. Admittedly it is not clear that the targeted 'superstitious' behaviour here actually reflected superstitious belief rather than, for example, social convention. Replication of this study for other potential indicators of paranormal belief is warranted. Keinan's finding nevertheless is supported by a card-guessing experiment by Case *et al.* (2004). In this study participants were relatively likely to resort to a superstitious strategy (using a psychic's prediction of the cards' identity rather than their own guesses) when the perceived likelihood of failure was high.

In any event, it seems that paranormal beliefs are activated when people with a need for control are in a stressful situation. More generally, paranormal beliefs may serve to enhance feelings of security in the face of a capricious and threatening world. Although people may realise they have little capacity for actual control over many life events, paranormal belief may engender some vague sense of optimism or *hope* that these events could be controlled, if only by supernatural or magical means. Indeed, people with a strong need for control but who feel that such control is beyond all hope may well be prone to depression (Burger, 1984; Mazure *et al.*, 2000; Wallace and Bergeman, 1997) or at least a low level of subjective well-being (DeNeve and Cooper, 1998). The proposed needs-serving role of paranormal beliefs thus is consistent with the theory of Taylor (1983; Taylor and Brown, 1988) and Fisher and Fisher (1993) that beliefs, whether realistic or delusory, can promote psychological well-being by acting as a buffer against the harsh realities of the world. The psychodynamic functions hypothesis is both buttressed and made more explicit by the empirical findings on the need for control in paranormal believers.

In searching for the origins of paranormal belief, therefore, it is pertinent to ask what prompts this need for control among paranormal believers. Now, it will be recalled that nearly all dimensions of paranormal belief are correlated with fantasy proneness and dissociative tendencies in general. Except perhaps in regard to a belief in witchcraft, this association does not appear to reflect parental encouragement of imagination during childhood (Makasovski and Irwin, 1999). This leaves the other major factor implicated in the development of fantasy proneness or dissociative tendencies: a history of traumatic childhood experiences, particularly physical abuse (Irwin, 1994c, 1999b; Lynn and Rhue, 1988; Sanders *et al.*, 1989; Wilson and Barber, 1983). On these grounds it may be proposed that childhood traumas constitute one of the developmental origins of paranormal belief.

This hypothesis is supported by data from Irwin (1992). In a sample of university students global paranormal belief correlated positively with the extent of intrafamilial physical abuse during childhood; the correlation with a collective index of childhood trauma also was positive, although in this case the statistical significance was borderline. In a constructive replication of this finding, Irwin (1994a) found stronger beliefs in witchcraft, superstitions and precognition among people who had grown up in an alcoholic household than among people who did not have this childhood background. Lawrence *et al.* (1995), Callaghan (2000) and Perkins (2001) also confirmed the correlation between global paranormal belief and a history of childhood trauma. A history of childhood trauma is reported to be common also among believers in extraterrestrial aliens and UFOs (Mack, 1994; Ring and Rosing, 1990), believers in astral travel (Bergstrom, 1999) and people who suddenly undergo a religious conversion or join a sect (Ullman, 1982). A study by Perkins and Allen (2006) focused specifically on the correlate of childhood physical abuse and found it to predict belief in psi, precognition and spiritualism, but not traditional religious beliefs, superstitiousness, or belief in extraordinary life forms.

Each of these studies relied on a retrospective assessment of the severity of childhood trauma. To avoid any methodological confound associated with this method of assessment, French and Kerman (1996) surveyed the paranormal beliefs of adolescents who were attending treatment units as identified victims of abuse. By comparison with a control group, the abused adolescents exhibited stronger paranormal belief.

The childhood traumas surveyed in the above studies often were severe and sustained. It is possible that a *single* experience of trauma may have a less extreme or less durable impact on paranormal belief. For example, Terr *et al.* (1997) interviewed school children who in 1986 had witnessed the explosion of the *Challenger* space shuttle which killed several astronauts including the children's teacher. When tested a few weeks after the traumatic experience, the children showed evidence of paranormal thinking, but this tendency tended to dissipate during the subsequent year. Thalbourne (personal communication, 9 September 1991) has suggested that *any* acute and severe suffering might turn a person's thoughts towards the paranormal. In any event, a history of either ongoing trauma or a series of different traumas may contribute to the development of enduring paranormal beliefs. Indeed, it seems the need for control and concomitant paranormal beliefs might be sustained by the occurrence of unpredictable events even after childhood. Jones *et al.* (1977) reported a positive relationship between global paranormal belief and the frequency of unpredictable changes in one's life during the previous year.

This is not to claim that all traumatised people endorse paranormal beliefs, nor even that only traumatised people become paranormal believers. Trauma might be merely one of a number of factors that can evoke a need for a sense of control and thence an attraction to paranormal belief. Without necessarily having any personal traumatic experience, people are aware that horrific events can occur in life. Without warning and seemingly at random, one could become a victim of any one of manifold instances of natural disaster, accident and violence (Fisher and Fisher, 1993; McKenna, 1993; Schumaker, 1990). Thus, even without a direct encounter with trauma, some people's insecurity in living in an apparently hostile world may continually kindle a need for control. Cognisance of these and other processes underlying the need for control might help to make the model of paranormal belief more comprehensive. Paranormal beliefs may contribute to what Greenberg *et al.* (1986) referred to as 'terror management', the creation of a buffer against the anxiety that may be evoked by an awareness of human vulnerability and ultimate mortality.

Nonetheless, the need for a sense of control, reality testing deficits and the transitory illusion of control over life events, are proposed as potential elements in a comprehensive model of paranormal belief. Further research into these speculations is called for, especially in the following respects.

First, it is not certain that all the above factors are pertinent to each and every dimension of paranormal belief. As noted in previous chapters, paranormal beliefs can differ in the pattern of their correlates and some consideration must therefore be given to the possibility that in order to accommodate all varieties of belief, an effective explanatory model may have to be relatively complex or, alternatively, slightly different models might be required for various subsets of paranormal beliefs. Second, there is a need for more precise identification of the ways in which the proposed factors interact with specific social and cultural contexts to yield the pattern of paranormal beliefs observed in any given individual. Several of these issues are pursued in Chapter 8, where a theoretical integration is attempted.

Chapter 8: Theoretical integration: a causal model of belief in scientifically unaccepted phenomena

In this the final chapter of the monograph I provide some theoretical integration of the diverse empirical evidence surveyed in the earlier chapters. More specifically, my principal task is to formulate a causal model of paranormal beliefs with a particular emphasis on the origins and psychological functions of these beliefs. In the course of this theoretical construction I revisit the issue of defining 'paranormal belief'. Later in the chapter I identify some pivotal issues for future scientific research into these beliefs.

A causal model of paranormal beliefs

A *causal model* of paranormal beliefs is a theoretical account that seeks to accommodate the known correlates of these beliefs in a diagrammatic representation of the fundamental psychological processes that underlie the development of the beliefs among the general population. Such a model differs crucially from a non-causal account. The latter would aim simply to systematise the known correlates of paranormal belief, would be largely descriptive and would not effectively signify nor incisively elucidate essential underlying processes. By contrast, a causal model is not intended merely to encompass the focal phenomenon's different facets and their predictors but is designed to capture or provide insight into the very processes whereby this phenomenon unfolds.

Broadly speaking, the discrete processes nominated in a causal model also have what might be termed a 'superordinate' quality; that is, each component process may not correspond precisely to a single observed correlate but rather would typically aggregate several cognate correlates in an endeavour to capture the essence of each distinct causal element of the model. For this reason the causal model to be expounded here does not have separate representations of peer group influence, gender, external locus of control, intolerance of ambiguity, fantasy proneness, parapsychological involvement and each and every one of the numerous other individually reported correlates of paranormal beliefs. The model focuses instead on specifying the dimensions generalised from the preceding analyses as conceptually the most instructive psychological correlates of paranormal beliefs. Where evidential foundations are not yet sufficient the model may make an occasional conceptual leap in order to stimulate further research into the origins and functions of paranormal beliefs.

Before explicating the model two types of intervening variables in a causal model must be described. A *mediating variable* is one that causally links one variable to another. By way of illustration, if a change in the variable X is deemed to cause a change in the variable Y, and this in turn causes a change in the variable Z (depicted diagrammatically as X→Y→Z), Y is said to 'mediate' the relationship between X and Z. A *moderator* is a variable that affects the strength (and perhaps even the sign) of the relationship between two variables but which in itself does not change; thus, a moderator might be said to be a catalyst for a relationship to occur. By way of illustration, gender may be a moderator of the relationship between parents' religious belief and that of their offspring if, for example, the impact of parental belief differs for sons versus daughters. Note here that while parental belief 'causes' the belief of the offspring, the gender of the offspring necessarily does not change during this process and thus gender is a moderator rather than a mediator of the relationship. Y as a moderator of the relationship between variables X and Z is depicted diagrammatically as follows:

$$X \rightarrow Z$$
$$\uparrow$$
$$Y$$

Note that the moderator Y lies outside the causal chain from X to Z but nonetheless governs the strength or quality of the causal link. In simple terms, a mediator explains *how* one variable is causally linked with another and a moderator governs *when* or *to what extent* the relationship obtains.

The causal model proposed here is represented diagrammatically in Figure 1. The evidence for the model is drawn from the survey of research undertaken in the preceding chapters of the monograph and will not be reiterated. The model is expounded progressively in the following sections.

Scientifically unaccepted beliefs

In Chapter 1 I devised a working definition of the term 'paranormal belief' as it is widely used by many researchers and the general public. Under this definition paranormal beliefs were delineated essentially as scientifically unaccepted beliefs and thus this domain was deemed to encompass endorsement of superstitions, psi processes, divinatory arts, esoteric systems of magic, New Age therapies, Eastern mystico–religious concepts, spiritism, traditional religious tenets and the existence of extraterrestrial aliens and cryptozoological creatures, as well as a wide variety of traditional beliefs of folklore (e.g., fairies, leprechauns, werewolves, vampires), beliefs advocated by small single-issue groups (e.g., a cargo cult, the Flat Earth Society) and beliefs associated with transient paranormal fads (e.g., the Bermuda Triangle). Adoption of this working definition enabled me to survey empirical findings on the correlates of paranormal belief in the widest possible context.

Notwithstanding the criterion of popular usage, however, it must be said that it is difficult to sustain a rigorous definition of paranormal belief that is any broader than a belief in the paranormal. Thus, strictly speaking, the term 'paranormal belief' should apply only to belief in events that in mainstream science are generally deemed to be scientifically *impossible*, that is, belief in phenomena that are widely viewed as contravening the 'basic limiting principles' of current scientific thinking (Broad, 1949) or confounding the core characteristics of fundamental ontological categories (Lindeman and Aarnio, 2006, 2007; Lindeman *et al.*, 2008; Lindeman and Saher, 2007). In this sense paranormal beliefs pertain to the subject matter of scientific parapsychology: psi processes (ESP and PK) and ostensibly psi-dependent phenomena (e.g., divinatory arts) as well as the notion of a non-material element of human existence (*viz.*, the spirit) and associated spiritist constructs (e.g., apparitions, reincarnation, astral projection). It is strongly recommended that researchers and other academic commentators define paranormal belief more specifically in terms of belief in phenomena that putatively are scientifically *impossible* rather than merely scientifically *unaccepted*. I concede this recommendation is bound to have little impact on popular usage of the term, but academics have a responsibility to be rather more rigorous in their terminology.

At the same time the empirical survey in this monograph strongly suggests there is extensive commonality among beliefs in scientifically unaccepted phenomena. Although factor–analytic studies imply the multidimensionality of this domain, there is a good deal of consistency in the demographic, cognitive and personality correlates of these beliefs (arguably with the exception of traditional religious beliefs, about which I comment later in this chapter). The empirical review thereby encourages the view that while scientifically impossible phenomena may be distinguished conceptually from other scientifically unaccepted phenomena, paranormal beliefs may legitimately be explained within the broader context of scientifically unaccepted beliefs. The model depicted in Figure 1 therefore carries the caption, 'A causal model of scientifically unaccepted beliefs'.

The model proposed here incorporates two distinct components of scientifically unaccepted beliefs (henceforth referred to as *SUBs*). The first component, labelled *Parapsychological Beliefs*, relates to belief in psi processes (ESP, PK) and phenomena that appear to depend explicitly or implicitly on such processes (e.g., fortune-telling, water divining), together with belief in a non-material dimension of human existence (as spiritistically rather than religiously conceived; Fuller, 2001) and phenomena implicating the existence of the human spirit (e.g., mediumship, astral projection, reincarnation). Thus, this component encompasses belief in phenomena studied by parapsychologists as putatively paranormal. In psychometric terms this component corresponds closely to Lange *et al.*'s (2000) factor of New Age Philosophy and probably also to the domain tapped by the *Australian Sheep–Goat Scale* (Thalbourne, 1995a; see also Lange and Thalbourne, 2002).

The second component of scientifically unaccepted beliefs is labelled *Belief in Black Magic* and pertains to belief in witchcraft, the efficacy of spells and incantations and the existence of the devil and of hell. This component is indexed psychometrically by Lange *et al.*'s (2000) factor of Traditional Paranormal Beliefs.

I pause briefly at this point to explain why the model does not subsume *Belief in Black Magic* under *Parapsychological Beliefs*. The factor–analytical evidence educed by Lange *et al.* (2000) clearly supports this differentiation of scientifically unaccepted beliefs, but some broader issues warrant acknowledgment. First, it must be said that although some rituals of black magic do appear to implicate paranormal processes, scientific parapsychologists generally do not accept that the former falls under their academic jurisdiction. Their stance is taken not because the parapsychological definition of the paranormal necessarily excludes the effects of witchcraft but, rather, because any interest shown by parapsychologists in such effects could subvert the objective of establishing parapsychology as a reputable scientific discipline (McClenon, 1984). A second and perhaps more fundamental issue is that beliefs in the devil and the existence of hell would not violate Broad's (1949) basic limiting principles and thereby these notions are *not* paranormal or parapsychological. To the extent that the constructs of the devil and hell are central to the characterisation of belief in black magic, there is in this respect a crucial conceptual distinction between the two factors of belief represented in the model. In short, belief in black magic may be deemed to relate more to the supernatural than to the paranormal as such. On each of these grounds it is argued that the two nominated components of scientifically unaccepted belief can be conceptually and empirically discriminated and are not seriously compromised by their slight semantic overlap. Thus, as indicated by the double-headed arrow in Figure 1, the model concedes that the components of scientifically unaccepted belief are statistically correlated, as observed by Lange *et al.* (2000); that is, people who endorse belief in black magic may be strongly inclined also to have some parapsychological (e.g., psi) beliefs, even if parapsychological believers may not be as consistent in their readiness to endorse the tenets of black magic.

The two above components are the only scientifically unaccepted beliefs explicitly represented in the model. As noted in Chapter 3, the multidimensionality of paranormal belief seems clear but the number of factors has yet to be ascertained definitively. To date, the best analysis (Lange *et al.*, 2000) of the broadest available questionnaire measure of paranormal belief (the *Revised Paranormal Belief Scale;* Tobacyk, 1988) adequately justifies the supposition of only two factors, New Age Philosophy and so-called Traditional Paranormal Beliefs. The present model therefore incorporates only two components of belief that are essentially isomorphic with those factors. It must be stressed, however, that there is no necessary implication here that additional factors will not be established in the future. The factors identified by Lange *et al.* do not incorporate, for example, beliefs in traditional Christian and other religious tenets (e.g., God), superstitions, extraterrestrial aliens, cryptozoological creatures, many New Age therapies and some traditional folkloric notions such as fairies. It remains for future researchers to show, first, that such beliefs can be indexed independently of differential item functioning and, second, that the proposed model would need to be expanded in order to accommodate these additional beliefs. The currently most parsimonious option, however, is to proceed on the assumption that there are just two distinct forms of SUB. This is the position adopted in the model shown in Figure 1.

It should be noted that although Parapsychological Beliefs and Belief in Black Magic are shown as discrete structures in the model, they cannot be imagined to exist independently of the person's various other beliefs. Although Zusne and Jones (1982, p. 186) speculated that some people may 'compartmentalise' their SUBs from other aspects of their lives, Irwin (2002) has reported some evidence to suggest that at least parapsychological beliefs typically are well integrated with the rest of the person's belief system. To depict these two belief structures as embedded in a broader belief system nevertheless would unduly complicate the model's graphical representation, so this underlying assumption will be taken here as axiomatic.

Activation of scientifically unaccepted beliefs

In most accounts of paranormal belief the formation of these beliefs would be the endpoint of the model; that is, paranormal beliefs would be the model's ultimate dependent variable. Under a more dynamic and, indeed, an ecologically more realistic approach, however, account should also be taken of the potential consequences of the endorsement of SUBs. One respect in which the present model realises this objective is by making a distinction between the *presence* of the two SUB structures in the person's belief system and the level of *activation* of these beliefs. A scientifically unaccepted belief is rather like a tuxedo that is taken out of the closet only when the occasion arises. Thus, for most of the time a person will not be (consciously or subconsciously) engaged in their parapsychological and black magical beliefs; even if one may be inclined to embrace ardently the concept of psi, for example, this belief is probably quiescent while one is deciding what to cook for dinner. When the prevailing context is appropriate, however, one or more of these beliefs may be activated so that they exert some degree of (conscious or subconscious) influence on the person's deliberations and/or observable behaviour. Such a circumstance is represented in Figure 1 by including two components labelled *Activated Parapsychological Beliefs* and *Activated Belief in Black Magic*.

The circumstances that govern the activation of a scientifically unaccepted belief are represented by the component, *Contextual Stress* (Figure 1). Broadly speaking, a stressful context that can activate a SUB will be one that induces a sense of vulnerability and perceived loss of personal control and a concomitant emotional state of some degree of anxiety or helplessness. Thus, the person may be experiencing mild cognitive dissonance (a threat to intellectual equanimity), a major emotional

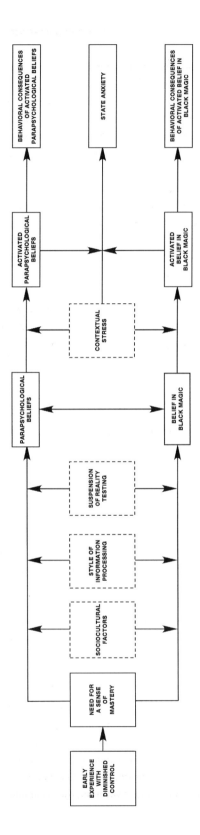

Fig. 1: *A causal model of scientifically unaccepted beliefs*

crisis in the face of a potential trauma, or some intermediate state of stress (Brugger *et al.*, 1999; Ellson, 1942; Gallagher and Lewis, 2001; Keinan, 1994, 2002; Padgett and Jorgenson, 1982; Selekler *et al.*, 2004; Shrimali and Broota, 1987; Sosis, 2007; Terr *et al.*, 1997; Wildta and Schultz-Venrath, 2004). By way of illustration, a person may have an anomalous experience such as receiving an unexpected phone call from a long-lost friend at the precise moment the person was reminiscing about the friend; the mild state of cognitive dissonance evoked by such an uncanny situation may then serve to activate a previously established belief in psi as the person tries to make sense of the experience. Near the more traumatic extreme, confrontation with a life-threatening illness may activate a belief in the protective power of a talisman habitually worn (and now desperately clutched) by the person.

The types of contextual stress that can activate a SUB may therefore vary in cognitive and affective *intensity* from one context to another. The stressor may also change in intensity within a single context: during a degenerative illness, for example, the activation of SUBs may increase progressively with the severity of deterioration (Wildta and Schultz-Venrath, 2004). In addition, the stressor may vary in *duration* from acute (e.g., a job interview) to ongoing (e.g., a difficult conjugal relationship). It should be noted, however, that many seemingly short-lived events may evoke stress that lasts for a substantial period and which serves to activate SUBs throughout much of this period. Thus, among the children who witnessed the death of their teacher in the *Challenger* explosion in 1986, Terr *et al.* (1997) observed an elevation of paranormal belief that in many cases persisted over much of the following year.

The state of contextual stress may or may not be something of which the person is conscious. On the one hand, it is possible that a SUB may be activated at times when the contextual stress becomes salient to the person; thoughts may then turn to the need for special powers. The seriously ill person clutching his or her talisman may well engage in conscious deliberation to the effect, 'My life is under serious threat, but then again, surely I will be saved from death if I protect myself by holding my magic charm'. Activation of belief in the talisman's power in this instance would be conscious. On the other hand, the activation of a SUB may commonly be a subconscious process (see also Kramer and Block, 2008). It certainly is not necessary for a SUB to emerge in the person's consciousness for it to be deemed active. Thus, the schoolchildren who witnessed the *Challenger* disaster might not have been *consciously* reasoning that they needed to have paranormal powers if they were to avoid the fate that had befallen their teacher. Indeed, in some instances consciousness of a SUB may be a consequence rather than a cause of the activation of the SUB. In any event, one should be hesitant to impute simplistic parallels between the activation of a SUB and a person's indulgence in a 'sustaining fantasy' (Zelin *et al.*, 1983).

In summary, contextual stress is a moderator of the link between scientifically unaccepted beliefs and their activated state. The status of contextual stress as a moderator is signified in Figure 1 by outlining this component in dashed lines.

Behavioural consequences of activated scientifically unaccepted beliefs

The present model goes beyond the mere formation of scientifically unaccepted beliefs to address also the possible behavioural consequences of SUB activation. The range of such behavioural consequences may be substantial. In part this may be due to a social value dubbed 'instrumental activism' by Parsons (1960, p. 172); that is, in contemporary Western society it is generally unacceptable to look like a passive fatalist and thus there is an implicit expectation that people should *do something* about the situations in which they find themselves, even if influence over such situations seemingly is not within one's capacity (see also Campbell, 1996; Presson, 1997).

A minimal behaviour arising from the SUB's activation is awareness of or deliberation about the SUB. Thus, the gambler may form an intense image of the desired outcome as the roulette wheel is spinning. On occasion, however, the activation of a SUB may lead to a motor (observable) behaviour rather than a purely mental response. Some of the ways in which parapsychological believers generally involve themselves in the paranormal were surveyed in Chapter 5 and include seeking entertainment with a paranormal theme, reading about paranormal or psychic phenomena, participating in courses on parapsychology or on psychic development, visiting professional psychics, or even practicing as a medium or psychic. Similar behavioural effects may be associated with the activation of a belief in black magic and may include, for example, experimentation with satanic practices. Possibly another behavioural consequence of SUB activation is that of interpreting anomalous experiences in parapsychological terms; the relationship between parapsychological beliefs and parapsychological experiences nevertheless is a complex issue and is addressed in more detail later in this chapter.

Some of these behaviours may well work to maintain the temporarily activated SUB in the longer term. Thus, in the mind of the believer an established SUB may be 'confirmed' by the subsequent occurrence of anomalous or seemingly paranormal experiences, by reading popularist accounts of the paranormal and by seeking comment from pro-paranormal authority figures. Similarly, the active avoidance of potentially contradictory information may impede disconfirmation of the SUB.

In psychology one's emotional state is also deemed a behaviour. In functional terms a theoretically important behavioural consequence of the activation of either type of SUB is a possible reduction of (state) anxiety in the face of contextual stress (see also Houran and Lange, 2004). In this respect SUBs may be deemed to operate as an adaptive behaviour or coping strategy. In formulating this hypothesis I do not mean to imply any necessary difference between believers and nonbelievers in state anxiety; people who do not subscribe to SUBs presumably have other coping strategies for dealing with contextual stress. Nonetheless, given that contextual stressors can activate scientifically unaccepted beliefs, it is appropriate here to specify some psychological benefit of SUB activation. The model therefore proposes this benefit to be reduced state anxiety. Although a contextual stressor may confront the person with evidence of the uncontrollability of the world, activation of a SUB may provide some reassurance that a degree of control might still be possible, if only at an intellectual or illusory level (Friedland *et al.*, 1992); this effect may be reflected in an attenuation of the person's anxiety level. More formally, the link between contextual stress and state anxiety is held to be moderated by the strength of a SUB's activation. The reduction of anxiety consequent to the activation of a SUB may serve in turn to reinforce the person's adherence to the belief.

Again, many of these behaviours might be *subconsciously* driven consequences of the activation of a SUB by some contextual stressor. Thus, people who endorse a SUB may not see themselves as responding to a contextually relevant belief at all but rather as simply acting in accordance with their 'sense of reality and truth' (Zusne and Jones, 1982, p. 197).

Cognitive and sociocultural processes underlying the formation of scientifically unaccepted beliefs

According to Humphrey (1995) paranormal beliefs are based essentially on what one is told by others rather than on personal experience (see also Patry and Pelletier, 2001). Contradicting this view is a survey by Blackmore (1984) which found that adults justified their paranormal beliefs more by personal experience (19 per cent) than by the experiences of other people (11 per cent) or media reports (11 per cent). The appeal to personal experiences in this context is documented also by Coll and Taylor (2004). Again, Houran (e.g., Houran *et al.*, 2001; Houran *et al.*, 2000) has argued that the two facets of scientifically unaccepted belief have fundamentally different modes of propagation, with parapsychological beliefs largely dependent on personal experience and belief in black magic ('traditional paranormal beliefs') more dependent on cultural reinforcement. The cognitive and sociocultural processes underlying the formation of SUBs nevertheless seem rather more complex than the views of Humphrey and Houran would allow and they therefore warrant closer examination.

Apart from the study of attributional processes, relatively little psychological research has been devoted to the study of cognitive processes associated with belief generation and evaluation. The following account draws substantially on the model formulated by Langdon and Coltheart (2000). Sensory mechanisms provide considerable information about the environment and the self for which the person requires an explanation. The desire for understanding of this information is especially the case in people with a need for a sense of mastery (Keinan and Sivan, 2001). The information occasionally may be discordant or anomalous and this can be the context for the generation of a SUB. Take, for example, the case of a personal anomalous experience (e.g., thinking of a long-lost friend immediately before receiving a phone call from that friend) or perhaps the more common instance of another person's claim (e.g., a media report or an acquaintance's narrative) of a paranormal phenomenon. Potential causal explanations of such incidents are generated through attributional processes (see Chapter 6), but these may be biased both by universal human dispositions and by the person's own idiosyncrasies. The narrative form in which the incident is mentally couched may also serve to bias the generation of potential causal explanations: it is difficult to describe these events to oneself without using such words as 'telepathy' and 'magic spell' and thereby sociocultural factors mould the form of the subsequently formulated SUB. In what Langdon and Coltheart denote as a 'normal' or nonpathological style of belief generation the person critically evaluates and ranks the plausibility of all the hypothetical explanations of the incident. That is, hypotheses may variously be examined in the light of prior personal experience, general knowledge and the input of authoritative others and similar sociocultural sources. These optional hypotheses thus are logically 'tested'; in the psychodynamic literature this process is known as *reality testing* and entails 'a set of perceptual, cognitive and sensorimotor acts that enables one to determine one's relationship with the external physical and social environments' (Reber, 1995, p. 640). The explanation that best survives reality testing may then be endorsed as a belief. Note that in the nonpathological case such a belief may always be subject to critical revision as further relevant information comes to hand.

As represented by Langdon and Coltheart (2000) the cognitive foundations of belief generation and evaluation clearly rely extensively on analytical–rational information processing. In a relatively small section of the population both types of SUB may be formed under such a process: that is, the SUBs may constitute what Sperber (1990) termed a reflective belief (see Chapter 1). Thus, academic parapsychologists and sceptics may develop their respective positions on the psi hypothesis through careful consideration of the relevant experimental literature in terms of culturally conveyed scientific standards of methodological adequacy (McConnell and Clark, 1980). Similarly, some people may form a belief in spiritism or in black magic through intense critical study of arcane texts and association with informed authorities who provide appropriate instruction in such matters. In these contexts SUBs depend pivotally on reasonably extensive critical analysis that reflects processes of cultural dissemination and induction in which the role of culturally signified authority is substantial. Further, the elementary SUBs here are likely to be embedded in a much more sophisticated belief system. A basic belief in the existence of the human spirit, for example, may be a mere fragment of an elaborate and far-ranging view of the fundamental nature of the spirit and of its significance for a philosophy of life and death.

Belief generation and evaluation of this highly analytical kind nevertheless are not characteristic of the formation of SUBs in the general population and although I acknowledge its occurrence, it is much too atypical to justify explicit depiction in Figure 1. I propose SUBs to arise in the 'average person' through a slightly different pattern of cognitive analysis. As Sperber would say, SUBs in the general population are intuitive beliefs formed essentially through 'spontaneous and unconscious perceptual and inferential processes' (Sperber, 1990, p. 35). This is evident in two principal respects. The first may be seen in the way people choose between the various hypothetical explanations for an anomalous incident: they opt for an intuitive-experiential interpretation at the expense of analytical–rational ones. Thus, the involvement of psi or a magical process is endorsed primarily because this is how the anomalous incident initially felt and not so much because the information is consistent with independent knowledge or with the opinions of mainstream scientists. SUBs therefore are most common in people with a habitual intuitive–experiential processing style (see Chapter 6), though of course even those people who usually rely on an analytical–rational processing style may sometimes suspend this strategy in the face of a striking personal anomalous experience. Second, when the preferred explanation is attested to primarily in terms of its intuitive appeal, the explanation might not then be subject to the usual rigorous processes of critical evaluation either at the time or when further relevant information subsequently becomes available. That is, SUBs in the general population typically are given scant critical testing by the person and, indeed, given their intuitive–experiential status, SUBs may be somewhat protected from such evaluation on an ongoing basis, with any inconsistent belief discarded and incompatible new information discounted. At least in these respects people who endorse SUBs therefore tend to show some deficit in reality testing (Irwin, 2003b, 2004). It must nevertheless be stressed that this deficit may well be specific to the context of belief generation (see Bell *et al.*, 2001); that is, paranormal believers may not necessarily present with reality-testing deficits in other contexts or with other characteristics of psychosis. In depicting paranormal believers to have reality-testing deficits we should keep in mind that all sorts of people may behave illogically in all sorts of contexts.

The cognitive processes described above are deemed to underlie the formation of both types of SUB in the general population. Consider the case of parapsychological beliefs. On the basis of intermittent intriguing extrinsic (e.g., media) reports of parapsychological phenomena and perhaps also in light of a vivid personal parapsychological experience a person may make a spontaneous subconscious inference about the paranormal nature of the world and the verbal (conscious) formulation of this inference may then be informed by concepts widely disseminated in the person's culture. By way of illustration, a given report might intuitively be taken to suggest the possibility of direct mind-to-mind communication and consequently the person may verbally formulate this inference in terms of such concepts as ESP or telepathy to which he or she has unwittingly been culturally exposed. Similarly, the notion of a non-material or spiritist element of human existence (without the elaborated structure of religious dogma) might be intuited from an apparitional experience or, more commonly, from hearing about other people's experiences of this sort.

Note that these parapsychological beliefs are relatively simple and unburdened by complex intellectual analysis. In their initial formation parapsychological beliefs are typically not subjected to any rigorous critical scrutiny; grounded in human (personal or vicarious) experience their paranormal nature is 'intuitively obvious' and accepted without rational analysis or consultation with informed others. Generally speaking, apart from the vicarious reports of the parapsychological experience itself, the only cultural input to the generation of the parapsychological belief is the mere name of the phenomenon underlying the belief (e.g., 'telepathy'). Some parapsychological believers may subsequently make an effort to read about the paranormal and in time might integrate their beliefs into a New Age type of worldview, but even in these instances the parapsychological beliefs might be subjected to little critical analysis.

In the general population, therefore, parapsychological beliefs typically arise spontaneously and are accepted uncritically. Parapsychological believers are probably not intrinsically deficient in the skills of critical analysis but they may be inclined to suspend such analysis in relation to beliefs attested by experience and to apply critical analysis more routinely only to other types of belief (see Merla-Ramos, 2000).

A similar account may be formulated for the development of belief in black magic among the general population. Note that in this context belief in black magic need not entail the endorsement of any comprehensive esoteric doctrine such as neo-pagan Wicca but merely a disposition towards elementary propositions such as the efficacy of spells and the existence of witches, the devil and hell. Most people who believe in black magic therefore have not pursued rigorous training and induction nor have they even given much scrutiny to the bases of these beliefs. Certainly there is some sociocultural input to the formation of belief in black magic, but at least in Western societies this input typically is unelaborated and unsophisticated; in most instances it may consist of little more than exposure during childhood to fairy tales about witches (Makasovski and Irwin, 1999) or casual exposure to the concepts of the devil and hell even in the absence of any systematic religious instruction. In any event, on hearing of a concept involving black magic some people may be inclined to rate its appeal largely on an intuitive–experiential basis and not to subject the concept to thorough critical analysis.

Information-processing style and suspension of reality testing therefore are crucially involved in the formation of SUBs and sociocultural factors may mould the precise form and name that these beliefs take (see Chapter 2). Each of these influences is represented as a moderator effect (depicted using dashed lines in Figure 1).

Motivational processes underlying the formation of scientifically unaccepted beliefs

In themselves the underlying cognitive processes do not provide a sufficient account of the formation of scientifically unaccepted beliefs. An essential concomitant of the cognitive processes described in the previous section is a psychological susceptibility to SUBs or the 'need to believe' (Krippner and

Winkler, 1996; Schumaker, 1990). As argued in Chapter 7, the need to endorse SUBs can best be understood from a psychodynamic perspective.

Under the present model the key motivational foundation of parapsychological belief may be characterised as a *Need for a Sense of Mastery* over life events (or, conversely, a fear of powerlessness). This idea is not new: precedents for this approach to paranormal belief may be found in the writings of Alcock (1981, p. 40), Frank (1977, pp. 556–7), Lillqvist and Lindeman (1998), Lindeman (1998), Marks and Kammann (1980, p. 156), Moody (1971/1974, p. 233), Schumaker (1990), Singer and Benassi (1981, p. 50) and Zusne and Jones (1982, p. 210). Specifically, under the model people who endorse SUBs have a need for a sense of mastery over their physical and social environment or for at least a sense of intellectual mastery over (i.e., understanding of) life events. As reported in Chapter 7, many psychologists (Anderson and Deuser, 1993; Fisher and Fisher, 1993; Flammer, 1995; Heider, 1958; Hobfoll *et al.*, 2002; Lefcourt, 1973; Rozin and Nemeroff, 1999; Shapiro *et al.*, 1996; Taylor, 1983; White, 1959) have argued that an assurance of order and meaning in the physical and social world is essential for emotional security and psychological adjustment. I propose that this basic human need drives the person's intuitive interpretations of many anomalous events and experiences in terms of parapsychological constructs. The formation of parapsychological beliefs enables the person to view such anomalous experiences as comprehensible and thereby the person gains mastery over the anomaly, at least intellectually.

This impression of mastery may be achieved in part by the activation of parapsychological beliefs that create a transitory 'illusion of control' (Langer, 1975; Presson and Benassi, 1996; Rudski and Edwards, 2007) in the face of events that are in reality not controllable by the individual. Parapsychological believers nevertheless do not function under a habitual delusion that they are in complete control of all facets of their life. On the contrary, believers still tend to see the world as more threatening than do nonbelievers (Sica *et al.*, 2002) and data on the relationship between paranormal beliefs and an external locus of control (see Chapter 5) indicate that they perceive much of their life to be governed by factors outside their control. A person's parapsychological beliefs therefore may serve as a coping strategy or adaptive buffer against the impression that aspects of the world are personally uncontrollable. In other words, parapsychological beliefs offer hope that seemingly uncontrollable events might possibly be controlled by the person, but at the same time the person appreciates that parapsychological control in a specific circumstance is not guaranteed. In addition, it is possible that the activation of a parapsychological belief may serve as a diversion from direct confrontation with the distressing knowledge that some events cannot be controlled (Callaghan and Irwin, 2003). Most fundamentally, however, parapsychological beliefs bring comfort to the person by providing a sense of understanding why these uncontrollable anomalous life events can occur. For the parapsychological believer the concepts of psi processes and the spiritist element of human existence illuminate many experiences and events that are potentially threatening to a perception of life as orderly and meaningful.

The motivation underlying the formation of belief in black magic is not well attested empirically, principally because this component of SUBs has been identified only recently as a distinct factor (Lange *et al.*, 2000). My reanalysis of the data reported by Irwin (2000b) suggested that both components of SUBs have the same pattern of predictors in the control domain, although the trend for belief in black magic was weak and did not quite reach statistical significance ($p < .08$). The need for a sense of mastery nevertheless seems as conceptually relevant to a belief in black magic as it does to parapsychological belief. On this basis and with the intention to encourage further research into the issue, the model posits the need for mastery as a motivational factor common to both SUBs.

Psychological origins of scientifically unaccepted beliefs

I turn now to the specific topic of the psychological origins of scientifically unaccepted beliefs. The need for a sense of mastery over life events is deemed to play an important role in this regard. A sense of mastery is a basic human need and to this extent Schumaker (1990) is correct in arguing that every person is susceptible to paranormal beliefs. On the other hand, there are marked individual differences in the need for mastery which I believe can accommodate much of the observed variation in the endorsement of SUBs across individuals.

The developmental bases of a need for a sense of mastery have been the focus of some research; a useful review of this literature is provided by Chorpita and Barlow (1998) and some thoughtful observations are made by Prilleltensky *et al.* (2001). Some people's childhood experiences may leave them with an unusually strong need for mastery which in turn may motivate them to form SUBs. One of the developmental factors associated with an enhanced need for mastery is childhood trauma, particularly abuse; as noted in Chapter 7, this is a well-established predictor of paranormal beliefs. That childhood trauma is the pivotal factor here, however, is unclear. It may be that the chaotic or unpredictable family environment in which childhood trauma tends to flourish is more fundamentally conducive to a pronounced need for mastery. Chorpita and Barlow (1998) and Schneewind (1995) have identified specific familial contexts that affect the development of a sense of control over life events. A belief that one has little such control is reported to be most prevalent in children who grow up with several older siblings; children whose parents behave inconsistently towards them; children whose parents are overprotective, intrusive, or authoritarian; and children whose parents are emotionally cold or rejecting and who obstruct the child from establishing a secure style of attachment. The trend in this literature seems to be that people with a greater need for mastery were in early childhood often put in situations over which they could not exercise sufficient autonomous control or, conversely, they were given too few opportunities for exercising autonomous control. Following Chorpita and Barlow (1998) I represent this factor in the model as *Early Experience with Diminished Control*. The significance of these early experiences for the development of SUBs is supported by the evidence relating to childhood trauma (see Chapter 7) and by the study by Granqvist and Hagekull (2001) which found an association between the intensity of New Age beliefs (see Appendix 14) and attachment insecurity. Initial empirical investigation (Roe and Bell, 2007; Watt *et al.*, 2007) suggests early experience with diminished control may predict the intensity of paranormal beliefs, although the relationship is not as strong as the present model might be taken to imply. Perhaps the development of a sense of mastery is more complex than envisaged by Chorpita and Barlow (1998) and Schneewind (1995).

The possibility should be acknowledged that this developmental context may also be influenced by many of the reported personality and other psychological correlates of paranormal belief, including schizotypy, fantasy proneness, dissociative tendencies, cognitive style, attributional style, subjective worldview and intolerance of ambiguity. To incorporate these effects would make the present model far too unwieldy and therefore they are not represented explicitly in Figure 1. At the same time, if these relationships are shown to be substantial they could have two important implications for the model. First, information-processing style might not be a moderator (as depicted in Figure 1) but rather a mediating variable in a more complex causal loop between *Early Experience with Diminished Control* and the respective SUB (see Janoff-Bulman, 1989). Second, the above relationships may call into question the very necessity of including *Need for a Sense of Mastery*. That is, it might be argued that this component is better replaced by some of the above variables as mediators between *Early Experience with Diminished Control* and the SUBs. At present it is a largely subjective judgment that incorporation of an explicitly motivational element enhances the explanatory value of the model, but further research may determine if this strategy best accommodates the data.

Summary of the model

For ease of exposition the model of scientifically unaccepted beliefs has been described progressively from the inside out. By way of a summary it is appropriate to recapitulate concisely and in correct temporal order the processes leading to the formation of SUBs and their behavioural consequences in the general population.

I propose that the fundamental developmental antecedent of SUBs is the child's substantial early experience with diminished control, which fosters an enduring need for a sense of mastery over life events. People who lack such a need do not feel so compelled to devise an explanation for the anomalous events they themselves encounter or about which they hear from others. A strong need for a sense of mastery, on the other hand, drives the formation of scientifically unaccepted beliefs. The specific SUBs that are created nevertheless are governed or moderated by both the person's information-processing style and the sociocultural setting. For example, one person may establish an intuitively–experientially grounded belief in clairvoyance or in the efficacy of magic spells;

less typically, another person may develop a more analytically–rationally oriented belief in the existence of psi or the power of the devil. The formation of a SUB with intuitive–experiential appeal also is marked by a suspension of reality testing so that alternative views are not countenanced or are dismissed peremptorily.

After a SUB is established within the person's system of beliefs, some effort may be made to ensure that the SUB is compatible with other cherished beliefs, thereby enabling a reasonably coherent or integrated belief system (e.g., a worldview). This process may entail modification of those beliefs that conflict with the more psychodynamically significant SUB or even entirely jettisoning a conflicting belief. Generally speaking, however, SUBs are relatively protected from direct critical scrutiny; that is, even after the formation of SUBs the person usually continues to inhibit the reality testing of these intuitively appealing beliefs. SUBs therefore have a favoured status within the person's belief system.

Confrontation by a contextual stressor may serve to activate the relevant SUBs, whether at a conscious or subconscious level. In this regard *the activation of a SUB is seen not so much as maladaptive behaviour but as an adaptive response.* The major functional significance of such activation is to attenuate the state of anxiety evoked by the stressor; indeed, the process of anxiety reduction may have a significant role in further reinforcing the intensity of the underlying belief. Other relevant behaviours may be instigated by the activation of the SUB. Thus, the person may be inspired to act upon the activated SUB and engage, for example, in SUB-associated rituals. In some instances these behaviours may function to maintain the SUB in the longer term, either by ostensibly confirming the SUB or by impeding its disconfirmation.

It should be noted that the proposed model has an explicitly interactionist perspective. The formation, activation and maintenance of a scientifically unaccepted belief in a given person are deemed to reflect interactions between psychological (cognitive, motivational and affective) dispositions and environmental stressors. This perspective adds to the complexity and the ecological realism of the model, although it may generate some empirical complications. A primary objective of the formulation of a theoretical model is, of course, to stimulate further research that will help to clarify the focal phenomenon. It is to the topic of future research that I now turn.

Issues for future empirical research

Where possible the causal model of scientifically unaccepted beliefs graphically represented in Figure 1 has been devised in light of the empirical findings surveyed in earlier chapters of the monograph. Most past research nevertheless has addressed the pertinence of specific causal factors in relative isolation. Assessment of the model as a whole would require a very substantial empirical investigation in which all the components of the model are indexed and statistically examined in terms of their nominated mediating or moderating role through a holistic method of analysis such as path analysis or structural equation modelling. By no means do I underestimate the logistical and statistical difficulties presented by such an investigation. At the same time the model also prompts some smaller-scale projects.

The developmental antecedents of SUBs warrant the considered attention of researchers. As was evident in the earlier chapters the current literature on this topic is far from comprehensive and, in particular, the contributions of parenting style, attachment style and familial structure in this context are not well attested. More important, much of the past research has utilised a retrospective approach, with participants being asked to recall features of their upbringing. This methodology may be severely constrained by the participants' memory and self-insight. There is a pressing need for prospective or longitudinal investigation of the development of SUBs, with relevant factors tapped directly over the course of that development. It is hoped that two specific components of the model, *Early Experience with Diminished Control* and *Need for a Sense of Mastery*, will offer researchers some guidance in their selection of variables for study within a longitudinal perspective.

Empirical consideration might be given also to the respects in which the developmental antecedents of the two SUBs might differ. *Early Experience with Diminished Control* generally encompasses the abusive and neglectful familial environments that are known to be correlated with parapsychological beliefs, but this is by no means uniformly so. Thus, a strong need for a sense of mastery may develop also in children whose parents are overprotective. Now, it is not inconceivable that an overprotected childhood is also an environment in which the child may often be read fairy tales and thereby exposed to some of the basic concepts of black magic (e.g., the wicked witch who casts spells). Should this be the case, children whose parents are overprotective may be rather more inclined to develop belief in black magic than they are to develop parapsychological beliefs. Such speculations may prove to be utterly erroneous but they do serve to caution that the two basic SUBs might yet be shown to have slightly different developmental antecedents. This can easily be tested.

Developmental issues other than childhood antecedents also may be explored. For example, it remains to be seen if the age-related differences found in cross-sectional studies (see Chapter 4) would be observed in a prospective longitudinal study and, if so, what might cause these changes. Certainly there are insufficient data on the precise developmental path of SUBs over the life span. Even a more detailed documentation of the structure of SUBs in specific age groups would be welcome.

Although the model has taken pains to specify in some detail the *formation* of SUBs, perhaps there are grounds for arguing that neither the model nor the associated empirical literature has taken sufficient account of processes entailed in the ongoing *maintenance* of established SUBs. People's apparent protection of their SUBs from extensive critical scrutiny is a matter for further research. To what extent are people aware that their SUBs are 'scientifically unaccepted' and how is such knowledge reconciled with the endorsement of SUBs? This issue bears fundamentally on the dynamics of a person's belief system and thus may have significant conceptual implications beyond the boundaries of paranormal belief. More generally, there is a need for more extensive empirical documentation of the cognitive and other behavioural strategies that may be used by believers and by disbelievers to 'confirm' their established views and to impede disconfirmation.

Arguably the greatest current obstacle to incisive research into SUBs is the lack of a measure that indexes the full range of scientifically unaccepted beliefs to a psychometrically satisfactory standard, namely, with well-attested reliability and validity and in the demonstrated absence of differential item functioning. The development of such an instrument is important to the effective differentiation of correlates across SUBs and fundamental to the determination of the factorial structure of SUBs. The present model posits only two types of SUB, parapsychological beliefs and belief in black magic, because Lange *et al.* (2000) identified only two validly indexed factors in the *Revised Paranormal Belief Scale* (see Appendix 9). The item pool for this analysis failed, however, to include items that effectively tapped belief in superstitions, UFOs and extraterrestrial aliens, cryptozoological creatures, traditional religious tenets, New Age therapies and many traditional folkloric notions. Even if many of these beliefs are not legitimately labelled 'paranormal' (see Lindeman and Aarnio, 2006, 2007; Lindeman and Saher, 2007), all are scientifically unaccepted beliefs and as such deserve scientific study. The construction of a fully comprehensive, psychometrically sound measure of SUBs and the determination of the factorial structure of this instrument (and thence of the domain of SUBs itself) are major and crucial projects for future research. There is scope also for empirical research to be more extensively driven by theoretically nominated or empirically identified factors of SUBs. Past research has tended either to treat paranormal beliefs in an inappropriately global manner or to take insufficient account of the possibility of different patterns of correlates across SUBs.

I would like to draw attention to a specific instance of the above issue which concerns traditional religious beliefs. Not only are these beliefs inadequately indexed by currently available measures but ideally there needs to be a clearer psychometric differentiation of these beliefs from both spiritist views (specifically, belief in the existence of the spirit) and the diabolical component of belief in black magic. In addition and rather more fundamentally, my review of the evidence raises some doubt about the likelihood that these beliefs could be accommodated by the present model: in several respects the pattern of their correlates differs from that of the other beliefs. In short, religious beliefs seem to be somehow different in kind from the other paranormal beliefs. This may be an obstacle to formulating a comprehensive account of SUBs. Perhaps the situation will be resolved as suggested in the previous paragraph, that is, through further empirical study. New data may show that the inclusion of traditional religious beliefs would require an expansion of my model, perhaps with a partially or even wholly distinct causal pathway for these beliefs. Such findings would not be a matter of major concern; given the diversity of scientifically unacceptable beliefs a *universal* explanation of the origins and the functions of SUBs may be an unduly optimistic expectation. Alternatively, an incisive conceptual analysis may demonstrate that traditional religious tenets are better classified as something other than a scientifically unacceptable belief and should therefore be excluded from the model. In any event, researchers in the future should certainly think more critically about subsuming traditional religious tenets under the broad rubric of paranormal belief.

Relatively little research has yet been undertaken into the extent to which the endorsement of a SUB has implications for the person's behaviour (see Chapter 5). That is, to what extent do people act upon their SUBs or, alternatively, to what extent are SUBs merely abstracted notions with scant practical significance for human behaviour? More generally, a new measure of SUBs usefully would address cognitive, affective and behavioural components of the beliefs; an interesting if somewhat simplistic step towards this goal is described by Hart (2008). Allied to this issue is the possibility of devising performance measures of SUB (see Subbotsky, 2001; Zapf, 1945a) or at least indices that bear more on actual behaviour than on mere verbal declarations of belief.

A related issue concerns the link between SUBs and personal parapsychological experiences. Although people may justify their paranormal beliefs in terms of personal experience (Blackmore, 1984), in many instances a person will endorse a paranormal belief without having had any personal experience of the associated phenomenon (Humphrey, 1995; Irwin, 1985b). In the *formation* of SUBs, therefore, it seems that one or two personal parapsychological or magical experiences may make some (albeit limited) contribution. Once SUBS are well established, however, the apparent direction of the association between experience and belief may be strongly reversed. Thus, some studies (Lange and Houran, 1998, 1999) have employed path analysis or a similar statistical technique to suggest that the predominant effect is for beliefs to evoke (reports of) personal parapsychological experience rather than vice versa. On the other hand, in a similar analysis the opposite trend was identified by Lawrence *et al.* (1995). Thus, as I have suggested elsewhere (Irwin, 1992, 1993) it is possible that putative parapsychological experiences serve additionally to reinforce underlying beliefs (see also Snow and Machalek, 1982). Further, it must be acknowledged that an anomalous or ostensibly parapsychological experience can arise even in disbelievers (Irwin, 1985b). These diverse processes deserve further comparative investigation with a view to determining if a complex causal loop between SUBs and personal parapsychological experiences might usefully be incorporated into the model.

One of the key propositions of the model concerns the role of contextual stress in activating SUBs. Following the lead of Dudley (1999b) and Keinan (2002), I urge that further research effort be devoted to this issue. Specific matters for investigation here include details of the correspondence between particular instances of contextual stressors and the SUBs they activate and the extent to which state anxiety evoked by contextual stress is reduced by the SUB activation. Attention might also be given to a more precise determination of the essential psychological qualities of the contextual stress that activates SUBs. The model characterises these qualities primarily in terms of a sense of vulnerability and perceived loss of personal control, with a concomitant state of anxiety or helplessness (see also Keinan, 1994, 2002). At the same time other commentators such as Dudley (1999b, 2000) and Beck and Miller (2001) have represented the impact of contextual stress more in terms of depressive symptoms. Rather more focused research should provide greater clarity on this issue.

Based on the two SUBs in the model, the model posits a reduction in state anxiety with SUB activation. Although the model does not yet formally encompass belief in superstitions it is feasible that some commentators would argue an attenuation of anxiety is unlikely to occur when a negative superstition is activated. That is, the activation of a superstition concerning good fortune (e.g., 'touch wood', 'cross your fingers') might well attenuate state anxiety but the activation of a superstitious belief about bad luck (e.g., 'On Friday the 13th misfortune will occur') may ostensibly *increase* state anxiety. Indeed, some recent empirical studies (Lewis and Gallagher, 2001; Lucey, 2001; Näyhä, 2002; Phillips *et al.*, 2001; Scanlon *et al.*, 1993; Voracek *et al.*, 2002; Yang *et al.*, 2008; Zebb and Moore, 2003; but see Radun and Summala, 2004) offer observations putatively implying the latter to be the case. Further, a fear of Friday the 13th is a clinically recognised phobia (with the grand title of 'paraskavedekatriaphobia'; Lewis and Gallagher, 2001). On this basis it might be asserted that the model's postulate of a reduction in state anxiety has limited generality.

A more searching consideration of the above example, however, suggests the possible value here of distinguishing between the *presence* of a SUB in a person's belief system and the *activation* of that SUB. First, it may be argued that in the case of a negative superstition the source of stress that evokes anxiety is the perception that current circumstances may be conducive to bad luck. In generating this perception some knowledge (e.g., 'Today is Friday the 13th') is passively moderated by the *presence* of a SUB ('On Friday 13th misfortune will occur') as an implicit or automatic cognitive process, so that the knowledge is anxiety arousing (as was implied by the findings of Lucey, 2001; Näyhä, 2002; Phillips *et al.*, 2001; Scanlon *et al.*, 1993; Voracek *et al.*, 2002; Yang *et al.*, 2008; Zebb and Moore, 2003). Second and by contrast, the *activation* of the SUB for this superstition may fundamentally reflect a deliberative or explicit attributional process, the establishment of a sense of understanding about the potential occurrence of misfortune, that (in accordance with the model) functions counteractively to reduce anxiety to some extent (e.g., 'If bad luck happens today it's not because I deserve it but rather because there is a universal tendency for bad things to be more likely on Friday the 13th'). Thus, the presence of a belief in a negative superstition may be a factor in the believer's nervousness that misfortune may be imminent, but the activation of the belief in the face of this stress may underlie the believer's feeling of intellectual mastery which helps to keep the evoked anxiety under a degree of control. The situation may of course be further complicated by the fact that contextual stress could also foster the activation of an even more stress-countering belief such as a positive superstition or a religious belief (e.g., 'A St. Christopher medal will ward off misfortune on one's travels'), with its own behavioural consequences ('I will carry my St. Christopher medal on Friday the 13th').

Whether or not the foregoing speculation is viable, it does reinforce the need to ascertain with greater qualitative and quantitative precision the cognitive processes entailed in the activation of a SUB as well as the cognitive significance of the presence of a SUB. In this context the psychological nature of negative superstitions calls for specific examination both empirically and conceptually (e.g., see Dagnall *et al.*, 2007b; Wiseman and Watt, 2004). A similar analysis may be applicable in relation to the two principal SUBs currently identified in the model. For example, the supernatural phenomena implicated in black magic might readily evoke fear in their adherents and, indeed, these beliefs' apparent sociocultural functions in non-technological societies have been deemed to rely strongly on this fear (Frazer, 1911; Seligman, 1975; Wilson, 1951). The perception of the phenomena here may be passively mediated by the black-magical beliefs or, more precisely, the concepts incorporated into the beliefs. Nonetheless, one may argue it is the phenomena that arouse anxiety, not the beliefs. In a similar vein parapsychological phenomena also may frighten many people (Gallagher *et al.*, 1994; Irwin, 1985a; Lange and Houran, 1998; Tart, 1982; Tart and Labore, 1986), but again the fundamental view advocated here is that *activation* of parapsychological beliefs does not cause anxiety; rather, confrontation with a phenomenon perceived to be paranormal may evoke anxiety and this anxiety may then be attenuated when activation of the corresponding SUB brings a sense of understanding or intellectual mastery over the situation. Much the same may apply in regard to the sceptic's parapsychological *disbelief:* exposure to an anomalous event may be disturbing but activation of the belief that 'the paranormal does not exist' brings a degree of reassurance.

It should be reiterated that observations by Näyhä (2002) and by Zebb and Moore (2003) of an apparent association between superstitiousness and high state anxiety do not contradict the model. The model does not posit lower state anxiety among paranormal believers than among nonbelievers. Rather, it proposes that when paranormal believers encounter a stressor their activation of a SUB may serve to reduce their anxiety below what it might otherwise have been. Nonbelievers may well use other coping mechanisms in the face of contextual stress, so the simple correlation between SUB endorsement and state anxiety does not bear directly upon the validity of the model.

Negative superstitions nevertheless warrant closer empirical scrutiny in relation to other beliefs. Perhaps there are functional distinctions between SUBs (such as superstitions) activated in the expectation of some event happening and SUBs (e.g., parapsychological beliefs) activated when an (anomalous) event is actually happening. Thus, the former context may allow greater scope for negative reinforcement of beliefs (Aeschleman *et al.*, 2003) whereas the latter context may engender positive reinforcement of beliefs.

An ostensible empirical anomaly that might be investigated is the apparent lack of a correlation between paranormal beliefs and *trait* anxiety (Irwin, 1995; Jones *et al.*, 1977; Perkins, 2001; Smith and Karmin, 2002; Tobacyk, 1982), that is, anxiety as a persistent disposition rather than a merely transitory state. Early experience with diminished control is proposed here to be an antecedent of SUBs and Chorpita and Barlow (1998) have argued that early experience with diminished control also is a factor in the development of trait anxiety. Why, then, are SUBs not associated with trait anxiety? Closer examination of the argument by Chorpita and Barlow reveals that they regard early experience with diminished control to foster a tendency to interpret life events as being beyond one's control and thus frequently to evoke state anxiety; by a process of conditioning, they argue, this pattern becomes ingrained. It is possible that the formation of SUBs serves to inhibit the conditioning process posited by Chorpita and Barlow. That is, when life events appear to be out of control, the believer's SUBs may be activated so as to reduce state anxiety, thereby making it less likely that anxiety will become conditioned as a habitual response to everyday life. This account should be subjected to empirical scrutiny. First, research may determine if Chorpita and Barlow's claimed link between early experience with diminished control and susceptibility to state anxiety is moderated by the presence of SUBs. Second, it may be possible to study the utility of SUB activation (or indeed any effective coping strategy) in helping to prevent frequently elicited state anxiety from becoming conditioned as trait anxiety.

It seems fair to say, therefore, that the causal model of scientifically unaccepted beliefs presented here is a fertile one for generating ideas for future empirical research. I hope that the model is found to be of value to researchers in this respect.

This monograph has addressed the definition of paranormal belief, some widely advocated theories of such belief and the available evidence that bears on each of these theories, culminating in the formulation of a detailed causal model of scientifically unaccepted beliefs. It is argued that the model serves to capture some of the evident complexities of the development of paranormal beliefs and in this respect it has promise for greater ecological validity than do earlier simplistic characterisations of paranormal believers variously as socially marginal, subjectively oriented, cognitively deficient, or psychologically dysfunctional. In itself the endorsement of paranormal belief evidently does not mark out a person as different in kind from others but, rather, it simply contributes to the manifold dimensions that help to define what it is to be human.

References

Aarnio, K. and Lindeman, M. (2005). Paranormal beliefs, education and thinking styles. *Personality and Individual Differences, 39,* 1227–36.

Abdel-Khalek, A. M. (2002). Age and sex differences for anxiety in relation to family size, birth order and religiosity among Kuwaiti adolescents. *Psychological Reports, 90,* 1031–6.

Abramson, L. Y., Seligman, M. E. P. and Teasdale, J. D. (1978). Learned helplessness in humans: critique and reformulation. *Journal of Abnormal Psychology, 87,* 49–74.

Aeschleman, S. R., Rosen, C. C. and Williams, M. R. (2003). The effect of non-contingent negative and positive reinforcement operations on the acquisition of superstitious behaviours. *Behavioural Processes, 61,* 37–45.

Alcock, J. E. (1975). *Some correlates of extraordinary belief.* Paper presented at the 36th Annual Meeting of the Canadian Psychological Association, Quebec.

Alcock, J. E. (1981). *Parapsychology: science or magic? A psychological perspective.* Elmsford, NY: Pergamon Press.

Alcock, J. E. (1995). The belief engine. *Skeptical Inquirer, 19* (3), 14–18.

Alcock, J. E. and Otis, L. P. (1980). Critical thinking and belief in the paranormal. *Psychological Reports, 46,* 479–482.

Allen, J. and Lester, D. (1994). Belief in paranormal phenomena and an external locus of control. *Perceptual and Motor Skills, 79,* 226.

Allison, N. (1996). *Do you believe? The relationship between paranormal beliefs and fantasy proneness.* Unpublished BSc thesis, University of Portsmouth, UK.

Almond, G. A., Appleby, R. S. and Sivan, E. (2003). *Strong religion: the rise of fundamentalisms around the world.* Chicago: University of Chicago Press.

Alprin, L. and Lester, D. (1995). Belief in reincarnation and locus of control. *Psychological Reports, 76,* 1018.

Altemeyer, B. and Hunsberger, B. (1997). *Amazing conversions: why some turn to faith and others abandon religion.* Amherst, NY: Prometheus Books.

Alvarado, K. A., Templer, D. I., Bresler, C. and Thomas-Dobson, S. (1995). The relationship of religious variables to death depression and death anxiety. *Journal of Clinical Psychology, 51,* 202–4.

American Psychiatric Association. (1994). *Diagnostic and statistical manual of mental disorders* (4th ed.). Washington, DC: American Psychiatric Association.

Anderson, C. A. and Deuser, W. E. (1993). The primacy of control in causal thinking and attributional style: an attributional functionalism perspective. In G. Weary, F. Gleicher and K. L. Marsh (Eds.), *Control motivation and social cognition* (pp. 94–121). New York: Springer-Verlag.

Anderson, J. (1988). *Trance mediums and schizophrenics: a psychological assessment and P300 analysis.* Unpublished master's thesis, University of New England, Armidale, Australia.

Andrews, L. and Lester, D. (1998). Manic-depressive tendencies and belief in life after death. *Psychological Reports, 82,* 1114.

Appelbaum, P. S., Robbins, P. C. and Roth, L. H. (1999). Dimensional approach to delusions: comparison across types and diagnoses. *American Journal of Psychiatry, 156,* 1938–43.

Appelle, S., Lynn, S. J. and Newman, L. (2000). Alien abduction experiences. In E. Cardeña, S. J. Lynn and S. Krippner (Eds.), *Varieties of anomalous experience: examining the scientific evidence* (pp. 253–82). Washington, DC: American Psychological Association.

Appleyard, B. (1992). *Understanding the present: science and the soul of modern man.* London: Pan Books.

Argue, A., Johnson, D. R. and White, L. K. (1999). Age and religiosity: evidence from a three-wave panel analysis. *Journal for the Scientific Study of Religion, 38,* 423–35.

Argyle, M. (2000). *Psychology and religion: an introduction.* London: Routledge.

Atkinson, R. P. (1994). Relationships of hypnotic susceptibility to paranormal beliefs and claimed experiences: implications for hypnotic absorption. *American Journal of Clinical Hypnosis, 37,* 34–40.

Auton, H. R., Pope, J. and Seeger, G. (2003). Isn't it strange: paranormal belief and personality traits. *Social Behavior and Personality, 31,* 711–13.

Ayeroff, F. and Abelson, R. P. (1976). ESP and ESB: belief in personal success at mental telepathy. *Journal of Personality and Social Psychology, 34,* 240–7.

Bader, C. (1999). When prophecy passes unnoticed: new perspectives on failed prophecy. *Journal for the Scientific Study of Religion, 38,* 119–31.

Bader, C. D. (2003). Supernatural support groups: who are the UFO abductees and ritual-abuse survivors? *Journal for the Scientific Study of Religion, 42,* 669–78.

Bainbridge, W. S. (1978). Chariots of the gullible. *Skeptical Inquirer, 3,* 33–48.

Bainbridge, W. S. (1983). Attitudes towards interstellar communication: an empirical study. *Journal of the British Interplanetary Society, 36,* 298–304.

Bainbridge, W. S. (2004). After the New Age. *Journal for the Scientific Study of Religion, 43,* 381–94.

Baldacchino, D. and Draper, P. (2001). Spiritual coping strategies: a review of the nursing research literature. *Journal of Advanced Nursing, 34,* 833–41.

Banziger, G. (1983). Normalizing the paranormal: short-term and long-term change in belief in the paranormal among older learners during a short course. *Teaching of Psychology, 10,* 212–14.

Barker, E. (1984). *The making of a Moonie: choice or brainwashing?* London: Blackwell.

Barker, E. (1989). *New religious movements: a practical introduction.* London: Her Majesty's Stationery Office (HMSO).

Barrett, J. B., Pearson, J., Muller, C. and Frank, K. A. (2007). Adolescent religiosity and school contexts. *Social Science Quarterly, 88,* 1024–37.

Bartholomew, R. E. (2001). *Little green men, meowing nuns and head-hunting panics: a study of mass psychogenic illness and social delusion.* Jefferson, NC: McFarland.

Bartholomew, R. E., Basterfield, K. and Howard, G. S. (1991). UFO abductees and contactees: psychopathology or fantasy proneness? *Professional Psychology: Research and Practice, 22,* 215–22.

Bartkowski, J. P. (1998). Claims-making and typifications of voodoo as a deviant religion: hex, lies and videotape. *Journal for the Scientific Study of Religion, 37,* 559–79.

Basterfield, K. and Thalbourne, M. A. (2002). Belief in and alleged experience of the paranormal in ostensible UFO abductees. *Australian Journal of Parapsychology, 2* (1), 2–18.

Bauer, H. H. (1996). Cryptozoology. In G. Stein (Ed.), *The encyclopaedia of the paranormal* (pp. 199–214). Amherst, NY: Prometheus Books.

Beck, R. and Miller, J. P. (2001). Erosion of belief and disbelief: effects of religiosity and negative affect on beliefs in the paranormal and supernatural. *Journal of Social Psychology, 141,* 277–87.

Belanger, A. F. (1944). An empirical study of superstitions and unfounded beliefs. *Proceedings of the Iowa Academy of Science, 51,* 355–9.

Bell, M. D., Greig, T. C., Bryson, G. and Kaplan, E. (2001). Patterns of object relations and reality testing deficits in schizophrenia: clusters and their symptom and personality correlates. *Journal of Clinical Psychology, 57,* 1353–67.

Beloff, J. (1977). Backward causation. *Parapsychology Review, 8* (1), 1–5.

Benassi, V. A., Sweeney, P. D. and Drevno, G. E. (1979). Mind over matter: perceived success at psychokinesis. *Journal of Personality and Social Psychology, 37,* 1377–86.

Bennett, G. (1987). *Traditions of belief: women and the supernatural.* London: Penguin.

Bergstrom, C. B. (1999). The development of belief in astral travel as an accommodation to childhood sexual abuse: a grounded theory. (Doctoral dissertation, Pepperdine University.) *Dissertation Abstracts International, 59* (11), 6059B.

Bevan, J. M. (1947). The relation of attitude to success in ESP scoring. *Journal of Parapsychology, 11,* 296–309.

Bever, E. (2002). Witchcraft, female aggression and power in the early modern community. *Journal of Social History, 35,* 955–88.

Beyer, P. (1994). *Religion and globalization.* London: Sage.

Beyerstein, B. L. (1998). The sorry state of scientific literacy in the industrialized democracies. *Learning Quarterly, 2* (2), 5–11.

Bhadra, B. H. (1966). The relationship of test scores to belief in ESP. *Journal of Parapsychology, 30,* 1–17.

Bhushan, R. and Bhushan, L. I. (1987). Superstition among college students. *Asian Journal of Psychology and Education, 19* (4), 11–16.

Blachowski, S. (1937). The magical behavior of children in relation to school. *American Journal of Psychology, 50,* 347–61.

Black, A. W. (1990). The sociology of religion in Australia. *Sociological Analysis, 51* (Sup.), S27–S41.

Blackmore, S. J. (1984). A postal survey of OBEs and other experiences. *Journal of the Society for Psychical Research, 52,* 225–44.

Blackmore, S. J. (1997). Probability misjudgment and belief in the paranormal: a newspaper survey. *British Journal of Psychology, 88,* 683–9.

Blackmore, S. [J.] and Moore, R. (1994). Seeing things: visual recognition and belief in the paranormal. *European Journal of Parapsychology, 10,* 91–103.

Blackmore, S. [J.] and Troscianko, T. (1985). Belief in the paranormal: probability judgements, illusory control and the 'chance baseline shift'. *British Journal of Psychology, 76,* 459–68.

Bleak, J. L. and Frederick, C. M. (1998). Superstitious behavior in sport: levels of effectiveness and determinants of use in three collegiate sports. *Journal of Sport Behavior, 21,* 1–15.

Blum, S. H. (1976). Some aspects of belief in prevailing superstitions. *Psychological Reports, 38,* 579–82.

Blum, S. H. and Blum, L. H. (1974). Dos and don'ts: an informal study of some prevailing superstitions. *Psychological Reports, 35,* 567–71.

Boy, D. (2002). Les Français et les para-sciences: vingt ans de mesures [The French and the parasciences: twenty years of measures]. *Revue Française de Sociologie, 43,* 35–45.

Boyce, T. E. and Geller, E. S. (2002). Using the Barnum effect to teach psychological research methods. *Teaching of Psychology, 29,* 316–18.

Brasher, B. E. (Ed.). (2001). *Encyclopaedia of fundamentalism.* New York: Routledge.

Braude, S. E. (1978). On the meaning of 'paranormal'. In J. Ludwig (Ed.), *Philosophy and parapsychology* (pp. 227–44). Buffalo, NY: Prometheus Books.

Bressan, P. (2002). The connection between random sequences, everyday coincidences and belief in the paranormal. *Applied Cognitive Psychology, 16,* 17–34.

Bressan, P., Kramer, P. and Germani, M. (2008). Visual attentional capture predicts belief in a meaningful world. *Cortex, 44,* 1299–306.

Broad, C. D. (1937). The philosophical implications of foreknowledge. *Proceedings of the Aristotelian Society, 16* (Sup.), 177–209.

Broad, C. D. (1949). The relevance of psychical research to philosophy. *Philosophy, 24,* 291–309.

Bromley, D. G. and Shupe, A. D. Jr. (1979). *Moonies in America: cult, church and crusade.* Beverly Hills, CA: Sage.

Brown, L. T., Ruder, V. G., Ruder, J. H. and Young, S. D. (1974). Stimulation seeking and the Change Seeker Index. *Journal of Consulting and Clinical Psychology, 42,* 311.

Brugger, P., Gamma, A., Muri, R., Schäfer, M. and Taylor, K. I. (1993). Functional hemispheric asymmetry and belief in ESP: toward a 'neuropsychology of belief'. *Perceptual and Motor Skills, 77,* 1299–308.

Brugger, P., Regard, M. and Landis, T. (1991). Belief in extrasensory perception and illusory control: a replication. *Journal of Psychology, 125,* 501–2.

Brugger, P., Regard, M., Landis, T., Cook, N., Krebs, D. and Niederberger, J. (1993). 'Meaningful' patterns in visual noise: effects of lateral stimulation and the observer's belief in ESP. *Psychopathology, 26,* 261–5.

Brugger, P., Regard, M., Landis, T. and Graves, R. E. (1995). The roots of meaningful coincidence. *Lancet, 345,* 1306–7.

Brugger, P., Regard, M., Landis, T. and Oelz, O. (1999). Hallucinatory experiences in extreme-altitude climbers. *Neuropsychiatry, Neuropsychology and Behavioral Neurology, 12,* 67–71.

Bunge, M. (1991). A skeptic's beliefs and disbeliefs. *New Ideas in Psychology, 9,* 131–49.

Burger, J. M. (1984). Desire for control, locus of control and proneness to depression. *Journal of Personality, 52,* 71–89.

Burger, J. M. (1992). *Desire for control: personality, social and clinical perspectives.* New York: Plenum Press.

Burger, J. M. and Cooper, H. M. (1979). The desirability of control. *Motivation and Emotion, 3,* 381–393.

Burger, J. M. and Lynn, A. L. (2005). Superstitious behavior among American and Japanese professional baseball players. *Basic and Applied Social Psychology, 27,* 71–6.

Caird, D. and Law, H. G. (1982). Non-conventional beliefs: their structure and measurement. *Journal for the Scientific Study of Religion, 21,* 152–63.

Caldwell, O. W. and Lundeen, G. E. (1932). What can be done regarding unfounded beliefs? *School and Society, 35,* 680–6.

Caldwell, O. W. and Lundeen, G. E. (1934). Further study of unfounded beliefs among junior high school pupils. *Teachers College Record, 36,* 35–52.

Callaghan, A. (2000). *The effect of coping style on paranormal belief.* Unpublished dissertation for the Graduate Diploma of Psychology, University of New England, Australia.

Callaghan, A. and Irwin, H. J. (2003). Paranormal belief as a psychological coping mechanism. *Journal of the Society for Psychical Research, 67,* 200–7.

Campbell, C. (1996). Half-belief and the paradox of ritual instrumental activism: a theory of modern superstition. *British Journal of Sociology, 47,* 151–66.

Canetti, D. and Pedahzur, A. (2002). The effects of contextual and psychological variables on extreme right-wing sentiments. *Social Behavior and Personality, 30,* 317–34.

Carr, S. M., Marshall, H. D., Johnstone, K. A., Pynn, L. M. and Stenson, G. B. (2002). How to tell a sea monster: molecular discrimination of large marine animals of the North Atlantic. *Biological Bulletin, 202,* 1–5.

Carver, C. S., Scheier, M. F. and Weintraub, J. K. (1989). Assessing coping strategies: a theoretically-based approach. *Journal of Personality and Social Psychology, 56,* 267–83.

Case, T. I., Fitness, J., Cairns, D. R. and Stevenson, R. J. (2004). Coping with uncertainty: superstitious strategies and secondary control. *Journal of Applied Social Psychology, 34,* 848–71.

Cavalli-Sforza, L. L., Feldman, M. W., Chen, K. and Dornbusch, S. M. (1982). Theory and observation in cultural transmission. *Science, 218,* 19–27.

Chadwick, P. D. J. and Lowe, C. F. (1990). Measurement and modification of delusional beliefs. *Journal of Consulting and Clinical Psychology, 58,* 225–32.

Charumathy, P. J. and Anantharaman, R. N. (1983). Personality and superstition. *Indian Journal of Clinical Psychology, 10,* 61–62.

Chequers, J., Joseph, S. and Diduca, D. (1997). Belief in extraterrestrial life, UFO-related beliefs and schizotypal personality. *Personality and Individual Differences, 23,* 519–21.

Chorpita, B. F. and Barlow, D. H. (1998). The development of anxiety: the role of control in the early environment. *Psychological Bulletin, 124,* 3–21.

Christopher, S., Fearon, J., McCoy, J. and Nobbe, C. (1971). Social deprivation and religiosity. *Journal for the Scientific Study of Religion, 10,* 385–92.

Claridge, G. (Ed.). (1997). *Schizotypy: implications for illness and health.* Oxford: Oxford University Press.

Clark, L. S. (2002). US adolescent religious identity, the media and the 'funky' side of religion. *Journal of Communication, 52,* 794–811.

Clark, L. S. (2003). *From angels to aliens: teenagers, the media and the supernatural.* New York: Oxford University Press.

Clarke, D. (1991a). Belief in the paranormal: a New Zealand survey. *Journal of the Society for Psychical Research, 57,* 412–25.

Clarke, D. (1991b). Students' beliefs and academic performance in an empathic course on the paranormal. *Journal of the Society for Psychical Research, 58,* 74–83.

Clarke, D. (1993). Self-actualization and paranormal beliefs: an empirical study. *Journal of the Society for Psychical Research, 59,* 81–8.

Clarke, D. (1995). Experience and other reasons given for belief and disbelief in paranormal and religious phenomena. *Journal of the Society for Psychical Research, 60,* 371–84.

Cohn, S. A. (1999). Second sight and family history: pedigree and segregation analyses. *Journal of Scientific Exploration, 13,* 351–72.

Coleman, L. and Clark, J. (1999). *Cryptozoology A to Z: The encyclopedia of loch monsters, Sasquatch, chupacabras and other authentic mysteries of nature.* New York: Simon and Schuster.

Coll, R. K. and Taylor, N. (2004). Probing scientists' beliefs: how open-minded are modern scientists? *International Journal of Science Education, 26,* 757–78.

Conklin, E. S. (1919). Superstitious belief and practice among college students. *American Journal of Psychology, 30,* 83–102.

Cook, L. (2002). *Do people's beliefs in ESP affect the way they evaluate evidence confirming or disconfirming their beliefs?* Unpublished BSc dissertation, University of Edinburgh.

Cook, S. W. and Heppner, P. P. (1997). A psychometric study of three coping measures. *Educational and Psychological Measurement, 57,* 906–23.

Copen, C. E. and Silverstein, M. (2008). *Journal of Comparative Family Studies, 39,* 59–72.

Cosgel, M. M. (2001). The commitment process in a religious commune: the Shakers. *Journal for the Scientific Study of Religion, 40,* 27–38.

Costa, P. T. and Widiger, T. A. (1994). *Personality disorders and the five-factor model of personality.* Washington, DC: American Psychological Association.

Cowan, D. E. and Bromley, D. G. (2008). *Cults and new religions: a brief history.* Malden, MA: Blackwell.

Crandall, J. E. (1985). Effects of favorable and unfavorable conditions on the psi-missing displacement effect. *Journal of the American Society for Psychical Research, 79,* 27–38.

Crockett, A. and Voas, D. (2006). Generations of decline: religious change in 20th century Britain. *Journal for the Scientific Study of Religion, 45,* 567–84.

Curtis, J. T. and Wilson, J. P. (1997). Sensation seeking and ESP test performance: a preliminary investigation. *Journal of the Society for Psychical Research, 62,* 1–21.

Dag, I. (1999). The relationships among paranormal beliefs, locus of control and psychopathology in a Turkish college sample. *Personality and Individual Differences, 26,* 723–37.

Dag, I. (2002). Kontrol Odagi Ölçegi (KOÖ): Ölçek gelistirme, güvenirlik ve geçerlik çalismasi [Locus of Control Scale: scale development, reliability and validity study]. *Türk Psikoloji Dergisi, 17* (49), 77–92.

Dagnall, N., Parker, A. and Munley, G. (2007a). Paranormal belief and reasoning. *Personality and Individual Differences, 43,* 1406–15.

Dagnall, N., Parker, A. and Munley, G. (2007b). Superstitious belief: negative and positive superstitions and psychological functioning. *European Journal of Parapsychology, 22,* 121–37.

Davies, M. F. (1985). Self-consciousness and paranormal belief. *Perceptual and Motor Skills, 60,* 484–6.

Davies, M. F. (1988). Paranormal beliefs in British and southern USA college students. *Psychological Reports, 62,* 163–6.

Davies, M. F. and Kirkby, H. E. (1985). Multidimensionality of the relationship between perceived control and belief in the paranormal: spheres of control and types of paranormal phenomena. *Personality and Individual Differences, 6,* 661–3.

Davis, G. A., Peterson, J. M. and Farley, F. H. (1974). Attitudes, motivation, sensation seeking and belief in ESP as predictors of real creative behavior. *Journal of Creative Behavior, 8,* 31–9.

de Barbenza, C. M. and de Vila, N. C. (1989). Creencia en fenomenos paranormals – Implicancias socioculturales [Belief in paranormal phenomena: sociocultural implications]. *Arquivos Brasileiros de Psicologia, 41* (3), 41–50.

de Vaus, D. and McAllister, I. (1987). Gender differences in religion: a test of the structural location theory. *American Sociological Review, 52,* 472–81.

Delpech, L. (1957). Preliminary study of attitudes. In *Proceedings of four conferences of parapsychological studies* (pp. 143–4). New York: Parapsychology Foundation.

Denes-Raj, V. and Epstein, S. (1994). Conflict between intuitive and rational processing: when people behave against their better judgment. *Journal of Personality and Social Psychology, 66,* 819–29.

DeNeve, K. M. and Cooper, H. (1998). The happy personality: a meta-analysis of 137 personality traits and subjective well-being. *Psychological Bulletin, 124,* 197–229.

Dew, R. E., Daniel, S. S., Armstrong, T. D., Goldston, D. B., Triplett, M. F. and Koenig, H. G. (2008). Religion/spirituality and adolescent psychiatric symptoms: A review. *Child Psychiatry and Human Development, 39,* 381–98.

Donahue, M. J. (1993). Prevalence and correlates of New Age beliefs in six Protestant denominations. *Journal for the Scientific Study of Religion, 32,* 177–84.

D'Onofrio, B. M., Eaves, L. J., Murrelle, L., Maes, H. H. and Spilka, B. (1999). Understanding biological and social influences on religious affiliation, attitudes and behaviors: a behavior genetic perspective. *Journal of Personality, 67,* 953–84.

Donovan, J. M. (1998). Reinterpreting telepathy as unusual experiences of empathy and charisma. *Perceptual and Motor Skills, 87,* 131–46.

Dresslar, F. B. (1907). Superstition and education. *University of California Publications: Education, 5,* 1–239.

Dresslar, F. B. (1910). Suggestions on the psychology of superstition. *American Journal of Insanity, 67,* 213–26.

Dudley, R. L. and Dudley, M. G. (1986). Transmission of religious values from parents to adolescents. *Review of Religious Research, 28,* 3–13.`

Dudley, R. T. (1999a). Effect of restriction of working memory on reported paranormal belief. *Psychological Reports, 84,* 313–16.

Dudley, R. T. (1999b). The effect of superstitious belief on performance following an unsolvable problem. *Personality and Individual Differences, 26,* 1057–64.

Dudley, R. T. (2000). The relationship between negative affect and paranormal belief. *Personality and Individual Differences, 28,* 315–21.

Dudley, R. T. (2002). Order effects in research on paranormal belief. *Psychological Reports, 90,* 665–6.

Dudley, R. T. and Whisnand, E. A. (2000). Paranormal belief and attributional style. *Psychological Reports, 86,* 863–4.

Dudycha, G. J. (1933). The superstitious beliefs of college students. *Journal of Abnormal and Social Psychology, 27,* 457–64.

Duncan, D. F., Donnelly, J. W. and Nicholson, T. (1992). Belief in the paranormal and religious belief among American college students. *Psychological Reports, 70,* 15–18.

Eckblad, M. and Chapman, L. (1983). Magical ideation as an indicator of schizotypy. *Journal of Consulting and Clinical Psychology, 51,* 215–25.

Edge, H. and Suryani, L. K. (2001, August). *Investigation of psychic beliefs in Bali.* Paper presented at the 44th Annual Convention of the Parapsychological Association, New York.

Edwards, E. D. (2001). A house that tries to be haunted: ghostly narratives in popular film and television. In J. Houran and R. Lange (Eds.), *Hauntings and poltergeists: multidisciplinary perspectives* (pp. 82–119). Jefferson, NC: McFarland.

Edwards, P. (1996). *Reincarnation: a critical examination.* Amherst, NY: Prometheus Books.

Egan, V., Auty, J., Miller, R., Ahmadi, S., Richardson, C. and Gargan, I. (1999). Sensational interests and general personality traits. *Journal of Forensic Psychiatry, 10,* 567–82.

Eilbert, L. and Schmeidler, G. R. (1950). A study of certain psychological factors in relation to ESP performance. *Journal of Parapsychology, 14,* 53–74.

Ejvegaard, R. and Johnson, M. (1981). Murderous ESP: a case of story fabrication. *European Journal of Parapsychology, 4,* 81–98.

Eliade, M. (1964). *Shamanism: archaic techniques of ecstasy* (W. R. Trask, Trans.). London: Routledge and Kegan Paul.

Ellis, A. (1962). *Reason and emotion in psychotherapy.* New York: Lyle Stuart.

Ellis, B. (2002). Why is a lucky rabbit's foot lucky? Body parts as fetishes. *Journal of Folklore Research, 39,* 51–84.

Ellson, D. G. (1942). Book publications in psychical research and spiritualism in wartime. *Journal of Abnormal and Social Psychology, 37,* 388–92.

Emery, E. (1996). The media and the paranormal. In G. Stein (Ed.), *The encyclopedia of the paranormal* (pp. 385–93). Amherst, NY: Prometheus Books.

Emme, E. E. (1940). Modification and origin of certain beliefs in superstition among 96 college students. *Journal of Psychology, 10,* 279–91.

Emme, E. E. (1941). Supplementary study of superstitious belief among college students. *Journal of Psychology, 12,* 183–4.

Emmons, C. F. and Sobal, J. (1981a). Paranormal beliefs: functional alternatives to mainstream religion? *Review of Religious Research, 22,* 301–12.

Emmons, C. F. and Sobal, J. (1981b). Paranormal beliefs: testing the marginality hypothesis. *Sociological Focus, 14,* 49–56.

Endler, N. S. and Parker, J. D. A. (1994). Assessment of multidimensional coping: task, emotion and avoidance strategies. *Psychological Assessment, 6,* 50–60.

Epstein, S. (1994). Integration of the cognitive and the psychodynamic unconscious. *American Psychologist, 49,* 709–24.

Epstein, S., Pacini, R., Denes-Raj, V. and Heier, H. (1996). Individual differences in intuitive–experiential and analytical–rational thinking styles. *Journal of Personality and Social Psychology, 71,* 390–405.

Erickson, J. A. (1992). Adolescent religious development and commitment: a structural equation model of the role of family, peer group and educational influences. *Journal for the Scientific Study of Religion, 31,* 131–52.

Esgate, A. E. and Groome, D. (2001). Probability and coincidence. In R. Roberts and D. Groome (Eds.), *Parapsychology: the science of unusual experience.* London: Arnold.

Eudell, E. and Campbell, J. B. (2007). Openness to experience and belief in the paranormal: a modified replication of Zingrone, Alvarado and Dalton (1998–9). *European Journal of Parapsychology, 22,* 166–74.

Evans, J. St. B. T., Barston, J. and Pollard, P. (1983). On the conflict between logic and belief in syllogistic reasoning. *Memory and Cognition, 11,* 295–306.

Fabricatore, A. N. (2002). Stress, religion and mental health: the role of religious coping (Doctoral dissertation, Saint Louis University). *Dissertation Abstracts International, 63* (4), 2053B.

Farha, B. and Steward, G. (2006). Paranormal beliefs: an analysis of college students. *Skeptical Inquirer, 30* (1), 37–40.

Farias, M., Claridge, G. and Lalljee, M. (2005). Personality and cognitive predictors of New Age practices and beliefs. *Personality and Individual Differences, 39,* 979–89.

Fichten, C. S. and Sunerton, B. (1983). Popular horoscopes and the 'Barnum effect'. *Journal of Psychology, 114,* 123–34.

Finch, S. E. (2002). *Daydream believers? Fantasy-proneness, transliminality and reality monitoring: a search for vulnerability factors in false memory creation.* Unpublished doctoral dissertation, Goldsmiths College, University of London.

Fishbein, M. and Ajzen, I. (1975). *Belief, attitude, intention and behavior: an introduction to theory and research.* Reading, MA: Addison-Wesley.

Fishbein, M. and Raven, B. H. (1967). The AB scales: an operational definition of belief and attitude. In M. Fishbein (Ed.), *Readings in attitude theory and measurement* (pp. 183–9). New York: Wiley.

Fisher, S. and Fisher, R. L. (1993). *The psychology of adaptation to absurdity: tactics of make-believe.* Hillsdale, NJ: Lawrence Erlbaum Associates.

Fishman, S. (1992). Relationships among an older adult's life review, ego integrity and death anxiety. *International Psychogeriatrics, 4* (Sup. 2), 267–77.

Fisman, S. and Fisman, R. (1999). Cultural influences on symptom presentation in childhood. *Journal of the American Academy of Child and Adolescent Psychiatry, 38,* 782–3.

Fitzpatrick, O. D. and Shook, S. L. (1994). Belief in the paranormal: does identity development during the college years make a difference? An initial investigation. *Journal of Parapsychology, 58,* 315–29.

Flammer, A. (1995). Developmental analysis of control beliefs. In A. Bandura (Ed.), *Self-efficacy in changing societies* (pp. 69–113). Cambridge: Cambridge University Press.

Flere, S. (2007). Gender and religious orientation. *Social Compass, 54,* 239–53.

Flynn, T. (1996). Photography (as it applies to the paranormal). In G. Stein (Ed.), *The encyclopedia of the paranormal* (pp. 515–27). Amherst, NY: Prometheus Books.

Fox, J. and Williams, C. (2000). Paranormal belief, experience and the Keirsey Temperament Sorter. *Psychological Reports, 86,* 1104–6.

Fox, J. W. (1992). The structure, stability and social antecedents of reported paranormal experiences. *Sociological Analysis, 53,* 417–31.

Fox, P. (1979). Social and cultural factors influencing beliefs about UFOs. In R. F. Haines (Ed.), *UFO phenomena and the behavioral scientist* (pp. 20–42). Metuchen, NJ: Scarecrow Press.

Francis, L. J. (1986). Denominational schools and pupil attitudes toward Christianity. *British Educational Research Journal, 12,* 145–52.

Francis, L. J. and Kaldor, P. (2002). The relationship between psychological well-being and Christian faith and practice in an Australian population sample. *Journal for the Scientific Study of Religion, 41,* 179–84.

Frank, J. D. (1977). Nature and functions of belief systems: humanism and transcendental religion. *American Psychologist, 32,* 555–9.

Frazer, J. G. (1911). *The golden bough: a study in magic and religion* (3rd ed.). London: Macmillan.

Frazier K. (1996). Committee for the Scientific Investigation of Claims of the Paranormal (CSICOP). In G. Stein (Ed.), *The encyclopedia of the paranormal* (pp. 168–81). Amherst, NY: Prometheus Books.

French, C. C. (1992). Factors underlying belief in the paranormal: do sheep and goats think differently? *The Psychologist, 5,* 295–9.

French, C. C. (2000). The media and the paranormal: A sceptic's view. *Magonia, 70,* 9–13.

French, C. C. and Kerman, M. K. (1996, December). *Childhood trauma, fantasy proneness and belief in the paranormal.* Paper presented at the Annual Conference of the British Psychological Society, London.

French, C. C., O'Donnell, H. and Williams, L. (2001, March). *Hypnotic susceptibility, paranormal belief and reports of 'crystal power'.* Paper presented at the Centenary Annual Conference of the British Psychological Society, Glasgow.

French, C. C., Rose, N. J. and Blackmore, S. J. (2002, August). *Paranormal belief and interpretations of sleep paralysis.* Paper presented at the 45th Annual Convention of the Parapsychological Association, Paris, France.

French, C. C., Santomauro, J., Hamilton, V., Fox, R. and Thalbourne, M. A. (2008). Psychological aspects of the alien contact experience. *Cortex, 44,* 1387–95.

Friedland, N., Keinan, G. and Regev, Y. (1992). Controlling the uncontrollable: effects of stress on illusory perceptions of controllability. *Journal of Personality and Social Psychology, 63,* 923–31.

Frith, C. D. and Done, D. J. (1989). Experiences of alien control in schizophrenia reflect a disorder in the central monitoring of action. *Psychological Medicine, 19,* 359–63.

Fry, M. D. (2000). A developmental analysis of children's and adolescents' understanding of luck and ability in the physical domain. *Journal of Sport and Exercise Psychology, 22,* 145–66.

Fuller, R. C. (2001). *Spiritual, but not religious: understanding unchurched America.* New York: Oxford University Press.

Gallagher, C., Kumar, V. K. and Pekala, R. J. (1994). The Anomalous Experiences Inventory: reliability and validity. *Journal of Parapsychology, 58,* 402–28.

Gallagher, T. J. and Lewis, J. M. (2001). Rationalists, fatalists and the modern superstitious: test-taking in introductory sociology. *Sociological Inquiry, 71,* 1–12.

Gallup, G., Jr. (Ed.) (1997). *The Gallup poll: public opinion, 1996.* Wilmington, DE: Scholarly Resources.

Garrett, H. E. and Fisher, T. R. (1926). The prevalence of certain popular misconceptions. *Journal of Applied Psychology, 10,* 411–20.

Gasde, I. and Block, R. A. (1998). Cult experience: psychological abuse, distress, personality characteristics and changes in personal relationships reported by former members of Church Universal and Triumphant. *Cultic Studies Journal, 15,* 192–221.

Genovese, J. E. C. (2005). Paranormal beliefs, schizotypy and thinking styles among teachers and future teachers. *Personality and Individual Differences, 39,* 93–102.

George, S. and Sreedhar, K. P. (2006). Globalisation and the prevalence of superstitious beliefs. *Journal of the Indian Academy of Applied Psychology, 32,* 337–43.

Gianotti, L. R. R., Faber, P. L. and Lehmann, D. (2002). EEG source locations after guessed random events in believers and skeptics of paranormal phenomena. *International Congress Series, 1232,* 439–41.

Gianotti, L. R. R., Mohr, C., Pizzagalli, D., Lehmann, D. and Brugger, P. (2001). Associative processing and paranormal belief. *Psychiatry and Clinical Neurosciences, 55,* 595–603.

Gill, A. (1994). All at sea? The survival of superstition. *History Today, 44* (12), 9–11.

Gilliland, A. R. (1930). A study of the superstitions of college students. *Journal of Abnormal and Social Psychology, 24*, 472–9.

Gilovich, T. (1991). *How we know what isn't so: the fallibility of human reason in everyday life.* New York: Free Press.

Gilovich, T., Griffin, D. and Kahneman, D. (Eds.) (2002). *Heuristics and biases: the psychology of intuitive judgment.* New York: Cambridge University Press.

Glicksohn, J. (1990). Belief in the paranormal and subjective paranormal experience. *Personality and Individual Differences, 11*, 675–83.

Glock, C. Y. (1964). The role of deprivation in the origin and evolution of religious groups. In R. Lee and M. E. Marty (Eds.), *Religion and social conflict* (pp. 24–36). New York: Oxford University Press.

Glock, C. Y. and Stark, R. (1965). *Religion and society in tension.* Chicago: Rand McNally.

Goode, E. (2000a). *Paranormal beliefs: a sociological introduction.* Prospect Heights, IL: Waveland Press.

Goode, E. (2000b). Two paranormalisms or two and a half? An empirical exploration. *Skeptical Inquirer, 24* (1), 29–35.

Göritz, A. S. and Schumacher, J. (2000). The WWW as a research medium: an illustrative survey on paranormal belief. *Perceptual and Motor Skills, 90*, 1195–206.

Gorsuch, R. L. (1980). Identifying the religiously committed person. In J. R. Tisdale (Ed.), *Growing edges in the psychology of religion* (pp. 7–17). Chicago: Nelson-Hall.

Gorsuch, R. L. (1984). Measurement: the boon and bane of investigating religion. *American Psychologist, 39*, 228–36.

Gould, R. L. (1921). Superstitions among Scottish college girls. *Pedagogical Seminary, 28*, 203–48.

Goulding, A. (2004). Schizotypy models in relation to subjective health and paranormal beliefs and experiences. *Personality and Individual Differences, 37*, 157–67.

Goulding, A. (2005). Healthy schizotypy in a population of paranormal believers and experients. *Personality and Individual Differences, 38*, 1069–83.

Goulding, A. and Parker, A. (2001). Finding psi in the paranormal: psychometric measures used in research on paranormal beliefs/experiences and in research on psi-ability. *European Journal of Parapsychology, 16*, 73–101.

Granqvist, P. and Hagekull, B. (1999). Religiousness and perceived childhood attachment: profiling socialized correspondence and emotional compensation. *Journal for the Scientific Study of Religion, 38*, 254–73.

Granqvist, P. and Hagekull, B. (2001). Seeking security in the New Age: on attachment and emotional compensation. *Journal for the Scientific Study of Religion, 40*, 527–45.

Granqvist, P., Ivarsson, T., Broberg, A. G. and Hagekull, B. (2007). Examining relations among attachment, religiosity and New Age spirituality using the Adult Attachment Interview. *Developmental Psychology, 43,* 590–601.

Gray, T. (1984). University course reduces belief in paranormal. *Skeptical Inquirer, 8,* 247–51.

Gray, T. (1985). Changing unsubstantiated belief: testing the ignorance hypothesis. *Canadian Journal of Behavioural Science, 17,* 263–70.

Gray, T. (1987). Educational experience and belief in paranormal phenomena. In F. B. Harrold and R. A. Eve (Eds.), *Cult archaeology and creationism: understanding pseudoscientific beliefs about the past* (pp. 21–33). Iowa City: University of Iowa Press.

Gray, T. (1990a). Gender differences in belief in scientifically unsubstantiated phenomena. *Canadian Journal of Behavioural Science, 22,* 181–90.

Gray, T. (1990b). Questionnaire format and item content affect level of belief in both scientifically unsubstantiated and substantiated phenomena. *Canadian Journal of Behavioural Science, 22,* 173–80.

Gray, T. and Mill, D. (1990). Critical abilities, graduate education (Biology vs. English) and belief in unsubstantiated phenomena. *Canadian Journal of Behavioural Science, 22,* 162–72.

Greeley, A. M. (1975). *The sociology of the paranormal: a reconnaissance.* Beverly Hills, CA: Sage.

Greenberg, J., Pyszczynski, T. and Solomon, S. (1986). The causes and consequences of a need for self-esteem: a terror management theory. In R. F. Baumeister (Ed.), *Public self and private self* (pp. 189–212). New York: Springer-Verlag.

Gregory, C. J. (1975). Changes in superstitious beliefs among college women. *Psychological Reports, 37,* 939–44.

Grey, W. (1988). Australia's credulity rating: bad or worse? *The Skeptic* (Australia), *8* (4), 35.

Greyson, B. (1977). Telepathy in mental illness: deluge or delusion? *Journal of Nervous and Mental Disease, 165,* 184–200.

Grimmer, M. R. (1992). Searching for security in the mystical: the function of paranormal beliefs. *Skeptical Inquirer, 16,* 173–6.

Grimmer, M. R. and White, K. D. (1986). Psychics and ESP: the role of population stereotypes. *Australian Psychologist, 21,* 405–11.

Grimmer, M. R. and White, K. D. (1990). The structure of paranormal beliefs among Australian psychology students. *Journal of Psychology, 124,* 357–70.

Grimmer, M. R. and White, K. D. (1992). Nonconventional beliefs among Australian science and nonscience students. *Journal of Psychology, 126,* 521–8.

Gross, P. R. and Levitt, N. (1994). *Higher superstition: the academic left and its quarrels with science.* Baltimore, MD: Johns Hopkins University Press.

Groth-Marnat, G. and Pegden, J. (1998). Personality correlates of paranormal belief: locus of control and sensation seeking. *Social Behavior and Personality, 26,* 291–6.

Groth-Marnat, G., Roberts, L. and Ollier, K. (1998–9). Hypnotizability, dissociation and paranormal beliefs. *Imagination, Cognition and Personality, 18*, 127–32.

Gunnoe, M. L. and Moore, K. A. (2002). Predictors of religiosity among youth aged 17–22: a longitudinal study of the National Survey of Children. *Journal for the Scientific Study of Religion, 41*, 613–22.

Hackney, C. H. and Sanders, G. S. (2003). Religiosity and mental health: a meta-analysis of recent studies. *Journal for the Scientific Study of Religion, 42*, 43–55.

Haight, J. (1979). Spontaneous psi cases: a survey and preliminary study of ESP, attitude and personality relationships. *Journal of Parapsychology, 43*, 179–204.

Hamilton, M. (2001). Who believes in astrology? Effect of favorableness of astrologically derived personality descriptions on acceptance of astrology. *Personality and Individual Differences, 31*, 895–902.

Hansen, G. P. (1992). CSICOP and the skeptics: an overview. *Journal of the American Society for Psychical Research, 86*, 19–63.

Happs, J. C. (1987). Conceptual conflict over pseudoscience: a case study involving teacher trainees and their belief in water divining. *The Skeptic* (Australia), 7 (2), 21–8.

Haraldsson, E. (1981). Some determinants of belief in psychical phenomena. *Journal of the American Society for Psychical Research, 75*, 297–309.

Haraldsson, E. (1985a). Interrogative suggestibility and its relationship with personality, perceptual defensiveness and extraordinary beliefs. *Personality and Individual Differences, 6*, 765–7.

Haraldsson, E. (1985b). Representative national surveys of psychic phenomena: Iceland, Great Britain, Sweden, USA and Gallup's multinational survey. *Journal of the Society for Psychical Research, 53*, 145–58.

Haraldsson, E., Gudmundsdottir, A., Ragnarsson, A., Loftsson, J. and Jonsson, S. (1977). National survey of psychical experiences and attitudes toward the paranormal in Iceland. In J. D. Morris, W. G. Roll and R. L. Morris (Eds.), *Research in parapsychology 1976* (pp. 182–6). Metuchen, NJ: Scarecrow Press.

Haraldsson, E. and Houtkooper, J. M. (1996). Traditional Christian beliefs, spiritualism and the paranormal: an Icelandic–American comparison. *International Journal for the Psychology of Religion, 6*, 51–64.

Harris, J. I., Schoneman, S. W. and Carrera, S. R. (2002). Approaches to religiosity related to anxiety among college students. *Mental Health, Religion and Culture, 5*, 253–65.

Hart, T. (2008, April). *Head vs. heart: dissection of paranormal beliefs.* Poster presented at the 36th Annual Western Pennsylvania Undergraduate Psychology Conference, Erie, PA, www.academics.rmu.edu/~paul/research/2008/headheart.pdf, retrieved 16 January 2009.

Hartman, P. A. (1976). Social dimensions of occult participation: the Gnostica study. *British Journal of Sociology, 27*, 169–83.

Hartman, S. E. (1999). Another view of the Paranormal Belief Scale. *Journal of Parapsychology, 63*, 131–41.

Hatton, K. (2001). Developmental origins of magical beliefs. *The Skeptic* (UK), *14* (1), 18–19.

Hay, D. and Morisy, A. (1978). Reports of ecstatic, paranormal, or religious experience in Great Britain and the United States: a comparison of trends. *Journal for the Scientific Study of Religion, 17,* 255–68.

Heard, K. V. and Vyse, S. A. (1998). Authoritarianism and paranormal beliefs. *Imagination, Cognition and Personality, 18,* 121–6.

Heider, F. (1958). *The psychology of interpersonal relations.* New York: Wiley.

Heintz, L. M. and Baruss, I. (2001). Spirituality in late adulthood. *Psychological Reports, 88,* 651–4.

Hergovich, A. (2003). Field dependence, suggestibility and belief in paranormal phenomena. *Personality and Individual Differences, 34,* 195–209.

Hergovich, A. (2004). The effect of pseudo-psychic demonstrations as dependent on belief in paranormal phenomena and suggestibility. *Personality and Individual Differences, 36,* 365–80.

Hergovich, A. and Arendasy, M. (2005). Critical thinking ability and belief in the paranormal. *Personality and Individual Differences, 38,* 1805–12.

Hergovich, A., Schott, R. and Arendasy, M. (2005). Paranormal belief and religiosity. *Journal of Parapsychology, 69,* 293–303.

Hergovich, A., Schott, R. and Arendasy, M. (2008). On the relationship between paranormal belief and schizotypy among adolescents. *Personality and Individual Differences, 45,* 19–125.

Hess, D. J. (1993). *Science in the New Age: the paranormal, its defenders and debunkers and American culture.* Madison, WI: University of Wisconsin Press.

Hillstrom, E. L. and Strachan, M. (2000). Strong commitment to traditional Protestant religious beliefs is negatively related to beliefs in paranormal phenomena. *Psychological Reports, 86,* 183–9.

Hirschfelder, G. (2001). Freitag der 13. – ein unglückstag? [Friday the 13th – a fateful day?]. *Zeitschrift für Volkskunde, 97,* 29–48.

Hobfoll, S. E., Schröder, K. E. E., Wells, M. and Malek, M. (2002). Communal versus individualistic construction of sense of mastery in facing life challenges. *Journal of Social and Clinical Psychology, 21,* 362–99.

Hodgson, R. and Davey, S. J. (1887). The possibilities of mal-observation and lapse of memory from a practical point of view. *Proceedings of the Society for Psychical Research, 4,* 381–495.

Hoge, D. R. and Roozen, D. A. (1979). Research on factors influencing church commitment. In D. R. Hoge and D. A. Roozen (Eds.), *Understanding church growth and decline: 1950–78* (pp. 42–68). New York: Pilgrim Press.

Holt, N. J., Simmonds-Moore, C. A. and Moore, S. L. (2008). Benign schizotypy: investigating differences between clusters of schizotype on paranormal belief, creativity, intelligence and mental health. Paper presented at the 51st Annual Convention of the Parapsychological Association, Winchester, England.

Horne, J. R. (1996). Morality and parapsychology. In M. Stoeber and H. Meynell (Eds.), *Critical reflections on the paranormal* (pp. 197–215). Albany, NY: State University of New York Press.

Houran, J. (1997). Tolerance of ambiguity and the perception of UFOs. *Perceptual and Motor Skills, 85,* 973–4.

Houran, J. (2001). Technical note: clarification on 'entity encounter experiences' and paranormal belief. *Journal of the Society for Psychical Research, 65,* 218–20.

Houran, J., Irwin, H. J. and Lange, R. (2001). Clinical relevance of the two-factor Rasch version of the Revised Paranormal Belief Scale. *Personality and Individual Differences, 31,* 371–82.

Houran, J., Kumar, V. K., Thalbourne, M. A. and Lavertue, N. E. (2002). Haunted by somatic tendencies: spirit infestation as psychogenic illness. *Mental Health, Religion and Culture, 5,* 119–33.

Houran, J. and Lange, R. (2001). Support for the construct validity of the two-factor conceptualization of paranormal belief: a complement to Thalbourne. *European Journal of Parapsychology, 16,* 53–60.

Houran, J. and Lange, R. (2004). Redefining delusion based on studies of subjective paranormal ideation. *Psychological Reports, 94,* 501–13.

Houran, J. and Thalbourne, M. A. (2001). Further study and speculation on the psychology of 'entity encounter experiences'. *Journal of the Society for Psychical Research, 65,* 26–37.

Houran, J., Thalbourne, M. A. and Ashe, D. D. (2000). Testing a psycho-anthropological view of paranormal belief and experience. *North American Journal of Psychology, 2,* 127–38.

Houran, J. and Williams, C. (1998). Relation of tolerance of ambiguity to global and specific paranormal experience. *Psychological Reports, 83,* 807–18.

Houran, J., Wiseman, R. and Thalbourne, M. A. (2002). Perceptual-personality characteristics associated with naturalistic haunt experiences. *European Journal of Parapsychology, 17,* 17–44.

Houtman, D. and Mascini, P. (2002). Why do churches become empty, while New Age grows? Secularization and religious change in the Netherlands. *Journal for the Scientific Study of Religion, 41,* 455–73.

Hume, D. (1777/1955). *Enquiries concerning the human understanding and concerning the principles of morals* (L. A. Selby-Bigge, Ed.). Oxford: Clarendon Press.

Humphrey, N. (1995). *Soul searching: human nature and supernatural belief.* London: Chatto and Windus.

Hunsberger, B. (1985). Religion, age, life satisfaction and perceived sources of religiousness: a study of older persons. *Journal of Gerontology, 40,* 615–20.

Hutton, R. (2000). *The triumph of the moon: a history of modern pagan witchcraft.* Oxford: Oxford University Press.

Hutton, R. (2007). The status of witchcraft in the modern world. *Pomegranate, 9,* 121–31.

Inglis, B. (1986). Retrocognitive dissonance. *Theta, 13/14* (1), 4–9.

Inglis, D. and Holmes, M. (2003). Highland and other haunts: ghosts in Scottish tourism. *Annals of Tourism Research, 30*, 50–63.

Institute for Research in Social Science. (1998). *Southern Focus Poll, Spring 1998.* Chapel Hill, NC: Author, University of Northern Carolina at Chapel Hill, www.irss.unc.edu/tempdocs/20:39:15:1.htm, retrieved 22 May 2001.

Irwin, H. J. (1985a). Fear of psi and attitude to parapsychological research. *Parapsychology Review, 16* (6), 1–4.

Irwin, H. J. (1985b). A study of the measurement and the correlates of paranormal belief. *Journal of the American Society for Psychical Research, 79*, 301–26.

Irwin, H. J. (1986). The relationship between locus of control and belief in the paranormal. *Parapsychological Journal of South Africa, 7*, 1–23.

Irwin, H. J. (1989). On paranormal disbelief: the psychology of the sceptic. In G. K. Zollschan, J. F. Schumaker and G. F. Walsh (Eds.), *Exploring the paranormal: perspectives on belief and experience* (pp. 305–12). Bridport, UK: Prism Press.

Irwin, H. J. (1990a). Fantasy proneness and paranormal beliefs. *Psychological Reports, 66*, 655–8.

Irwin, H. J. (1990b). Parapsychology courses and students' belief in the paranormal. *Journal of the Society for Psychical Research, 56*, 266–72.

Irwin, H. J. (1991a). The reasoning skills of paranormal believers. *Journal of Parapsychology, 55*, 281–300.

Irwin, H. J. (1991b). A study of paranormal belief, psychological adjustment and fantasy proneness. *Journal of the American Society for Psychical Research, 85*, 317–31.

Irwin, H. J. (1992). Origins and functions of paranormal belief: the role of childhood trauma and interpersonal control. *Journal of the American Society for Psychical Research, 86*, 199–208.

Irwin, H. J. (1993). Belief in the paranormal: a review of the empirical literature. *Journal of the American Society for Psychical Research, 87*, 1–39.

Irwin, H. J. (1994a). Childhood trauma and the origins of paranormal belief: a constructive replication. *Psychological Reports, 74*, 107–11.

Irwin, H. J. (1994b). Paranormal belief and proneness to dissociation. *Psychological Reports, 75*, 1344–6.

Irwin, H. J. (1994c). Proneness to dissociation and traumatic childhood events. *Journal of Nervous and Mental Disease, 182*, 456–60.

Irwin, H. J. (1995). Las creencias paranormales y las funciones emocionales [Paranormal belief and emotional functioning]. *Revista Argentina de Psicologia Paranormal, 6*, 69–76.

Irwin, H. J. (1997). An empirically-derived typology of paranormal believers. *European Journal of Parapsychology, 13*, 1–14.

Irwin, H. J. (1999a). *An introduction to parapsychology* (3rd ed.). Jefferson, NC: McFarland.

Irwin, H. J. (1999b). Pathological and nonpathological dissociation: the relevance of childhood trauma. *Journal of Psychology: Interdisciplinary and Applied, 133,* 157–64.

Irwin, H. J. (1999c). Review of E. Goode, 'Paranormal beliefs: a sociological introduction'. *Journal of the American Society for Psychical Research, 93,* 217–23.

Irwin, H. J. (2000a). Age and sex differences in paranormal beliefs: a response to Vitulli, Tipton and Rowe (1999). *Psychological Reports, 86,* 595–6.

Irwin, H. J. (2000b). Belief in the paranormal and a sense of control over life. *European Journal of Parapsychology, 15,* 68–78.

Irwin, H. J. (2000c). The luck of the paranormal believer. *International Journal of Parapsychology, 11* (2), 79–95.

Irwin, H. J. (2001a). Age and sex differences in paranormal beliefs after controlling for differential item functioning. *European Journal of Parapsychology, 16,* 102–6.

Irwin, H. J. (2001b). The relationship between dissociative tendencies and schizotypy: An artifact of childhood trauma? *Journal of Clinical Psychology, 57,* 331–42.

Irwin, H. J. (2002). Proneness to self-deception and the two-factor model of paranormal belief. *Journal of the Society for Psychical Research, 66,* 80–7.

Irwin, H. J. (2003a). Paranormal beliefs and the maintenance of assumptive world views. *Journal of the Society for Psychical Research, 67,* 18–25.

Irwin, H. J. (2003b). Reality testing and the formation of paranormal beliefs. *European Journal of Parapsychology, 18,* 15–27.

Irwin, H. J. (2004). Reality testing and the formation of paranormal beliefs: a constructive replication. *Journal of the Society for Psychical Research, 68,* 143–52.

Irwin, H. J. (2007). The measurement of superstitiousness as a component of paranormal belief: some critical reflections. *European Journal of Parapsychology, 22,* 95–120.

Irwin, H. J. and Green, M. J. (1998–99). Schizotypal processes and belief in the paranormal: a multidimensional study. *European Journal of Parapsychology, 14,* 1–15.

Irwin, H. J. and Young, J. M. (2002). Intuitive versus reflective processes in the formation of paranormal beliefs. *European Journal of Parapsychology, 17,* 45–53.

Jahoda, G. (1970). Supernatural beliefs and changing cognitive structures among Ghanaian university students. *Journal of Cross-Cultural Psychology, 1,* 115–30.

Jang, S. J. and Johnson, B. R. (2003). Strain, negative emotions and deviant coping among African Americans: a test of general strain theory. *Journal of Quantitative Criminology, 19,* 79–105.

Janoff-Bulman, R. (1989). Assumptive worlds and the stress of traumatic events: applications of the schema construct. *Social Cognition, 7,* 113–36.

Jawanda, J. S. (1968). Superstition and personality. *Journal of Psychological Researches, 12* (1), 21–4.

Jenkins, R. (2007). The transformations of Biddy Early: from local reports of magical healing to globalised New Age fantasies. *Folklore, 18,* 162–82.

Joesting, J. and Joesting, R. (1969). Torrance's Creative Motivation Inventory and its relationship to several personality variables. *Psychological Reports, 24,* 30.

Johnson, D. C. (1997). Formal education vs. religious belief: soliciting new evidence with multinomial logit modeling. *Journal for the Scientific Study of Religion, 36,* 231–46.

Johnson, R. D. and Jones, C. H. (1984). Attitudes toward the existence and scientific investigation of extrasensory perception. *Journal of Psychology, 117,* 19–22.

Johnston, J. C., de Groot, H. P. and Spanos, N. P. (1995). The structure of paranormal belief: a factor–analytic investigation. *Imagination, Cognition and Personality, 14,* 165–174.

Jones, E. and Watson, J. P. (1997). Delusion, the overvalued idea and religious beliefs: a comparative analysis of their characteristics. *British Journal of Psychiatry, 170,* 381–6.

Jones, W. H. and Russell, D. (1980). The selective processing of belief disconfirming information. *European Journal of Social Psychology, 10,* 309–12.

Jones, W. H., Russell, D. W. and Nickel, T. W. (1977). Belief in the Paranormal Scale: an objective instrument to measure belief in magical phenomena and causes. *Journal Supplement Abstract Service, Catalog of Selected Documents in Psychology, 7,* 100 (MS 1577).

Jorgensen, P. (1995). Delusional beliefs: definition and classification. *Nordic Journal of Psychiatry, 49,* 459–64.

Joukhador, J., Blaszczynski, A. and MacCallum, F. (2004). Superstitious beliefs in gambling among problem and non-problem gamblers: preliminary data. *Journal of Gambling Studies, 20,* 171–80.

Jueneman, F. B. (2001). The making of a myth. *Research and Development, 43* (4), 9–10.

Jupp, J. (2008). Belief and disbelief in Australia. *Dialogue: Journal of the Academy of the Social Sciences in Australia, 27 (2),* 6–15.

Kahler, L. F. (2001). *The effect of paranormal beliefs on performance following an unsolvable problem.* Unpublished dissertation for the Graduate Diploma of Psychology, University of New England, Australia.

Kahneman, D. and Tversky, A. (1972). Subjective probability: a judgment of representativeness. *Cognitive Psychology, 3,* 430–54.

Katz, D. (1960). The functional approach to the study of attitudes. *Public Opinion Quarterly, 24,* 163–204.

Kay, A. C., Gaucher, D., Napier, J. L., Callan, M. J. and Laurin, K. (2008). God and the government: testing a compensatory control mechanism for the support of external systems. *Journal of Personality and Social Psychology, 95,* 18–35.

Keinan, G. (1994). Effects of stress and tolerance of ambiguity on magical thinking. *Journal of Personality and Social Psychology, 67,* 48–55.

Keinan, G. (2002). The effects of stress and desire for control on superstitious behavior. *Personality and Social Psychology Bulletin, 28,* 102–8.

Keinan, G. and Sivan, D. (2001). The effects of stress and desire for control on the formation of causal attributions. *Journal of Research in Personality, 35,* 127–37.

Kelly, I. W. (1998). Why astrology doesn't work. *Psychological Reports, 82,* 527–46.

Kennedy, J. L. (1939). Changes in attitude toward 'telepathy' and 'clairvoyance' during a 25-year period. *Psychological Bulletin, 36,* 649–50 (abstract).

Killen, P., Wildman, R. W. and Wildman, R. W. II (1974). Superstitiousness and intelligence. *Psychological Reports, 34,* 1158.

Kim, A. E. (2005). Nonofficial religion in South Korea: prevalence of fortunetelling and other forms of divination. *Review of Religious Research, 46,* 284–302.

Kintlerová, T. (2000). Osobnostne charakteristiky clenov siekt a kultov [Personality characteristics of members of sects and cults]. *Ceskoslovenská Psychologie, 44,* 180–9.

Klare, R. (1990). Ghosts make news: how four newspapers report psychic phenomena. *Skeptical Inquirer, 14,* 363–71.

Klass, P. J. (2001). UFOs: an innocent myth turned evil. In P. Kurtz (Ed.), *Skeptical odysseys: personal accounts by the world's leading paranormal inquirers* (pp. 123–9). Amherst, NY: Prometheus Books.

Kline, P. (1974). Factors influencing supernatural beliefs among Indian university students. *Indian Journal of Psychology, 49,* 127–138.

Knowlson, T. S. (1930/1998). *The origins of popular superstitions.* Twickenham, England: Senate.

Kramer, T. and Block, L. (2008). Conscious and nonconscious components of superstitious beliefs in judgment and decision making. *Journal of Consumer Research, 34,* 783–93.

Krippner, S. (1962). Creativity and psychic phenomena. *Indian Journal of Parapsychology, 4,* 1–20.

Krippner, S. and Winkler, M. (1996). The 'need to believe'. In G. Stein (Ed.), *The encyclopedia of the paranormal* (pp. 441–54). Amherst, NY: Prometheus Books.

Kristensen, K. B. (1999). The influence of religious affiliation and religious orientation on beliefs in science, religion and the paranormal (Doctoral dissertation, Brigham Young University). *Dissertation Abstracts International, 59* (11), 6057B.

Kuban, G. J. (1997). Sea-monster or shark? An analysis of a supposed plesiosaur carcass netted in 1977. *Reports of the National Center for Science Education, 17* (3), 16–28.

Kumar, V. K. and Pekala, R. J. (2001). Relation of hypnosis-specific attitudes and behaviors to paranormal beliefs and experiences: a technical review. In J. Houran and R. Lange (Eds.), *Hauntings and poltergeists: multidisciplinary perspectives* (pp. 260–79). Jefferson, NC: McFarland.

Kumar, V. K., Pekala, R. J. and Cummings, J. (1993). Sensation seeking, drug use and reported paranormal beliefs and experiences. *Personality and Individual Differences, 14,* 685–91.

Kurtz, P. (1985a). Introduction: more than a century of psychical research. In P. Kurtz (Ed.), *A skeptic's handbook of parapsychology* (pp. xi–xxiv). Buffalo, NY: Prometheus Books.

Kurtz, P. (1985b). The responsibilities of the media and paranormal claims. *Skeptical Inquirer, 9,* 357–62.

Kurtz, P. (1996). Skepticism and the paranormal. In G. Stein (Ed.), *The encyclopedia of the paranormal* (pp. 684–701). Amherst, NY: Prometheus Books.`

Kurtz, P. (1999). Why do people believe or disbelieve? Letting science answer the question. *Free Inquiry, 19* (3), 23–7.

Lack, S. A., Kumar, V. K. and Arevalo, S. (2003). Fantasy proneness, creative capacity and styles of creativity. *Perceptual and Motor Skills, 96,* 19–24.

Lamont, P. (2007). Paranormal belief and the avowal of prior scepticism. *Theory and Psychology, 17,* 681–96.

Lang, G. and Ragvald, L. (1998). Spirit-writing and the development of Chinese cults. *Sociology of Religion, 59,* 309–28.

Langdon, R. and Coltheart, M. (2000). The cognitive neuropsychology of delusions. In M. Coltheart and M. Davies (Eds.), *Pathologies of belief* (pp. 183–216). Oxford: Blackwell.

Lange, R. and Houran, J. (1997). Death anxiety and the paranormal: the primacy of belief over experience. *Journal of Nervous and Mental Disease, 185,* 584–6.

Lange, R. and Houran, J. (1998). Delusions of the paranormal: a haunting question of perception. *Journal of Nervous and Mental Disease, 186,* 637–45.

Lange, R. and Houran, J. (1999). The role of fear in delusions of the paranormal: a haunting question of perception. *Journal of Nervous and Mental Disease, 187,* 159–66.

Lange, R., Irwin, H. J. and Houran, J. (2000). Top-down purification of Tobacyk's Revised Paranormal Belief Scale. *Personality and Individual Differences, 29,* 131–56.

Lange, R., Irwin, H. J. and Houran, J. (2001). Objective measurement of paranormal belief: a rebuttal to Vitulli. *Psychological Reports, 88,* 641–4.

Lange, R. and Thalbourne, M. A. (2002). Rasch scaling paranormal belief and experience: structure and semantics of Thalbourne's Australian Sheep–Goat Scale. *Psychological Reports, 91,* 1065–73.

Langer, E. J. (1975). The illusion of control. *Journal of Personality and Social Psychology, 32,* 311–28.

Lanternari, V. (1963). *The religions of the oppressed: a study of modern messianic cults* (L. Sergio, Trans.). London: MacGibbon and Kee.

Lawrence, E. and Peters, E. (2004). Reasoning in believers in the paranormal. *Journal of Nervous and Mental Disease, 192,* 727–33.

Lawrence, T. R. (1993, August). *Gathering in the sheep and the goats: a meta-analysis of forced-choice sheep–goat ESP studies, 1947–93*. Paper presented at the 36th Annual Convention of the Parapsychological Association, Toronto, Canada.

Lawrence, T. R. (1995). How many factors of paranormal belief are there? A critique of the Paranormal Belief Scale. *Journal of Parapsychology, 59*, 3–25.

Lawrence, T. R. and De Cicco, P. (1997). The factor structure of the Paranormal Belief Scale: more evidence in support of the Oblique Five. *Journal of Parapsychology, 61*, 243–251.

Lawrence, T. [R.], Edwards, C., Barraclough, N., Church, S. and Hetherington, F. (1995). Modelling childhood causes of paranormal belief and experience: Childhood trauma and childhood fantasy. *Personality and Individual Differences, 19*, 209–15.

Lawrence, T. R., Roe, C. A. and Williams, C. (1997). Confirming the factor structure of the Paranormal Beliefs Scale: big orthogonal seven or oblique five? *Journal of Parapsychology, 61*, 13–31.

Layton, B. D. and Turnbull, B. (1975). Belief, evaluation and performance on an ESP task. *Journal of Experimental Social Psychology, 11*, 166–79.

Lazarus, R. S. and Folkman, S. (1984). *Stress, appraisal and coping*. New York: Springer.

Leeds, S. M. (1995). Personality, belief in the paranormal and involvement with satanic practices among young adult males: Dabblers versus gamers. *Cultic Studies Journal, 12*, 148–65.

Leeser, J. and O'Donohue, W. (1999). What is a delusion? Epistemological dimensions. *Journal of Abnormal Psychology, 108*, 687–94.

Lefcourt, H. M. (1973). The function of the illusions of control and freedom. *American Psychologist, 28*, 417–25.

Lehman, H. C. and Fenton, N. (1929). The prevalence of certain misconceptions and superstitions among college students before and after a course in psychology. *Education, 50*, 485–94.

Lehman, H. C. and Witty, P. A. (1928). Sex differences in credulity. *Journal of Abnormal and Social Psychology, 23*, 356–68.

Lehrer, E. L. and Chiswick, C. U. (1993). Religion as a determinant of marital stability. *Demography, 30*, 385–404.

Lenzenweger, M. F., Clarkin, J. F., Kernberg, O. F. and Foelsch, P. A. (2001). The Inventory of Personality Organization: psychometric properties, factorial composition and criterion relations with affect, aggressive dyscontrol, psychosis proneness and self-domains in a nonclinical sample. *Psychological Assessment, 13*, 577–91.

Leonhard, D. and Brugger, P. (1998). Creative, paranormal and delusional thought: a consequence of right hemisphere semantic activation? *Neuropsychiatry, Neuropsychology and Behavioral Neurology, 11*, 177–83.

Lerner, M. J. (1980). *The belief in a just world: a fundamental delusion*. New York: Plenum Press.

Lester, D. (1993). Paranormal beliefs and psychoticism. *Personality and Individual Differences, 14,* 739.

Lester, D. and Monaghan, K. (1995). Belief in paranormal phenomena and personality. *Perceptual and Motor Skills, 81,* 114.

Lester, D., Thinschmidt, J. S. and Trautman, L. A. (1987). Paranormal belief and Jungian dimensions of personality. *Psychological Reports, 61,* 182.

Lett, J. (1992). The persistent popularity of the paranormal. *Skeptical Inquirer, 16,* 381–8.

Levin, J. S., Taylor, R. J. and Chatters, L. M. (1994). Race and gender differences in religiosity among older adults: findings from four national surveys. *Journal of Gerontology, 49* (Sup.), S137–45.

Levitt, E. E. (1952). Superstitions: twenty-five years ago and today. *American Journal of Psychology, 65,* 443–9.

Lewis, C. M. (2002). *Investigating students' belief in the paranormal.* Unpublished master's thesis, University of Wisconsin at Stout, www.uwstout.edu/lib/thesis/2002/2002lewisc.pdf, retrieved 13 January 2009.

Lewis, J. M. and Gallagher, T. J. (2001). The salience of Friday the 13th for college students. *College Student Journal, 35,* 216–22.

Lewis, J. R. (2001). *The encyclopedia of cults, sects and new religions* (2nd ed.). Amherst, NY: Prometheus Books.

Lewis, V. C. (1974). A psychological analysis of faith. *Journal of Psychology and Theology, 2,* 97–103.

Lilienfeld, S. O., Lohr, J. M. and Morier, D. (2001). The teaching of courses in the science and pseudoscience of psychology: useful resources. *Teaching of Psychology, 28,* 182–91.

Lillqvist, O. and Lindeman, M. (1998). Belief in astrology as a strategy for self-verification and coping with negative life-events. *European Psychologist, 3,* 202–8.

Lindeman, M. (1998). Motivation, cognition and pseudoscience. *Scandinavian Journal of Psychology, 39,* 257–65.

Lindeman, M. and Aarnio, K. (2006). Paranormal beliefs: their dimensionality and correlates. *European Journal of Personality, 20,* 585–602.

Lindeman, M. and Aarnio, K. (2007). Superstitious, magical and paranormal beliefs: an integrative model. *Journal of Research in Personality, 41,* 731–44.

Lindeman, M., Cederström, S., Simola, P., Simula, A., Ollikainen, S. and Riekki, T. (2008). Sentences with core knowledge violations increase the size of N400 among paranormal believers. *Cortex, 44,* 2307–15.

Lindeman, M. and Saher, M. (2007). Vitalism, purpose and superstition. *British Journal of Psychology, 98,* 33–4.

Loewenthal, K. M., MacLeod, A. K. and Cinnirella, M. (2002). Are women more religious than men? Gender differences in religious activity among different religious groups in the UK. *Personality and Individual Differences, 32,* 133–9.

Lord, E. (1958). The impact of education on non-scientific beliefs in Ethiopia. *Journal of Social Psychology, 47,* 339–53.

Loughland, C. M. and Williams, L. M. (1997). A cluster analytic study of schizotypal trait dimensions. *Personality and Individual Differences, 23,* 877–83.

Lucey, B. M. (2001). Friday the 13th: international evidence. *Applied Economics Letters, 8,* 577–9.

Lundeen, G. E. and Caldwell, O. W. (1930). A study of unfounded beliefs among high-school seniors. *Journal of Educational Research, 22,* 257–73.

Lynn, S. J. and Rhue, J. W. (1988). Fantasy proneness: hypnosis, developmental antecedents and psychopathology. *American Psychologist, 43,* 35–44.

MacDonald, D. A. (2000). Spirituality: description, measurement and relation to the Five Factor Model of personality. *Journal of Personality, 68,* 153–97.

MacDonald, D. A. and Holland, D. (2002). Spirituality and complex partial epileptic-like signs. *Psychological Reports, 91,* 785–92.

MacDougall, C. D. (1983). *Superstition and the press.* Buffalo, NY: Prometheus Books.

Mack, J. E. (1994). *Abduction: human encounters with aliens.* New York: Scribner's.

Maguire, B. and Weatherby, G. A. (1998). The secularization of religion and television commercials. *Sociology of Religion, 59,* 171–8.

Maher, B. A. and Spitzer, M. (1993). Delusions. In P. B. Sutker and H. E. Adams (Eds.), *Comprehensive handbook of psychopathology* (2nd ed.) (pp. 263–93). New York: Plenum Press.

Makasovski, T. and Irwin, H. J. (1999). Paranormal belief, dissociative tendencies and parental encouragement of imagination in childhood. *Journal of the American Society for Psychical Research, 93,* 233–47.

Maller, J. B. and Lundeen, G. E. (1933). Sources of superstitious beliefs. *Journal of Educational Research, 26,* 321–43.

Maller, J. B. and Lundeen, G. E. (1934). Superstition and emotional maladjustment. *Journal of Educational Research, 27,* 592–617.

Maltby, J. and Day, L. (2001). Spiritual involvement and belief: the relationship between spirituality and Eysenck's personality dimensions. *Personality and Individual Differences, 30,* 187–92.

Manschreck, T. C. (1995). Pathogenesis of delusions. *Psychiatric Clinics of North America, 18,* 213–29.

Markovsky, B. and Thye, S. R. (2001). Social influence on paranormal beliefs. *Sociological Perspectives, 44,* 21–44.

Marks, A. D. G., Hine, D. W., Blore, R. L. and Phillips, W. J. (2008). Assessing individual differences in adolescents' preference for rational and experiential cognition. *Personality and Individual Differences, 44,* 42–52.

Marks, D. F. (1986). Investigating the paranormal. *Nature, 320,* 119–24.

Marks, D. and Kammann, R. (1980). *The psychology of the psychic.* Buffalo, NY: Prometheus Books.

Martin, G. (1998). Generational differences among New Age travellers. *Sociological Review, 46,* 735–56.

Martin, T. F., White, J. M. and Perlman, D. (2003). Religious socialization: a test of the channeling hypothesis of religious influence on adolescent faith maturity. *Journal of Adolescent Research, 18,* 169–87.

Mason, O., Claridge, G. and Williams, L. (1997). Questionnaire measurement. In G. Claridge (Ed.), *Schizotypy: implications for illness and health* (pp. 19–37). Oxford: Oxford University Press.

Matthews, M. (1996). Science, religion and education: editorial. *Science and Education, 5,* 91–9.

Matthews, R. and Blackmore, S. (1995). Why are coincidences so impressive? *Perceptual and Motor Skills, 80,* 1121–2.

Matute, H. (1994). Learned helplessness and superstitious behavior as opposite effects of uncontrollable reinforcement in humans. *Learning and Motivation, 25,* 216–32.

Matute, H. (1995). Human reactions to uncontrollable outcomes: further evidence for superstitions rather than helplessness. *Quarterly Journal of Experimental Psychology, B: Comparative and Physiological Psychology, 48,* 142–57.

Mauskopf, S. H. and McVaugh, M. R. (1980). *The elusive science: origins of experimental psychical research.* Baltimore: Johns Hopkins University Press.

Maxwell-Stuart, P. G. (2001). *Witchcraft: a history.* Stroud, UK: Tempus.

Maynard, E. A., Gorsuch, R. L. and Bjorck, J. P. (2001). Religious coping style, concept of God and personal religious variables in threat, loss and challenge situations. *Journal for the Scientific Study of Religion, 40,* 65–74.

Mazur, A. (2008). *Implausible beliefs in the bible, astrology and UFOs.* New Brunswick, NJ: Transaction Publishers.

Mazure, C. M., Bruce, M. L., Maciejewski, P. K. and Jacobs, S. C. (2000). Adverse life events and cognitive-personality characteristics in the prediction of major depression and antidepressant response. *American Journal of Psychiatry, 157,* 896–903.

McAllister, I. (1988). Religious change and secularization: the transmission of religious values in Australia. *Sociological Analysis, 49,* 249–63.

McBeath, M. K. (1985). Psi and sexuality. *Journal of the Society for Psychical Research, 53,* 65–77.

McBeath, M. K. and Thalbourne, M. A. (1985, February). *Type A personality and its relationship to belief in psi.* Paper presented at the 12th Annual Conference of the Southeastern Regional Parapsychological Association, Duke University, Durham, NC.

McBurney, D. H. (1976). ESP in the psychology curriculum. *Teaching of Psychology, 3,* 66–9.

McClearn, D. G. (2004). Interest in sports and belief in sports superstitions. *Psychological Reports, 94,* 1043–7.

McClenon, J. (1982). A survey of elite scientists: their attitudes toward ESP and parapsychology. *Journal of Parapsychology, 46*, 127–52.

McClenon, J. (1984). *Deviant science: the case of parapsychology.* Philadelphia, PA: University of Pennsylvania Press.

McClenon, J. (1990). Chinese and American anomalous experiences: the role of religiosity. *Sociological Analysis, 51*, 53–67.

McClenon, J. (1993). Surveys of anomalous experience in Chinese, Japanese and American samples. *Sociology of Religion, 54*, 295–302.

McClenon, J. (2000). Content analysis of an anomalous memorate collection: testing hypotheses regarding universal features. *Sociology of Religion, 61*, 155–69.

McConnell, R. A. and Clark, T. K. (1980). Training, belief and mental conflict within the Parapsychological Association. *Journal of Parapsychology, 44*, 245–68.

McCreery, C. and Claridge, G. (2002). Healthy schizotypy: the case of out-of-the-body experiences. *Personality and Individual Differences, 32*, 141–54.

McGarry, J. J. and Newberry, B. H. (1981). Beliefs in paranormal phenomena and locus of control: a field study. *Journal of Personality and Social Psychology, 41*, 725–36.

McKenna, F. P. (1993). It won't happen to me: unrealistic optimism or illusion of control? *British Journal of Psychology, 84*, 39–50.

McKinnon, A. M. (2003). The religious, the paranormal and church attendance: a response to Orenstein. *Journal for the Scientific Study of Religion, 42*, 299–303.

McMullen, T. (1978). A basic confusion in the concept of 'psi phenomena'. In J. P. Sutcliffe (Ed.), *Conceptual analysis and method in psychology: essays in honour of W. M. O'Neil* (pp. 15–20). Sydney: Sydney University Press.

Merla-Ramos, M. (2000). Belief and reasoning: the effects of beliefs on syllogistic reasoning (Doctoral dissertation, Long Island University, 1999). *Dissertation Abstracts International, 61* (1), 558B.

Merriam, S. B., Courtenay, B. and Baumgartner, L. (2003). On becoming a witch: learning in a marginalized community of practice. *Adult Education Quarterly, 53*, 170–88.

Merritt, R. D. and Waldo, T. G. (2000). MMPI code types and the fantasy prone personality. *Assessment, 7*, 87–95.

Messer, W. S. and Griggs, R. A. (1989). Student belief and involvement in the paranormal and performance in introductory psychology. *Teaching of Psychology, 16*, 187–91.

Meyer, P. (1986). Ghostboosters: the press and the paranormal. *Columbia Journalism Review, 24* (6), 38–41.

Miller, L., Weissman, M., Gur, M. and Greenwald, S. (2002). Adult religiousness and history of childhood depression: eleven-year follow-up study. *Journal of Nervous and Mental Disease, 190*, 86–93.

Miller, R. M. (1929). Superstitions among college students. *Sociology and Social Research, 13*, 361–5.

Minot, C. S. (1887). First report of the Committee on Experimental Psychology. *Proceedings of the American Society for Psychical Research, 1*, 218–23.

Mirowsky, J. (1995). Age and sense of control. *Social Psychology Quarterly, 58*, 31–43.

Moberg, D. O. (1972). Religion and the aging family. *The Family Coordinator, 21*, 47–60.

Mohammadi, S. D. and Honarmand, M. M. (2007). Relationship between religiousness and locus of control and the role of gender differences. *Psychological Research, 9* (3–4), 47–64.

Mol, H. (1985). *The faith of Australians.* Sydney: Allen and Unwin.

Moody, E. J. (1971/1974). Urban witches. In E. A. Tiryakian (Ed.), *On the margin of the visible: sociology, the esoteric and the occult* (pp. 223–34). New York: Wiley.

Moon, M. L. (1975). Artists contrasted with non-artists concerning belief in ESP: A poll. *Journal of the American Society for Psychical Research, 69*, 161–6.

Moore, R. L. (1977). *In search of white crows: spiritualism, parapsychology and American culture.* New York: Oxford University Press.

Morier, D. and Keeports, D. (1994). Normal science and the paranormal: the effect of a scientific method course on students' beliefs. *Research in Higher Education, 35*, 443–53.

Morneau, D. M., MacDonald, D. A., Holland, C. J. and Holland, D. C. (1996). A confirmatory study of the relation between self-reported complex partial epileptic signs, peak experiences and paranormal beliefs. *British Journal of Clinical Psychology, 35*, 627–30.

Morrison, A. P. and Wells, A. (2003). A comparison of metacognitions in patients with hallucinations, delusions, panic disorder and non-patient controls. *Behaviour Research and Therapy, 41*, 251–6.

Moss, S. and Butler, D. C. (1978). The scientific credibility of ESP. *Perceptual and Motor Skills, 46*, 1063–79.

Mueller, C. W. and Johnson, W. T. (1975). Socioeconomic status and religious participation. *American Sociological Review, 40*, 785–800.

Munro, G. D. and Munro, J. E. (2000). Using daily horoscopes to demonstrate expectancy confirmation. *Teaching of Psychology, 27*, 114–16.

Murphy, G. (1963). Creativity and its relation to extrasensory perception. *Journal of the American Society for Psychical Research, 57*, 203–14.

Murphy, K. and Lester, D. (1976). A search for correlates of belief in ESP. *Psychological Reports, 38*, 82.

Musch, J. and Ehrenberg, K. (2002). Probability misjudgment, cognitive ability and belief in the paranormal. *British Journal of Psychology, 93*, 169–77.

Musick, M. and Wilson, J. (1995). Religious switching for marriage reasons. *Sociology of Religion, 56*, 257–70.

Nadon, R., Laurence, J. and Perry, C. (1987). Multiple predictors of hypnotic susceptibility. *Journal of Personality and Social Psychology, 53*, 948–60.

Nambi, S. K., Prasad, J., Singh, D., Abraham, V., Kuruvilla, A. and Jacob, K. S. (2002). Explanatory models and common mental disorders among patients with unexplained somatic symptoms attending a primary care facility in Tamil Nadu. *National Medical Journal of India, 15,* 331–5.

National Science Foundation. (2002). *Science and engineering indicators, 2002.* Arlington, VA: National Science Foundation.

Näyhä, S. (2002). Traffic deaths and superstition on Friday the 13th. *American Journal of Psychiatry, 159,* 2110–1.

Nelson, G. K. (1968). The concept of cult. *Sociological Review, 16,* 351–62.

Neppe, V. M. (1981). A study of the incidence of subjective paranormal experience. *Parapsychological Journal of South Africa, 2* (1), 15–37.

Newby, R. W. and Davis, J. B. (2004). Relationships between locus of control and paranormal beliefs. *Psychological Reports, 94,* 1261–6.

Newman, L. S. and Baumeister, R. F. (1996). Toward an explanation of the UFO abduction phenomenon: hypnotic elaboration, extraterrestrial sadomasochism and spurious memories. *Psychological Inquiry, 7,* 99–126.

Newport, F. and Strausberg, M. (2001, June). *Gallup poll release: Americans' belief in psychic and paranormal phenomena is up over last decade,* www.gallup.com/poll/releases/pr010608.asp, retrieved 12 June 2001.

Ni, H., Simile, C. and Hardy, A. M. (2002). Utilization of complementary and alternative medicine by United States adults. *Medical Care, 40,* 353–8.

Nixon, H. K. (1925). Popular answers to some psychological questions. *American Journal of Psychology, 36,* 418–23.

Northcote, J. (2007). *The paranormal and the politics of truth: a sociological account.* Charlottesville, VA: Imprint Academic.

Novella, S. and Bloomberg, D. (1999). Scientific skepticism, CSICOP and the local groups. *Skeptical Inquirer, 23* (4), 44–6.

O'Connor, T. P., Hoge, D. R. and Alexander, E. (2002). The relative influence of youth and adult experiences on personal spirituality and church involvement. *Journal for the Scientific Study of Religion, 41,* 723–32.

Okamoto, Y. (1988). The attitude and behavior toward superstitions and proverbs [in Japanese]. *Japanese Journal of Psychology, 59,* 106–12.

O'Keeffe, C. and Villejoubert, G. (2002, August). *Probability of coincidences and paranormal belief.* Paper presented at the 45th Annual Convention of the Parapsychological Association, Paris, France.

Opie, I. and Tatem, M. (Eds.) (1989). *A dictionary of superstitions.* Oxford: Oxford University Press.

Orenstein, A. (2002). Religion and paranormal belief. *Journal for the Scientific Study of Religion, 41,* 301–11.

Osarchuk, M. and Tatz, S. J. (1973). Effect of induced fear of death on belief in afterlife. *Journal of Personality and Social Psychology, 27,* 256–60.

Oskamp, S. (1977). *Attitudes and opinions.* Englewood Cliffs, NJ: Prentice Hall.

Otis, L. (1979). Selective exposure to the film Close Encounters. *Journal of Psychology, 101,* 293–5.

Otis, L. P. and Alcock, J. E. (1982). Factors affecting extraordinary belief. *Journal of Social Psychology, 118,* 77–85.

Otis, L. P. and Kuo, E. C. Y. (1984). Extraordinary beliefs among students in Singapore and Canada. *Journal of Psychology, 116,* 215–26.

Owen, A. (1990). *The darkened room: women, power and spiritualism in late Victorian England.* Philadelphia, PA: University of Pennsylvania Press.

Ozorak, E. W. (1989). Social and cognitive influences on the development of religious beliefs and commitment in adolescence. *Journal for the Scientific Study of Religion, 28,* 448–63.

Pacini, R. and Epstein, S. (1999). The relation of rational and experiential information processing styles to personality, basic beliefs and the ratio-bias phenomenon. *Journal of Personality and Social Psychology, 76,* 972–87.

Padgett, V. R., Benassi, V. A. and Singer, B. F. (1981). Belief in ESP among psychologists. In K. Frazier (Ed.), *Paranormal borderlands of science* (pp. 66–7). Buffalo, NY: Prometheus Books.

Padgett, V. R. and Jorgenson, D. O. (1982). Superstition and economic threat: Germany, 1918–40. *Personality and Social Psychology Bulletin, 8,* 736–41.

Page, J. (1935). Superstition and personality. *Journal of Educational Psychology, 26,* 59–64.

Palmer, J. (1971). Scoring in ESP tests as a function of belief in ESP. I. The sheep–goat effect. *Journal of the American Society for Psychical Research, 65,* 373–408.

Pargament, K. I. (1997). *The psychology of religion and coping: theory, research, practice.* New York: Guilford Press.

Pargament, K. I., Grevengoed, N., Kennell, J., Newman, J., Hathaway, W. and Jones, W. (1988). Religion and the problem solving process: three styles of coping. *Journal for the Scientific Study of Religion, 27,* 90–104.

Parker, A. (2000). An experimental study of the influences of magical ideation and sense of meaning on the attribution of telepathic experience. *Journal of Mental Imagery, 24,* 97–110.

Parnell, J. (1988). Measured personality characteristics of persons who claim UFO experiences. *Psychotherapy in Private Practice, 6,* 159–65.

Parsons, T. (1960). *Structure and process in modern societies.* Glencoe, IL: Free Press.

Pasachoff, J. M., Cohen, R. J. and Pasachoff, N. W. (1970). Belief in the supernatural among Harvard and West African university students. *Nature, 227,* 971–2.

Patry, A. L. and Pelletier, L. G. (2001). Extraterrestrial beliefs and experiences: an application of the theory of reasoned action. *Journal of Social Psychology, 141,* 199–217.

Pavlos, A. J. (1982). *The cult experience*. Westport, CT: Greenwood Press.

Peatman, J. G. and Greenspan, I. (1935). The reliability of a questionnaire on superstitious beliefs of elementary school children. *Journal of Abnormal and Social Psychology, 30*, 208–21.

Peatman, J. G. and Greenspan, I. (1936). An analysis of results obtained from a questionnaire on superstitious beliefs of elementary school children. *Journal of Abnormal and Social Psychology, 30*, 502–7.

Pekala, R. J., Kumar, V. K. and Cummings, J. (1992). Types of high hypnotically-susceptible individuals and reported attitudes and experiences of the paranormal and the anomalous. *Journal of the American Society for Psychical Research, 86*, 135–50.

Peltzer, K. (2002). Paranormal beliefs and personality among black South African students. *Social Behavior and Personality, 30*, 391–7.

Peltzer, K. (2003). Magical thinking and paranormal beliefs among secondary and university students in South Africa. *Personality and Individual Differences, 35*, 1419–26.

Perkins, S. L. (2001). Paranormal beliefs: developmental antecedents, perceived control and defensive coping (Doctoral dissertation, Long Island University). *Dissertation Abstracts International, 61* (11), 6145B.

Perkins, S. L. and Allen, R. (2006). Childhood physical abuse and differential development of paranormal belief systems. *Journal of Nervous and Mental Disease, 194*, 349–55.

Persinger, M. A. (1987). *The neuropsychological bases of god beliefs*. New York: Praeger.

Persinger, M. A. and Makarec, K. (1991–2). Interactions between temporal lobe signs, imaginings, beliefs and gender: their effect upon logical inference. *Imagination, Cognition and Personality, 11*, 149–66.

Persinger, M. A. and Richards, P. (1991). Tobacyk's Paranormal Belief Scale and temporal lobe signs: sex differences in the experiences of ego-alien intrusions. *Perceptual and Motor Skills, 73*, 1151–6.

Peters, E., Day, S., McKenna, J. and Orbach, G. (1999). Delusional ideation in religious and psychotic populations. *British Journal of Clinical Psychology, 38*, 83–96.

Peters, E. R., Joseph, S. A. and Garety, P. A. (1999). Measurement of delusional ideation in the normal population: Introducing the PDI (Peters *et al.* Delusions Inventory). *Schizophrenia Bulletin, 25*, 553–76.

Peters, J. L. (1916). Superstitions among American girls. *Pedagogical Seminary, 23*, 445–51.

Peterson, C., Semmel, A., von Baeyer, C., Abramson, L. Y., Metalsky, G. I. and Seligman, M. E. P. (1982). The Attributional Style Questionnaire. *Cognitive Therapy and Research, 6*, 287–300.

Peterson, C. C. (1978). Locus of control and belief in self-oriented superstitions. *Journal of Social Psychology, 105*, 305–6.

Peterson, P. C. (2002). Religion in The X-Files. *Journal of Media and Religion, 1,* 181–96.

Phillips, D. P., Liu, G. C., Kwok, K., Jarvinen, J. R., Zhang, W. and Abramson, I. S. (2001). The Hound of the Baskervilles effect: natural experiment on the influence of psychological stress on timing of death. *British Medical Journal, 323,* 1443–6.

Pizzagalli, D., Lehmann, D. and Brugger, P. (2001). Lateralized direct and indirect semantic priming effects in subjects with paranormal experiences and beliefs. *Psychopathology, 34,* 75–80.

Pizzagalli, D., Lehmann, D., Gianotti, L., Koenig, T., Tanaka, H., Wackerman, J. and Brugger, P. (2000). Brain electric correlates of strong belief in paranormal phenomena: intracerebral EEG source and regional Omega complexity analyses. *Psychiatry Research: Neuroimaging Section, 100,* 139–54.

Plug, C. (1975). An investigation of superstitious belief and behaviour. *Journal of Behavioural Sciences, 2,* 169–78.

Plug, C. (1976). The psychology of superstition: a review. *Psychologia Africana, 16,* 93–115.

Polzella, D. J., Popp, R. J. and Hinsman, M. C. (1975). *ESP?* Paper presented at a meeting of the American Psychological Association, Chicago.

Power, T. L. and Smith, S. M. (2008). Predictors of fear of death and self-mortality: an Atlantic Canadian perspective. *Death Studies, 32,* 253–72.

Powers, F. F. (1931). The influence of intelligence and personality traits upon false beliefs. *Journal of Social Psychology, 2,* 490–3.

Preece, P. F. W. and Baxter, J. H. (2000). Scepticism and gullibility: the superstitious and pseudo-scientific beliefs of secondary school students. *International Journal of Science Education, 22,* 1147–56.

Presson, P. K. (1997). The multidimensionality of illusory judgments: reexamination of illusion of control research (Doctoral dissertation, University of New Hampshire). *Dissertation Abstracts International, 58* (4), 2180B.

Presson, P. K. and Benassi, V. A. (1996). Illusion of control: a meta-analytic review. *Journal of Social Behavior and Personality, 11,* 493–510.

Prilleltensky, I., Nelson, G. and Peirson, L. (2001). The role of power and control in children's lives: an ecological analysis of pathways toward wellness, resilience and problems. *Journal of Community and Applied Social Psychology, 11,* 143–158.

Radford, E. and Radford, M. A. (1949). *Encyclopaedia of superstitions.* New York: Philosophical Library.

Radun, I. and Summala, H. (2004, November 16). Females do not have more injury road accidents on Friday the 13th. *BMC Public Health, 4,* 54.

Raine, A., Reynolds, C., Lencz, T., Scerbo, A., Triphon, N. and Kim, D. (1994). Cognitive-perceptual, interpersonal and disorganized features of schizotypal personality. *Schizophrenia Bulletin, 20,* 191–201.

Randall, T. M. (1990). Belief in the paranormal declines: 1977–87. *Psychological Reports, 66,* 1347–51.

Randall, T. M. (1991). Is supernaturalism a part of authoritarianism? *Psychological Reports, 68*, 685–6.

Randall, T. M. (1997). Paranormal Short Inventory. *Perceptual and Motor Skills, 84*, 1265–6.

Randall, T. M. and Desrosiers, M. (1980). Measurement of supernatural belief: sex differences and locus of control. *Journal of Personality Assessment, 44*, 493–8.

Randi, J. (1992, April 13). Help stamp out absurd beliefs. *Time, 139* (15), 80.

Rattet, S. L. and Bursik, K. (2001). Investigating the personality correlates of paranormal belief and precognitive experience. *Personality and Individual Differences, 31*, 433–44.

Rawcliffe, D. H. (1959). *Illusions and delusions of the supernatural and the occult.* New York: Dover.

Reber, A. S. (1995). *The Penguin dictionary of psychology* (2nd ed.). London: Penguin Books.

Redden, G. (2002). The New Agents: personal transfiguration and radical privatization in New Age self-help. *Journal of Consumer Culture, 2*, 33–52.

Reimer, S. H. (1995). A look at cultural effects on religiosity: a comparison between the United States and Canada. *Journal for the Scientific Study of Religion, 34*, 445–57.

Reiss, S. (2000). Why people turn to religion: a motivational analysis. *Journal for the Scientific Study of Religion, 39*, 47–52.

Rhine, J. B. (1934). *Extra-sensory perception.* Boston: Boston Society for Psychic Research.

Rice, T. W. (2003). Believe it or not: religious and other paranormal beliefs in the United States. *Journal for the Scientific Study of Religion, 42*, 95–106.

Richet, C. (1923). *Thirty years of psychical research: being a treatise on metapsychics* (S. DeBrath, Trans.). New York: Macmillan.

Ring, K. and Rosing, C. J. (1990). The Omega Project: a psychological survey of persons reporting abductions and other UFO encounters. *Journal of UFO Studies, 2*, 59–98.

Roberts, M. J. and Seager, P. B. (1999). Predicting belief in paranormal phenomena: a comparison of conditional and probabilistic reasoning. *Applied Cognitive Psychology, 13*, 443–50.

Roccas, S., Sagiv, L., Schwartz, S. H. and Knafo, A. (2002). The Big Five personality factors and personal values. *Personality and Social Psychology Bulletin, 28*, 789–801.

Rodeghier, M., Goodpaster, J. and Blatterbauer, S. (1991). Psychosocial characteristics of abductees: results from the CUFOS abduction project. *Journal of UFO Studies, 3*, 59–90.

Roe, C. A. (1998). Belief in the paranormal and attendance at psychic readings. *Journal of the American Society for Psychical Research, 92*, 25–51.

Roe, C. A. (1999). Critical thinking and belief in the paranormal: a re-evaluation. *British Journal of Psychology, 90,* 85–98.

Roe, C. A. and Bell, C. (2003). *Paranormal belief and perceived control over life events.* Unpublished manuscript, University College Northampton.

Roe, C. A. and Bell, C. (2007). Paranormal belief, anxiety and perceived control over life events. Paper presented at the 50th Annual Convention of the Parapsychological Association, Halifax, Canada.

Roe, C. A. and Morgan, C. L. (2002). Narcissism and belief in the paranormal. *Psychological Reports, 90,* 405–11.

Roff, L. L., Butkeviciene, R. and Klemmack, D. L. (2002). Death anxiety and religiosity among Lithuanian health and social service professionals. *Death Studies, 26,* 731–42.

Rogers, P., Davis, T. and Fisk, J. (in press). Paranormal belief and susceptibility to the conjunction fallacy. *Applied Cognitive Psychology.*

Rogers, P., Qualter, P. and Phelps, G. (2007). The mediating and moderating effects of loneliness and attachment style on belief in the paranormal. *European Journal of Parapsychology, 22,* 138–65.

Rogers, P., Qualter, P., Phelps, G. and Gardner, K. (2006). Belief in the paranormal, coping and emotional intelligence. *Personality and Individual Differences, 41,* 1089–105.

Roig, M., Bridges, K. R., Renner, C. H. and Jackson, C. R. (1998). Belief in the paranormal and its association with irrational thinking controlled for context effects. *Personality and Individual Differences, 24,* 229–36.

Romm, E. G. (1977). When you give a closet occultist a PhD, what kind of research can you expect? *Humanist, 37* (3), 12–15.

Roney-Dougal, S. (1984). 'Occult' conference questionnaire. *Journal of the Society for Psychical Research, 52,* 379–82.

Roney-Dougal, S. M. (1987). A comparison of psi and subliminal perception: Exploratory and follow-up studies. *Journal of the American Society for Psychical Research, 81,* 141–81.

Ross, C. A. (1994). Commentary on 'Positive associations among dichotic listening errors, complex partial epileptic-like signs and paranormal beliefs'. *Journal of Nervous and Mental Disease, 182,* 57–9.

Royalty, J. (1995). The generalizability of critical thinking: paranormal beliefs versus statistical reasoning. *Journal of Genetic Psychology, 156,* 477–88.

Rozin, P. and Nemeroff, C. (1999). Magic and superstition. In R. A. Wilson and F. C. Keil (Eds.), *The MIT encyclopedia of the cognitive sciences* (pp. 503–5). Cambridge, MA: MIT Press.

Rudski, J. (2001). Competition, superstition and the illusion of control. *Current Psychology, 20,* 68–84.

Rudski, J. (2003a). The illusion of control, superstitious belief and optimism. *Current Psychology, 22,* 306–15.

Rudski, J. (2003b). What does a 'superstitious' person believe? Impressions of participants. *Journal of General Psychology, 130*, 431–45.

Rudski, J.M. and Edwards, A. (2007). Malinowski goes to college: factors influencing students' use of ritual and superstition. *Journal of General Psychology, 134*, 389–403.

Russell, D. and Jones, W. H. (1980). When superstition fails: reactions to disconfirmation of paranormal beliefs. *Personality and Social Psychology Bulletin, 6*, 74–83.

Saethre, E. (2007). Close encounters: UFO beliefs in a remote Australian Aboriginal community. *Journal of the Royal Anthropological Institute, 13*, 901–15.

Salter, C. A. and Routledge, L. M. (1971). Supernatural beliefs among graduate students at the University of Pennsylvania. *Nature, 232*, 278–9.

Sanders, B., McRoberts, G. and Tollefson, C. (1989). Childhood stress and dissociation in a college population. *Dissociation, 2*, 17–23.

Sanghera, S. (2002, October 8). Paranormal TV: Surveys edition. *Financial Times* (London), 26.

Sappington, A. A. (1990). The independent manipulation of intellectually and emotionally based beliefs. *Journal of Research in Personality, 24*, 487–509.

Saucer, P. R., Cahoon, D. D. and Edmonds, E. M. (1992). The Paranormal Belief Scale and the Atheistic Ideation Reference Scale as predictors of hypnotic susceptibility. *Psychology, 29*, 44–6.

Saunders, D. R. (1968). I. Factor analysis of UFO-related attitudes. *Perceptual and Motor Skills, 27*, 1207–18.

Saunders, D. R. and Van Arsdale, P. (1968). II. Points of view about UFOs: a multidimensional scaling study. *Perceptual and Motor Skills, 27*, 1219–38.

Saunders, G. (1983). Schools and popular media tend to foster belief in the paranormal. *The Skeptic* (Australia), *3* (3), 10–13.

Scanlon, T. J., Luben, R. N., Scanlon, F. L. and Singleton, N. (1993). Is Friday the 13th bad for your health? *British Medical Journal, 307*, 1584–6.

Scheibe, K. E. (1970). *Beliefs and values.* New York: Holt, Rinehart and Winston.

Scheidt, R. J. (1973). Belief in supernatural phenomena and locus of control. *Psychological Reports, 32*, 1159–62.

Schlitz, M. J. (1994). Women, power and the paranormal: a cultural critique. In L. Coly and R. A. White (Eds.), *Women and parapsychology: proceedings of an international conference* (pp. 157–74). New York: Parapsychology Foundation.

Schmeidler, G. R. (1985). Belief and disbelief in psi. *Parapsychology Review, 16* (1), 1–4.

Schmeidler, G. R. (1971). Parapsychologists' opinions about parapsychology, 1971. *Journal of Parapsychology, 35*, 208–218.

Schmeidler, G. R. and McConnell, R. A. (1958). *ESP and personality patterns.* New Haven: Yale University Press.

Schmeidler, G. R. and Murphy, G. (1946). The influence of belief and disbelief in ESP upon individual scoring levels. *Journal of Experimental Psychology, 36,* 271–6.

Schneewind, K. A. (1995). Impact of family processes on control beliefs. In A. Bandura (Ed.), *Self-efficacy in changing societies* (pp. 114–48). Cambridge: Cambridge University Press.

Schofield, K. and Claridge, G. (2007). Paranormal experiences and mental health: schizotypy as an underlying factor. *Personality and Individual Differences, 43,* 1908–16.

Schouten, S. A. (1983). Attitude about technology and belief in ESP. *Psychological Reports, 53,* 358.

Schriever, F. (1998). *Grenzbereiche der realitätserfassung: ein erklärungsmodell auf der basis individueller lebenserfahrungen* [Reality construction on the fringes: an explanatory model based on individual experiences]. Berlin: Retriever.

Schriever, F. (2000). Are there different cognitive structures behind paranormal beliefs? *European Journal of Parapsychology, 15,* 46–67.

Schulter, G. and Papousek, I. (2008). Believing in paranormal phenomena: relations to asymmetry of body and brain. *Cortex, 44,* 1326–35.

Schumaker, J. F. (1990). *Wings of illusion: the origin, nature and future of paranormal belief.* Buffalo, NY: Prometheus Books.

Schutz, W. C. (1978). *FIRO Awareness Scales manual.* Palo Alto, CA: Consulting Psychologists Press.

Schuyler, J. (1939). A study of the unfounded beliefs of defective delinquents. *Journal of Criminal Psychopathology, 1,* 127–48.

Scott, E. (1996). Scientific creationism. In G. Stein (Ed.), *The encyclopedia of the paranormal* (pp. 670–9). Amherst, NY: Prometheus Books.

Scriven, M. (1962). The frontiers of psychology: psychoanalysis and parapsychology. In R. G. Colodny (Ed.), *Frontiers of science and philosophy* (pp. 79–129). Pittsburgh, PA: University of Pittsburgh Press.

Sebastian, K. A. and Mathew, V. G. (2001). The development of a psi inventory. *Psychological Studies, 46,* 88–93.

Sedler, M. J. (1995). Understanding delusions. *Psychiatric Clinics of North America, 18,* 251–62.

Selekler, H. M., Erdogan, S., Iseri, P. and Komsuoglu, S. (2004). The sociodemographic findings, beliefs and behaviours of the patients admitted to Kocaeli University, Faculty of Medicine, Epilepsy Section. *Seizure: European Journal of Epilepsy, 13,* 438–40.

Seligman, K. (1948/1975). *Magic, supernaturalism and religion.* St Albans, UK: Paladin.

Seligman, M. E. P., Abramson, L. Y., Semmel, A. and von Baeyer, C. (1979). Depressive attributional style. *Journal of Abnormal Psychology, 88,* 242–7.

Shapiro, D. H. Jr., Schwartz, C. E. and Astin, J. A. (1996). Controlling ourselves, controlling our world: psychology's role in understanding positive and negative consequences of seeking and gaining control. *American Psychologist, 51,* 1213–30.

Sharps, M. J., Matthews, J. and Asten, J. (2006). Cognition and belief in paranormal phenomena: Gestalt/feature-intensive processing theory and tendencies toward ADHD, depression and dissociation. *Journal of Psychology, 140*, 579–90.

Sheaffer, R. (1996). Unidentified flying objects (UFOs). In G. Stein (Ed.), *The encyclopedia of the paranormal* (pp. 767–77). Amherst, NY: Prometheus Books.

Sheils, D. (1978). A cross-cultural study of beliefs in out-of-the-body experiences. *Journal of the Society for Psychical Research, 49*, 697–741.

Sheils, D. and Berg, P. (1977). A research note on sociological variables related to belief in psychic phenomena. *Wisconsin Sociologist, 14*, 24–31.

Shermer, M. (1997). *Why people believe weird things: pseudoscience, superstition and other confusions of our time.* New York: Freeman.

Sherwood, S. (1999). Relationship between childhood hypnagogic, hypnopompic and sleep experiences, childhood fantasy proneness and anomalous experiences and beliefs: an exploratory WWW survey. *Journal of the American Society for Psychical Research, 93*, 167–97.

Shimazono, S. (1999). 'New Age movement' or 'New Spirituality movements and culture'? *Social Compass, 46*, 121–33.

Shneidman, E. S. (1973). *Deaths of man.* New York: Quadrangle.

Shrimali, S. and Broota, K. D. (1987). Effect of surgical stress on belief in God and superstition: an *in situ* investigation. *Journal of Personality and Clinical Studies, 3*, 135–8.

Sica, C., Novara, C. and Sanavio, E. (2002). Culture and psychopathology: superstition and obsessive–compulsive cognitions and symptoms in a non-clinical Italian sample. *Personality and Individual Differences, 32*, 1001–12.

Siegel, K. Anderman, S. J. and Schrimshaw, E. W. (2001). Religion and coping with health-related stress. *Psychology and Health, 16*, 631–53.

Simmonds, C. A. (2001). *Investigating schizotypy as an anomaly-prone personality.* Unpublished doctoral dissertation, Leicester University.

Simmonds, C. A. and Roe, C. A. (2000, August). *Personality correlates of anomalous experiences, perceived ability and beliefs: schizotypy, temporal lobe signs and gender.* Paper presented at the 43rd Annual Convention of the Parapsychological Association, Freiburg, Germany.

Simón, A. (1979). Systematic replication of Saunders' (1968) attitude factors. *Perceptual and Motor Skills, 48*, 1199–210.

Singer, B. and Benassi, V. A. (1981). Occult beliefs. *American Scientist, 69*, 49–55.

Singer, M. T. and Lalich, J. (1995). *Cults in our midst.* San Francisco: Jossey-Bass.

Sjöberg, L. and Wåhlberg, A. (2002). Risk perception and New Age beliefs. *Risk Analysis, 22*, 751–64.

Skirda, R. J. and Persinger, M. A. (1993). Positive associations among dichotic listening errors, complex partial epileptic-like signs and paranormal beliefs. *Journal of Nervous and Mental Disease, 181*, 663–7.

Smith, C., Faris, R., Denton, M. L. and Regnerus, M. (2003). Mapping American adolescent subjective religiosity and attitudes of alienation toward religion: a research report. *Sociology of Religion, 64*, 111–33.

Smith, H. (1992). *The world's religions* (rev. ed.). San Francisco: Harper.

Smith, J. C. and Karmin, A. D. (2002). Idiosyncratic reality claims, relaxation dispositions and ABC relaxation theory: happiness, literal Christianity, miraculous powers, metaphysics and the paranormal. *Perceptual and Motor Skills, 95*, 1119–28.

Smith, M. D., Foster, C. L. and Stovin, G. (1998). Intelligence and paranormal belief: examining the role of context. *Journal of Parapsychology, 62*, 65–77.

Smith, V. C. (1930). Science methods and superstition. *School and Society, 31*, 66–8.

Snel, F. W. J. J., van der Sijde, P. C. and Wiegant, F. A. C. (1995). Cognitive styles of believers and disbelievers in paranormal phenomena. *Journal of the Society for Psychical Research, 60*, 251–7.

Snow, D. A. and Machalek, R. (1982). On the presumed fragility of unconventional beliefs. *Journal for the Scientific Study of Religion, 21*, 15–26.

Sobal, J. and Emmons, C. F. (1982). Patterns of belief in religious, psychic and other paranormal phenomena. *Zetetic Scholar, No. 9*, 7–17.

Sosis, R. (2007). Psalms for safety: magico-religious responses to threats of terror. *Current Anthropology, 48*, 903–11.

Spanos, N. P., Cross, P. A., Dickson, K. and DuBreuil, S. C. (1993). Close encounters: an examination of UFO experiences. *Journal of Abnormal Psychology, 102*, 624–32.

Sparks, G. G. (2001). The relationship between paranormal beliefs and religious beliefs. *Skeptical Inquirer, 25* (5), 50–6.

Sparks, G. G., Hansen, T. and Shah, R. (1994). Do televised depictions of paranormal events influence viewers' beliefs? *Skeptical Inquirer, 18*, 386–95.

Sparks, G. G. and Miller, W. (2001). Investigating the relationship between exposure to television programs that depict paranormal phenomena and beliefs in the paranormal. *Communication Monographs, 68*, 98–113.

Sparks, G. G., Nelson, C. L. and Campbell, R. G. (1997). The relationship between exposure to televised messages about paranormal phenomena and paranormal beliefs. *Journal of Broadcasting and Electronic Media, 41*, 345–59.

Sparks, G. G. and Pellechia, M. (1997). The effect of news stories about UFOs on readers' UFO beliefs: the role of confirming or disconfirming testimony from a scientist. *Communication Reports, 10*, 165–72.

Sparks, G. G., Pellechia, M. and Irvine, C. (1997). Does television news about UFOs affect viewers' UFO beliefs? An experimental investigation. *Communication Quarterly, 46*, 284–94.

Sparks, G. G., Sparks, C. W. and Gray, K. (1995). Media impact on fright reactions and belief in UFOs: the potential role of mental imagery. *Communication Research, 22*, 3–23.

Sperber, D. (1990). The epidemiology of beliefs. In C. Fraser and G. Gaskell (Eds.), *The social psychological study of widespread beliefs* (pp. 25–44). Oxford: Clarendon Press.

Spiegel, D. and Cardeña, E. (1991). Disintegrated experience: the dissociative disorders revisited. *Journal of Abnormal Psychology, 100,* 366–78.

Spilka, B., Minton, B., Sizemore, D. and Stout, L. (1977). Death and personal faith: a psychometric investigation. *Journal for the Scientific Study of Religion, 16,* 169–78.

Stanovich, K. E. (1989). Implicit philosophies of mind: the Dualism Scale and its relation to religiosity and belief in extrasensory perception. *Journal of Psychology, 123,* 5–23.

Stark, R. (1964). Class, radicalism and religious involvement in Great Britain. *American Sociological Review, 29,* 698–706.

Stark, R. and Bainbridge, W. S. (1980). Toward a theory of religion: religious commitment. *Journal for the Scientific Study of Religion, 19,* 114–28.

Stein, G. (Ed.). (1996). *The encyclopedia of the paranormal.* Amherst, NY: Prometheus Books.

Stevenson, I. (1977). Reincarnation: field studies and theoretical issues. In B. B. Wolman (Ed.), *Handbook of parapsychology* (pp. 631–63). New York: Van Nostrand Reinhold.

Stuart-Hamilton, I., Nayak, L. and Priest, L. (2006). Intelligence, belief in the paranormal, knowledge of probability and aging. *Educational Gerontology, 32,* 173–84.

Subbotsky, E. (2001). Causal explanations of events by children and adults: can alternative causal modes coexist in one mind? *British Journal of Developmental Psychology, 19,* 23–45.

Subbotsky, E. (2004). Magical thinking in judgments of causation: can anomalous phenomena affect ontological causal beliefs in children and adults? *British Journal of Developmental Psychology, 22,* 123–52S.

Sullivan, C. (1982). On 'Patterns of belief in religious, psychic and other paranormal phenomena'. *Zetetic Scholar, 10,* 147–9.

Sutherland, S. (1992). *Irrationality: the enemy within.* London: Constable.

Svensen, S. G., White, K. D. and Caird, D. (1992). Replications and resolutions: dualistic belief, personality, religiosity and paranormal belief in Australian students. *Journal of Psychology, 126,* 445–7.

Swartling, G. and Swartling, P. G. (1992). Psychiatric problems in ex-members of Word of Life. *Cultic Studies Journal, 9,* 78–88.

Sweeney, P. D., Benassi, V. A. and Drevno, G. (1980, September). *Transience of illusory control.* Paper presented at a meeting of the American Psychological Association, Montreal, Canada.

Tart, C. T. (1982). The controversy about psi: two psychological theories. *Journal of Parapsychology, 46,* 313–20.

Tart, C. T. and Labore, C. M. (1986). Attitudes toward strongly functioning psi: a preliminary survey. *Journal of the American Society for Psychical Research, 80,* 163–73.

Taylor, A. and MacDonald, D. A. (1999). Religion and the Five Factor Model of personality: an exploratory investigation using a Canadian university sample. *Personality and Individual Differences, 27,* 1243–59.

Taylor, J. H., Eve, R. A. and Harrold, F. B. (1995). Why creationists don't go to psychic fairs: differential sources of pseudoscientific beliefs. *Skeptical Inquirer, 19* (6), 23–8.

Taylor, N. M. (2001). Utilizing religious schemas to cope with mental illness. *Journal of Religion and Health, 40,* 383–8.

Taylor, S. E. (1983). Adjustment to threatening events: a theory of cognitive adaptation. *American Psychologist, 38,* 1161–73.

Taylor, S. E. and Brown, J. D. (1988). Illusion and well-being: a social psychological perspective on mental health. *Psychological Bulletin, 103,* 193–210.

TenDam, H. (1990). *Exploring reincarnation* (A. E. J. Wils, Trans.). London: Arkana.

Ter Keurst, A. J. (1939). Comparative differences between superstitious and non-superstitious children. *Journal of Experimental Education, 7,* 261–7.

Terr, L. C., Bloch, D. A., Michel, B. A., Shi, H., Reinhardt, J. A. and Metayer, S. (1997). Children's thinking in the wake of Challenger. *American Journal of Psychiatry, 154,* 744–51.

Thalbourne, M. A. (1981). Extraversion and the sheep–goat variable: a conceptual replication. *Journal of the American Society for Psychical Research, 75,* 105–19.

Thalbourne, M. A. (1984). Some correlates of belief in psychical phenomena: a partial replication of the Haraldsson findings. *Parapsychology Review, 15* (2), 13–15.

Thalbourne, M. A. (1985). Are believers in psi more prone to schizophrenia? [Summary]. In R. A. White and J. Solfvin (Eds.), *Research in parapsychology 1984* (pp. 85–8). Metuchen, NJ: Scarecrow Press.

Thalbourne, M. A. (1994). Belief in the paranormal and its relationship to schizophrenia-relevant measures: a confirmatory study. *British Journal of Clinical Psychology, 33,* 78–80.

Thalbourne, M. A. (1995a). Further studies of the measurement and correlates of belief in the paranormal. *Journal of the American Society for Psychical Research, 89,* 233–47.

Thalbourne, M. A. (1995b). Psychological characteristics of believers in the paranormal: a replicative study. *Journal of the American Society for Psychical Research, 89,* 153–64.

Thalbourne, M. A. (1996). Belief in life after death: psychological origins and influences. *Personality and Individual Differences, 21,* 1043–5.

Thalbourne, M. A. (1997). Testing the McBeath hypothesis: relation of sexual orientation and belief in the paranormal. *Psychological Reports, 81,* 890.

Thalbourne, M. A. (1998). Transliminality: further correlates and a short measure. *Journal of the American Society for Psychical Research, 92,* 402–419.

Thalbourne, M. A. (1998–99). The sheep–goat variable and mystical experience: their relationship and their levels in a special population. *European Journal of Parapsychology, 14,* 80–88.

Thalbourne, M. A. (1999). Dualism and the sheep–goat variable: a replication and extension. *Journal of the Society for Psychical Research, 63,* 213–16.

Thalbourne, M. A. (2000). Transliminality and creativity. *Journal of Creative Behavior, 34,* 193–202.

Thalbourne, M. A. (2001). Measures of the sheep–goat variable, transliminality and their correlates. *Psychological Reports, 88,* 339–50.

Thalbourne, M. A. (2003). Theism and belief in the paranormal. *Journal of the Society for Psychical Research, 67,* 208–210.

Thalbourne, M. A., Bartemucci, L., Delin, P. S., Fox, B. and Nofi, O. (1997). Transliminality: its nature and correlates. *Journal of the American Society for Psychical Research, 91,* 305–31.

Thalbourne, M. A., Beloff, J., Delanoy, D. and Jungkuntz, J. (1983). Some further tests of the extraverted sheep versus introverted goats hypothesis [Summary]. In W. G. Roll, J. Beloff and R. A. White (Eds.), *Research in parapsychology 1982* (pp. 199–200). Metuchen, NJ: Scarecrow Press.

Thalbourne, M. A. and Delin, P. S. (1993). A new instrument for measuring the sheep–goat variable: its psychometric properties and factor structure. *Journal of the Society for Psychical Research, 59,* 172–86.

Thalbourne, M. A. and Delin, P. S. (1994). A common thread underlying belief in the paranormal, creative personality, mystical experience and psychopathology. *Journal of Parapsychology, 58,* 3–38.

Thalbourne, M. A., Dunbar, K. A. and Delin, P. S. (1995). An investigation into correlates of belief in the paranormal. *Journal of the American Society for Psychical Research, 89,* 215–31.

Thalbourne, M. A. and French, C. C. (1995). Paranormal belief, manic-depressiveness and magical ideation: a replication. *Personality and Individual Differences, 18,* 291–2.

Thalbourne, M. A. and French, C. C. (1997). The sheep–goat variable and belief in non-paranormal anomalous phenomena. *Journal of the Society for Psychical Research, 62,* 41–5.

Thalbourne, M. A. and Haraldsson, E. (1980). Personality characteristics of sheep and goats. *Personality and Individual Differences, 1,* 180–5.

Thalbourne, M. A. and Hensley, J. H. (2001). Religiosity and belief in the paranormal. *Journal of the Society for Psychical Research, 65,* 47.

Thalbourne, M. A. and Houran, J. (2000). Transliminality, the Mental Experience Inventory and tolerance of ambiguity. *Personality and Individual Differences, 28,* 853–63.

Thalbourne, M. A. and Houtkooper, J. M. (2002). Religiosity/spirituality and belief in the paranormal: a German replication. *Journal of the Society for Psychical Research, 66,* 113–15.

Thalbourne, M. A. and Nofi, O. (1997). Belief in the paranormal, superstitiousness and intellectual ability. *Journal of the Society for Psychical Research, 61,* 365–71.

Thalbourne, M. A. and O'Brien, R. (1999). Belief in the paranormal and religious variables. *Journal of the Society for Psychical Research, 63,* 111–23.

The word cryptozoology. (2002, September 7). *New Scientist, 175* (2359), 51.

Thompson, E. H. and Remmes, K. R. (2002). Does masculinity thwart being religious? An examination of older men's religiousness. *Journal for the Scientific Study of Religion, 41,* 521–32.

Tilley, J. R. (2003). Secularization and aging in Britain: does family formation cause greater religiosity? *Journal for the Scientific Study of Religion, 42,* 269–78.

Tobacyk, J. [J.] (1982). Paranormal belief and trait anxiety. *Psychological Reports, 51,* 861–2.

Tobacyk, J. [J.] (1983a). Death threat, death concerns and paranormal belief. *Death Education, 7,* 115–24.

Tobacyk, J. [J.] (1983b). Paranormal beliefs, interpersonal trust and social interest. *Psychological Reports, 53,* 229–30.

Tobacyk, J. J. (1983c). Reduction in paranormal belief among participants in a college course. *Skeptical Inquirer, 8,* 57–61.

Tobacyk, J. [J.] (1984). Paranormal belief and college grade point average. *Psychological Reports, 54,* 217–18.

Tobacyk, J. J. (1985a). The Paranormal Belief Scale and social desirability. *Psychological Reports, 57,* 624.

Tobacyk, J. J. (1985b). Paranormal beliefs and identity achievement. *Psychological Reports, 56,* 26.

Tobacyk, J. J. (1985c). Paranormal beliefs, alienation and anomie in college students. *Psychological Reports, 57,* 844–6.

Tobacyk, J. J. (1988). *A revised Paranormal Belief Scale.* Unpublished manuscript, Louisiana Tech University, Ruston, LA.

Tobacyk, J. J. (1995). What is the correct dimensionality of paranormal beliefs? A reply to Lawrence's critique of the Paranormal Belief Scale. *Journal of Parapsychology, 59,* 27–46.

Tobacyk, J. [J.] and Milford, G. (1983). Belief in paranormal phenomena: Assessment instrument development and implications for personality functioning. *Journal of Personality and Social Psychology, 44,* 1029–37.

Tobacyk, J. [J.], Miller, M. J. and Jones, G. (1984). Paranormal beliefs of high school students. *Psychological Reports, 55,* 255–61.

Tobacyk, J. [J.], Miller, M., Murphy, P. and Mitchell, T. (1988). Comparisons of paranormal beliefs of black and white university students from the Southern United States. *Psychological Reports, 63,* 492–4.

Tobacyk, J. J. and Mitchell, T. E. (1987). Out-of-body experience status as a moderator of effects of narcissism on paranormal beliefs. *Psychological Reports, 60*, 440–2.

Tobacyk, J. J., Nagot, E. and Miller, M. (1988). Paranormal beliefs and locus of control: a multidimensional examination. *Journal of Personality Assessment, 52*, 241–6.

Tobacyk, J. J. and Pirttilä-Backman, A. (1992). Paranormal beliefs and their implications in university students from Finland and the United States. *Journal of Cross-Cultural Psychology, 23*, 59–71.

Tobacyk, J. [J.], Pritchett, G. and Mitchell, T. (1988). Paranormal beliefs in late-adulthood. *Psychological Reports, 62*, 965–6.

Tobacyk, J. [J.] and Shrader, D. (1991). Superstition and self-efficacy. *Psychological Reports, 68*, 1387–8.

Tobacyk, J. [J.] and Thomas, A. (1997). How the big orthogonal seven is really the oblique seven. *Journal of Parapsychology, 61*, 337–42.

Tobacyk, J. J. and Tobacyk, Z. S. (1992). Comparisons of belief-based personality constructs in Polish and American university students: paranormal beliefs, locus of control, irrational beliefs and social interest. *Journal of Cross-Cultural Psychology, 23*, 311–25.

Tobacyk, J. J., Wells, D. H. and Miller, M. M. (1998). Out-of-body experience and personality functioning. *Psychological Reports, 82*, 481–2.

Tobacyk, J. J. and Wilkinson, L. V. (1990). Magical thinking and paranormal beliefs. *Journal of Social Behavior and Personality, 5* (4), Special Issue, 255–64.

Tobacyk, J. J. and Wilkinson, L. V. (1991). Paranormal beliefs and preference for games of chance. *Psychological Reports, 68*, 1088–90.

Todd, M. and Brown, C. (2003). Characteristics associated with superstitious behavior in track and field athletes: are there NCAA divisional level differences? *Journal of Sport Behavior, 26*, 168–87.

Torgler, B. (2007). Determinants of superstition. *Journal of Socio-Economics, 36*, 713–33.

Tumminia, D. G. (2002). In the dreamtime of the saucer people: sense-making and interpretative boundaries in a contactee group. *Journal of Contemporary Ethnography, 31*, 675–705.

Tupper, V. and Williams, R. J. (1986). Unsubstantiated beliefs among beginning psychology students: 1925, 1952, 1983. *Psychological Reports, 58*, 383–8.

Ullman, C. (1982). Cognitive and emotional antecedents of religious conversion. *Journal of Personality and Social Psychology, 43*, 183–92.

Valentine, W. L. (1936). Common misconceptions of college students. *Journal of Applied Psychology, 20*, 633–58.

Van de Castle, R. L. and White, R. A. (1955). A report on a sentence completion form of sheep–goat attitude scale. *Journal of Parapsychology, 19*, 171–9.

Verdoux, H., van Os, J., Maurice-Tison, S., Gay, B., Salamon, R. and Bourgeois, M. (1998). Is early adulthood a critical developmental stage for psychosis proneness? A survey of delusional ideation in normal subjects. *Schizophrenia Research, 29,* 247–54.

Vicklund, O. U. (1940). The elimination of superstition in junior high school science. *Science Education, 24,* 93–9.

Vitulli, W. F. (1997). Beliefs in parapsychological events or experiences among college students in a course in experimental parapsychology. *Perceptual and Motor Skills, 85,* 2734.

Vitulli, W. F. (2000). Rejoinder to Irwin's (2000) 'Age and sex differences in paranormal beliefs: a response to Vitulli, Tipton and Rowe (1999)'. *Psychological Reports, 87,* 699–700.

Vitulli, W. F. and Luper, S. L. (1998). Sex differences in paranormal beliefs among undergraduate college students. *Perceptual and Motor Skills, 87,* 475–83.

Vitulli, W. F., Tipton, S. M. and Rowe, J. L. (1999). Beliefs in the paranormal: age and sex differences among elderly persons and undergraduate students. *Psychological Reports, 85,* 847–55.

Voracek, M., Fisher, M. L. and Sonneck, G. (2002). Solar eclipse and suicide. *American Journal of Psychiatry, 159,* 1247–8.

Vyse, S. A. (1997). *Believing in magic: the psychology of superstition.* New York: Oxford University Press.

Wagner, M. E. (1928). Superstitions and their social and psychological correlatives among college students. *Journal of Educational Sociology, 2,* 26–36.

Wagner, M. W. and Ratzeburg, F. H. (1987). Hypnotic suggestibility and paranormal belief. *Psychological Reports, 60,* 1069–70.

Walker, G. C. (2000). Secular eschatology: beliefs about afterlife. *Omega: Journal of Death and Dying, 41,* 5–22.

Walker, W. R., Hoekstra, S. J. and Vogl, R. J. (2002). Science education is no guarantee of skepticism. *Skeptic, 9* (3), 24–27.

Wallace, K. A. and Bergeman, C. S. (1997). Control and the elderly: goodness-of-fit. *International Journal of Aging and Human Development, 45,* 323–39.

Waller, N. G., Kojetin, B. A., Bouchard, T. J., Lykken, D. T., McGue, M. and Tellegen, A. (1990). Genetic and environmental influences on religious interests, attitudes and values: a study of twins reared apart and together. *Psychological Science, 1,* 138–42.

Walter, T. and Waterhouse, H. (1999). A very private belief: reincarnation in contemporary England. *Sociology of Religion, 60,* 187–97.

Warren, D. I. (1970). Status inconsistency theory and flying saucer sightings. *Science, 170,* 599–603.

Watt, C. and Baker, I. S. (2002). Remote facilitation of attention focusing with psi-supportive versus psi-unsupportive experimenter suggestions. *Journal of Parapsychology, 66,* 151–68.

Watt, C., Watson, S. and Wilson, L. (2007). Cognitive and psychological mediators of anxiety: evidence from a study of paranormal belief and perceived childhood control. *Personality and Individual Differences, 43,* 335–43.

Watt, C. and Wiseman, R. (2002). Experimenter differences in cognitive correlates of paranormal belief and in psi. *Journal of Parapsychology, 66*, 371–85.

Weiner, B. (1980). *Human motivation.* New York: Holt, Rinehart and Winston.

Weiner, B. (1986). *An attributional theory of motivation and emotion.* New York: Springer-Verlag.

Weinstein, S. and Graves, R. E. (2002). Are creativity and schizotypy products of a right hemisphere bias? *Brain and Cognition, 49*, 138–51.

Wesp, R. and Montgomery, K. (1998). Developing critical thinking through the study of paranormal phenomena. *Teaching of Psychology, 25*, 275–8.

Westman, A. S., Brackney, B. E. and Bylski, N. C. (1992). Religious beliefs are socialised in the same way as are other beliefs. *Psychological Reports, 70*, 1107–10.

Westrum, R. [M.] (1977). Social intelligence about anomalies: the case of UFOs. *Social Studies of Science, 7*, 271–302.

Westrum, R. M. (1979). Witnesses of UFOs and other anomalies. In R. F. Haines (Ed.), *UFO phenomena and the behavioral scientist* (pp. 89–112). Metuchen, NJ: Scarecrow Press.

White, R. (1959). Motivation reconsidered: the concept of competence. *Psychological Review, 66*, 297–333.

Whitelaw, H. and Laslett, H. R. (1932). A further study of acceptance of popular misbeliefs among college students. *Kadelpian Review, 11*, 297–300.

Wierzbicki, M. (1985). Reasoning errors and belief in the paranormal. *Journal of Social Psychology, 125*, 489–94.

Wildta, B. T. T. and Schultz-Venrath, U. (2004). Magical ideation – Defense mechanism or neuropathology? A study with multiple sclerosis patients. *Psychopathology, 37*, 141–4.

Willging, B. T. and Lester, D. (1997). Paranormal beliefs and personality scores of high school students. *Perceptual and Motor Skills, 85*, 938.

Williams, E., Francis, L. J. and Robbins, M. (2006). Attitude toward Christianity and paranormal belief among 13- to 16-year-old students. *Psychological Reports, 99*, 266.

Williams, E., Francis, L. J. and Robbins, M. (2007). Personality and paranormal belief: A study among adolescents. *Pastoral Psychology, 56*, 9–14.

Williams, L. (1989). *An exploratory study of the relationship between paranormal belief, magical ideation and schizotypy.* Unpublished Honours thesis, University of New England, Armidale, Australia.

Williams, L. (1995). Belief in the paranormal: its relationship with schizotypy and cognitive style. *Australian Parapsychological Review*, No. 20, 8–10.

Williams, L. M. and Irwin, H. J. (1991). A study of paranormal belief, magical ideation as an index of schizotypy and cognitive style. *Personality and Individual Differences, 12*, 1339–48.

Williams, R. N., Taylor, C. B. and Hintze, W. J. (1989). The influence of religious orientation on belief in science, religion and the paranormal. *Journal of Psychology and Theology, 17*, 352–9.

Wilson, K. and French, C. C. (2006). The relationship between susceptibility to false memories, dissociativity and paranormal belief and experience. *Personality and Individual Differences, 41*, 1493–502.

Wilson, K. M. and Frank, M. L. (1990). Persistence of paranormal beliefs. *Psychological Reports, 67*, 946.

Wilson, M. H. (1951). Witch beliefs and social structure. *American Journal of Sociology, 56*, 307–13.

Wilson, S. C. and Barber, T. X. (1983). The fantasy-prone personality: implications for understanding imagery, hypnosis and parapsychological phenomena. In A. A. Sheikh (Ed.), *Imagery: current theory, research and application* (pp. 340–87). New York: Wiley.

Windholz, G. and Diamant, L. (1974). Some personality traits of believers in extraordinary phenomena. *Bulletin of the Psychonomic Society, 3*, 125–6.

Wink, P., Ciciolla, L., Dillon, M. and Tracy, A. (2007). Religiousness, spiritual seeking and personality: findings from a longitudinal study. *Journal of Personality, 75*, 1051–70.

Wiseman, R. (2003). *UK superstition survey.* (Unpublished manuscript, University of Hertfordshire), http://www.richardwiseman.com/resources/superstition_report.pdf, retrieved 19 January 2009.

Wiseman, R., Greening, E. and Smith, M. (2003). Belief in the paranormal and suggestion in the seance room. *British Journal of Psychology, 94*, 285–97.

Wiseman, R. and Morris, R. L. (1995). Recalling pseudo-psychic demonstrations. *British Journal of Psychology, 86*, 113–25.

Wiseman, R. and Schlitz, M. (1997). Experimenter effects and the remote detection of staring. *Journal of Parapsychology, 61*, 197–208.

Wiseman, R., Seager, P. and Smith, M. D. (1997, August). *Eyewitness testimony for 'seance room' phenomena.* Paper presented at the 40th Annual Convention of the Parapsychological Association, Brighton, UK.

Wiseman, R. and Smith, M. D. (2002). Assessing the role of cognitive and motivational biases in belief in the paranormal. *Journal of the Society for Psychical Research, 66*, 157–66.

Wiseman, R. and Watt, C. (2002, August). *Belief in the paranormal, cognitive ability and extrasensory perception: the role of experimenter effects.* Paper presented at the 45th Annual Convention of the Parapsychological Association, Paris, France.

Wiseman, R. and Watt, C. (2004). Measuring superstitious belief: why lucky charms matter. *Personality and Individual Differences, 37*, 1533–41.

Wiseman, R. and Watt, C. (2006). Belief in psychic ability and the misattribution hypothesis: a qualitative review. *British Journal of Psychology, 97*, 323–38.

Wolfradt, U. (1997). Dissociative experiences, trait anxiety and paranormal beliefs. *Personality and Individual Differences, 23*, 15–19.

Wolfradt, U., Oubaid, V., Straube, E. R., Bischoff, N. and Mischo, J. (1999). Thinking styles, schizotypal traits and anomalous experiences. *Personality and Individual Differences, 27*, 821–30.

Womack, M. (1992). Why athletes need ritual: a study of magic among professional athletes. In S. Hoffman (Ed.), *Sport and religion* (pp. 191–202). Champaign, IL: Human Kinetics.

Wong-McDonald, A. and Gorsuch, R. L. (2000). Surrender to God: an additional coping style? *Journal of Psychology and Theology, 28,* 149–61.

Woolley, J. D., Boerger, E. A. and Markman, A. B. (2004). A visit from the Candy Witch: factors influencing young children's belief in a novel fantastical being. *Developmental Science, 7,* 456–68.

Wuthnow, R. (1976). Astrology and marginality. *Journal for the Scientific Study of Religion, 15,* 157–68.

Yang, C. H., Huang, Y. T., Janes, C., Lin, K. C. and Lu, T. H. (2008). Belief in ghost month can prevent drowning deaths: a natural experiment on the effects of cultural beliefs on risky behaviours. *Social Science and Medicine, 66,* 1990–8.

Yip, K. (2003). Traditional Chinese religious beliefs and superstitions in delusions and hallucinations of Chinese schizophrenic patients. *International Journal of Social Psychiatry, 49,* 97–111.

Zapf, R. M. (1938). Superstitions of junior high school pupils. Part II. Effect of instruction on superstitious beliefs. *Journal of Educational Research, 31,* 481–96.

Zapf, R. M. (1945a). Comparisons of responses to superstitions on a written test and in actual situations. *Journal of Educational Research, 39,* 13–24.

Zapf, R. M. (1945b). Relationship between belief in superstitions and other factors. *Journal of Educational Research, 38,* 561–79.

Za'vour, G. I. (1972). Superstitions among certain groups of Lebanese Arab students in Beirut. *Journal of Cross-Cultural Psychology, 3,* 273–82.

Zebb, B. J. and Moore, M. C. (2003). Superstitiousness and perceived anxiety control as predictors of psychological distress. *Journal of Anxiety Disorders, 17,* 115–130.

Zeidner, M. and Beit-Hallahmi, B. (1988). Sex, ethnic and social class differences in parareligious beliefs among Israeli adolescents. *Journal of Social Psychology, 128,* 333–43.

Zelin, M. L., Bernstein, S. B., Heijn, C., Jampel, R. M., Myerson, P. G., Adler, G., Buie, D. H. and Rizzuto, A. M. (1983). The Sustaining Fantasy Questionnaire: measurement of sustaining functions of fantasies in psychiatric inpatients. *Journal of Personality Assessment, 47,* 427–39.

Zimmer, T. A. (1984). Social psychological correlates of possible UFO sightings. *Journal of Social Psychology, 123,* 199–206.

Zingrone, N. L. (1994). Images of woman as medium: power, pathology and passivity in the writings of Frederic Marvin and Cesare Lombroso. In L. Coly and R. A. White (Eds.), *Women and parapsychology: proceedings of an international conference* (pp. 90–123). New York: Parapsychology Foundation.

Zuckerman, M., Bone, R. N., Neary, R., Mangelsdorff, D. and Brustman, B. (1972). What is the sensation seeker? Personality trait and experience correlates of the Sensation-Seeking Scales. *Journal of Consulting and Clinical Psychology, 39,* 308–21.

Zusne, L. and Jones, W. H. (1982). *Anomalistic psychology: a study of extraordinary phenomena of behavior and experience.* Hillsdale, NJ: Lawrence Erlbaum Associates.

Zusne, L. and Jones, W. H. (1989). *Anomalistic psychology: a study of magical thinking* (2nd ed.). Hillsdale, NJ: Lawrence Erlbaum Associates.

Appendices

Some historically significant measures of paranormal belief

Appendix 1

Nixon's Superstitions Scale
(Nixon, 1925)

Below are a number of statements. Some of them you may consider true, some of them false. If you think a statement is substantially true, draw a circle around T; if the statement is false, then a circle around F. Where it seems debatable, mark as seems to you nearest right.

1.	The number of man's senses is five.	T F
2.	A child comes into the world with an instinctive knowledge of good and evil. This is his conscience and is born in him.	T F
3.	Certain lines in a person's hand foretell his future.	T F
4.	If you will stare at a person's back you can make him turn around. This is a form of telepathy.	T F
5.	It really is unlucky to have anything to do with the number 13.	T F
6.	A man's character can be read by noting the size and location of special developments of his head.	T F
7.	People with greenish eyes are not as trustworthy as people with blue or black eyes.	T F
8.	An expectant mother by fixing her mind on a subject can influence the character of her unborn child.	T F
9.	Women are inferior to men in intelligence.	T F
10.	People born under the influence of certain planets show the influence in their characters.	T F
11.	Intelligence can be increased by training.	T F
12.	Long, slender hands indicate an artistic nature.	T F
13.	Beginning an undertaking on Friday is almost certain to bring bad luck.	T F
14.	If a man but had faith enough he could heal a broken limb instantly.	T F
15.	Many eminent men have been feeble-minded as children.	T F
16.	Some animals are as intelligent as the average human.	T F
17.	No defect of body or mind can hold us back if we have enough will power.	T F
18.	Adults sometimes become feeble-minded from overstudy.	T F
19.	All men are created equal in capacity for achievement.	T F
20.	The marriage of cousins is practically certain to result in children of inferior intelligence.	T F

21. Especially intelligent children are likely to be weak and retarded physically.   T F

22. The study of mathematics is valuable because it gives one a logical mind.   T F

23. A square jaw is a sign of will power.   T F

24. You can estimate an individual's intelligence pretty closely by just looking at his face.   T F

25. A high forehead indicates intellectual superiority.   T F

26. Fear is unnatural. It is a bad habit.   T F

27. Women are by nature purer and better than men.   T F

28. A person who does not look you in the eye is likely to be dishonest.   T F

29. Man is superior because his conduct is very largely guided by reason.   T F

30. Any physical or mental disease can be contracted by thinking about it.   T F

Scoring

A superstitiousness score is computed as the number of items for which the response is 'True'.

Appendix 2

Gilliland's Revision of Nixon's Superstitions Scale
(Gilliland, 1930)

Below are a number of statements. Some of them you may consider true, some of them false. If you think a statement is substantially true, draw a circle around T; if the statement is false, then a circle around F. Where there is doubt mark as seems to you nearer right.

1.   The number of man's senses is limited to five.   T F

2.*   Psychology is the study of human behavior.   T F

3.*   The opposite of red is green.   T F

4.   A child comes into the world with an instinctive knowledge of good and evil.   T F
      This is his conscience and is born in him.

5.*   Periods of illness appear longer than they really are at the time and shorter   T F
      than it really was in retrospection.

6.   Certain lines in a person's hand foretell his future.   T F

7.   If you will stare at a person's back you can make him turn around. This is a   T F
      form of telepathy.

8.   It really is unlucky to have anything to do with the number 13.   T F

9.*   Sensations exist in pure form only at birth or as an abstraction.   T F

10.* Perceptions very seldom change even in childhood.   T F

11.   A man's character can be read by noting the size and location of special   T F
      developments of his head.

12.   People with greenish eyes are not as trustworthy as people with blue or black   T F
      eyes.

13.   An expectant mother by fixing her mind on a subject can influence the   T F
      character of her unborn child.

14.   Women are inferior to men in intelligence.   T F

15.* Some people can learn fifteen to twenty times as rapidly as others.   T F

16.   People born under the influence of certain planets show the influence in   T F
      their characters.

17.   Intelligence can be increased by training.   T F

18.   Long, slender hands indicate an artistic nature.   T F

19.   Beginning an undertaking on Friday is almost certain to bring bad luck.   T F

20.   If a man but had faith enough he could heal a broken limb instantly.   T F

21.* A square box looks higher than it is wide.   T F

22.	Many eminent men have been feeble-minded as children.	T	F
23.*	There is never an active movement of the body which is not produced by a nervous current.	T	F
24.	You can estimate an individual's intelligence pretty closely by just looking at his face.	T	F
25.	Some animals are as intelligent as the average human.	T	F
26.	No defect of body or mind can hold us back if we have enough will power.	T	F
27.	Adults sometimes become feeble-minded from overstudy.	T	F
28.	All men are created equal in capacity for achievement.	T	F
29.*	We ordinarily have forgotten half of what we have learned in twenty-four hours afterwards.	T	F
30.	The marriage of cousins is practically certain to result in children of inferior intelligence.	T	F
31.	Especially intelligent children are likely to be weak and retarded physically.	T	F
32.	The study of mathematics is valuable because it gives one a logical mind.	T	F
33.	A square jaw is a sign of will power.	T	F
34.*	All ideas probably originate in the gray matter of the brain.	T	F
35.	A high forehead indicates intellectual superiority.	T	F
36.	A person who does not look you in the eye is likely to be dishonest.	T	F
37.	Women are by nature purer and better than men.	T	F
38.	Fear is unnatural. It is a bad habit.	T	F
39.	Man is superior to animals because his conduct is mostly guided by reason.	T	F
40.	Any physical or mental disease can be contracted by thinking about it.	T	F

*These are merely 'buffer' items and are not scored.

Scoring

A superstitiousness score is computed as the number of (non-asterisked) items for which the response is 'True'.

Appendix 3

Sentence Completion Test of ESP Belief
(Van de Castle and White, 1955)

Below you will find a series of incomplete sentences which you are to complete by writing down the *first* words that come to your mind after reading the phrase. Don't be concerned with grammatical correctness. For the purposes of this survey that is not important. What is wanted is your immediate response after reading each item. Put down the first word or words that come to your mind.

1.   I believe that hunches often...
2.   Stories we hear about telepathy...
3.   Clairvoyance might sometimes...
4.   The scientific evidence for parapsychology...
5.   People who are skeptical of ESP are...
6.   The idea of telepathy...
7.   There seems little doubt that ESP...
8.   A careful study of parapsychology would show...
9.   It is impossible for ESP...

Scoring

For each item a score of 1 is assigned if the completed sentence signifies a negative attitude toward ESP, a score of 2 for a neutral position and a score of 3 for a positive orientation toward ESP. The scores are then summed across the 9 items. Respondents who score above 19 are labeled 'sheep' (ESP believers) and those who score below 17 are designated 'goats' (disbelievers).

Reproduced with permission of authors and publisher from:
Van de Castle, R. L. and White, R. A. (1955). A report on a sentence completion form of sheep–goat attitude scale. *Journal of Parapsychology, 19,* 171–9. © Journal of Parapsychology 1955

Appendix 4

Attitude to ESP
(Bhadra, 1966)

1.	Have you ever come to know in advance that you are going to receive a particular letter on a particular day?	Yes No
2.	Have you ever come to know in advance that someone whom you have not thought of for years is going to call you?	Yes No
3.	Have you ever had a dream which later came true?	Yes No
4.	Are you consistently lucky at whatever you do?	Yes No
5.	Have you ever suspected that a person will fall sick or meet with an accident or die and this has actually happened?	Yes No
6.	Have you ever tried in a card game or playing with dice or couries to score in a definite way, i.e., expecting to get one, two, or three to appear and succeeded?	Yes No
7.	If you have observed some of the above incidents coming true, please mark any of the reasons given which you think is correct.	Mere chance or luck Coincidence Special gift or ESP
8.	If you try and get more correct scores [in a card-guessing ESP test], for example, out of 25 trials you score 10 or 15 as correct and this is repeated consistently throughout your trials, what reasons can you give?	It is luck It is coincidence It is a special gift or ESP
9.	If some people get only chance scores, some others still less and some others more than chance, what reasons can you give for the people who score more than chance expectation?	Luck Coincidence Special gift or ESP
10.	Do you consider that the existence of ESP or the special gift is...	Impossible Possible Certain
11.	Which statement is the best expression of your belief about your own ESP ability?	No possibility I have ESP Possibly I have ESP Believe I have ESP
12.	If you take the [ESP] card test can you score...	Below chance At chance Above chance

Scoring

For details on how the above items are used to categorize 'sheep' (believers) and 'goats' (disbelievers), see Bhadra (1966).

Reproduced with permission of authors and publisher from:
Bhadra, B. H. (1966). The relationship of test scores to belief in ESP. *Journal of Parapsychology, 30,* 1–17. © Journal of Parapsychology 1966

Appendix 5

Belief in the Paranormal Scale
(Jones, Russell and Nickel, 1977)

For each item indicate your level of agreement using the following scale.

1	2	3	4	5
strongly disagree	disagree	undecided	agree	strongly agree

1. I believe psychic phenomena are real and should become a part of psychology and be studied scientifically.

2.* All UFO sightings are either other forms of physical phenomena (such as weather balloons) or simply hallucinations.

3. I am convinced the Abominable Snowman of Tibet really exists.

4. I firmly believe that ghosts or spirits do exist.

5. Black magic really exists and should be dealt with in a serious manner.

6. Witches and warlocks do exist.

7.* Only the uneducated or the demented believe in the supernatural and the occult.

8. Through psychic individuals it is possible to communicate with the dead.

9. I believe the Loch Ness monster of Scotland exists.

10. I believe that once a person dies his spirit may come back from time to time in the form of ghosts.

11. Some individuals are able to levitate (lift objects) through mysterious mental forces.

12. I believe that many special persons throughout the world have the ability to predict the future.

13.* The idea of being able to tell the future through the means of palm reading represents the beliefs of foolish and unreliable persons.

14. I am firmly convinced that reincarnation has been occurring throughout history and that it will continue to occur.

15. I firmly believe that, at least on some occasions, I can read another person's mind via ESP (extrasensory perception).

16. ESP is an unusual gift that many persons have and should not be confused with the elaborate tricks used by entertainers.

17.* Ghosts and witches do not exist outside the realm of imagination.

18. Supernatural phenomena should become part of scientific study, equal in importance to physical phenomena.

19.* All of the reports of 'scientific proof' of psychic phenomena are strictly sensationalism with no factual basis.

20. Through the use of mysterious formulas and incantations it is possible to cast spells on individuals.

21. With proper training anyone could learn to read other people's minds.

22. It is advisable to consult your horoscope daily.

23. Plants can sense the feelings of humans through a form of ESP.

24. ESP has been scientifically proven to exist.

25. There is a great deal we have yet to understand about the mind of man, so it is likely that many phenomena (such as ESP) will one day be proven to exist.

*Responses to these items are reversed for scoring purposes.

Scoring

Sum the responses over the 25 items.

Appendix 6

Supernaturalism Scale
(Randall and Desrosiers, 1980)

Below you will find a number of statements of opinion. Since these are opinions and not statements of fact, there are no right or wrong answers. For each statement of public opinion please indicate *how strongly* you agree or disagree with that statement, using the following scale.

1	2	3	4	5	6
strongly disagree	disagree somewhat	disagree slightly	agree slightly	agree somewhat	agree strongly

1.† Every child should have some type of formal religious training.

2.†* Religion probably has done more to hurt the generation gap than to help it.

3. It is probably true that certain people can predict the future quite accurately.

4. It is often possible to make valid personality judgments about people by knowing their astrological sign.

5.† The best way to rehabilitate a criminal is to help him find religion.

6. It is possible for certain people to have a mental power to manipulate others.

7.* Basically, there is no truth to the belief that the Earth is being watched by extraterrestrial beings, or 'spacemen'.

8.* For the most part, people who claim to be psychics are in reality very good actors.

9.† Belief in a Supreme Being is essential for human existence.

10. In spite of what the 'experts' think, there is more to magic than quick hands and fast talking.

11.* With regard to one's health, it is always best to place confidence in the ability of a trained physician rather than to tamper with the unknown, like so called Faith Healing.

12. It is quite possible for planetary forces to control personality traits.

13. Contrary to scientific opinion, there is some validity to fortune telling.

14. In spite of the laws of science, some people can use their psychic powers to make objects move.

15.* Rather than to rely on astrology, it might benefit one more to rely on the opinion of trained, professional counselors.

16. Plants, although not as sophisticated as humans, do have a way to respond or communicate.

17.* As a general rule, a fortune teller's predictions which come true are a result of coincidence.

18.* Generally speaking, people who live their lives according to astrological predictions are basically insecure or naïve.

19.* Regardless of what you might read in the magazines, people who actually believe in 'magical' ritual ceremonies are just wasting their time.

20.* As a general rule, UFO sightings can best be explained as overreactions by people to naturally occurring events.

21.†* Religious training often does as much harm as good for a child's development of morals.

22.* For the most part, most fortune teller's predictions are general and vague. It is just the situation that makes them believable.

23. It is more than likely that UFOs are visits from superior beings who could have control over the planet Earth.

24.* For the most part, people who believe that music and talking can influence the growth of plants are deceiving themselves.

25.† Without religion the world would probably be in a state of total disruption.

26.* For the most part, the study of astrology is not a very efficient way of dealing with life.

27.* In spite of what some people say, the full moon has no 'special powers' to make people act peculiar.

28. Generally speaking, people who believe that only sun, soil and water influence the proper growth of a plant are not being realistic.

29.†* Religious people are just as responsible as atheists for much of the evil in society.

30. In spite of what many people think, card reading, for example tarot cards, can tell a lot about a person and their future.

31. If people were really honest, they would admit that there are ways of curing that modern medicine cannot explain.

32. Cosmic forces (like astrology) can still influence people's lives even though they don't believe in it.

33. The experience of 'déjà vu', or having vague feelings of reliving a past experience, is probably a memory of a previous life.

34.* Although some people believe there still are people who can actually put a hex on or cast a love spell on someone, such belief is only superstition.

35.* Matters of health are far too important to be risked at the hands of an unlicensed 'healer'.

36. Contrary to scientific belief, some people can make contact with the dead.

37.†* Religion is probably responsible for a lot of the problems of adolescents.

38. Generally, the way people turn out in life is dependent upon the position of the planets and stars at the time of their birth.

39.* Most people who believe in the predictions of a fortune teller are usually of low self-direction.

40.* There is nothing more to the belief in reincarnation than just people who are afraid of dying.

† These items on religious belief are buffer items that should be scored separately.

* These items are reversed for scoring.

Scoring

Supernaturalism = sum of responses to the 32 non-buffer items

(Religious belief = sum of responses to the 8 buffer items)

Appendix 7

Extraordinary Beliefs Inventory
(Otis and Alcock, 1982)

Using the numbers as indicated below, please put a number next to each item to best represent your own opinion. Please don't be too technical in interpreting the questions. They are not meant to be subtle or tricky in any way.

7	6	5	4	3	2	1
strongly agree	agree	slightly agree	undecided	slightly disagree	disagree	strongly disagree

1. There is a real phenomenon known as *psychokinesis* (the ability to move objects by the power of the mind).

2. Miracles are performed by the power of God, even today.

3. Finding a four leaf clover brings good luck.

4. The Loch Ness monster exists.

5. A Supreme Being exists.

6. Many of the stories of mysterious psychical happenings are true.

7. Some people can actually foretell your future by looking at the lines in your palm.

8. The Abominable Snowman exists.

9. There is a life after death.

10. Psychics possess a mysterious ability to know things about a person's past and future.

11. The spirits of people who have died can sometimes communicate with the living.

12. There is such a thing as astral projection (where the body remains behind while the spirit travels).

13. Everyone has an immortal soul.

14. Misfortunes tend to come in threes.

15. There are such things as ghosts.

16. Some people who describe themselves as witches have special magical powers.

17. After walking under a ladder bad luck will follow.

18. There are such things as *poltergeists* (spirits which signal their presence by moving objects or making noises).

19. There is such a thing as *extrasensory perception* (ESP).

20. A black cat crossing your path sometimes brings bad luck.

21. Some buildings are haunted.

22. God has given some people the power to heal the sick.

23. Some people have a mysterious ability to accurately predict such things as natural disasters, election results, political assassinations, etc.

24. God sometimes or always answers prayers.

25. There is such a thing as *levitation* (raising the body through mental power).

26. There is much truth in *astrology*.

27. There is such a thing as *telepathy* (communication directly from mind to mind).

28. Every person has an aura (a mysterious energy field, usually invisible, surrounding the body).

29. Heaven and Hell exist.

30. Good luck charms sometimes help to bring good luck.

Scoring

Belief in luck = mean of items 3, 14, 17, 20, 30.

Belief in spirits = mean of items 11, 15, 16, 18, 21.

Belief in religion = mean of items 2, 5, 9, 13, 22, 24, 29.

Belief in psychic phenomena = mean of items 1, 6, 10, 12, 19, 25, 27, 28.

Belief in creatures = mean of items 4, 8.

Belief in fortune telling = mean of items 7, 23, 26.

Appendix 8

Paranormal Belief Scale
(Tobacyk and Milford, 1983)

Please put a number next to each item to indicate how much you agree or disagree with that item. Use the numbers as indicated below. There are no right or wrong answers. This is a sample of your own beliefs and attitudes.

1	2	3	4	5
strongly disagree	disagree	undecided	agree	strongly agree

1. The soul continues to exist though the body may die.

2. Some individuals are able to levitate (lift) objects through mental forces.

3. Black magic really exists.

4. Black cats can bring bad luck.

5. Your mind or soul can leave your body and travel (astral projection).

6. The Abominable Snowman of Tibet exists.

7. Dreams can provide information about the future.

8. There is a Devil.

9. Psychokinesis, the movement of objects through psychic powers, does exist.

10. Witches do exist.

11. If you break a mirror, you will have bad luck.

12. During altered states, such as sleep or trances, the spirit can leave the body.

13. The Loch Ness monster of Scotland exists.

14. Some people have the ability to predict the future.

15. I believe in God.

16. A person's thoughts can influence the movement of a physical object.

17. Voodoo is a real method to use paranormal powers.

18. The number '13' is unlucky.

19. Reincarnation does occur.

20. Big Foot does exist.

21.* The idea of predicting the future is foolish.

22. There is a heaven and a hell.

23.* Mind reading is not possible.

24. There are actual cases of Voodoo Death.

25. It is possible to communicate with the dead.

*Items 21 and 23 are reversed for scoring.

Scoring

Traditional religious belief = mean of items 1, 8, 15, 22.

Psi = mean of items 2, 9, 16, 23.

Witchcraft = mean of items 3, 10, 17, 24.

Superstition = mean of items 4, 11, 18.

Spiritualism = mean of items 5, 12, 19, 25.

Extraordinary life forms = mean of items 6, 13, 20.

Precognition = mean of items 7, 14, 21.

Reproduced with permission of authors and publisher from:

Tobacyk, J. and Milford, G. (1983). Belief in paranormal phenomena: assessment instrument development and implications for personality functioning. *Journal of Personality and Social Psychology, 44,* 1029–37. Copyright © 1983 by the American Psychological Association 1983. Adapted with permission.

Appendix 9

Revised Paranormal Belief Scale
(Tobacyk, 1988)

Please put a number next to each item to indicate how much you agree or disagree with that item. Use the numbers as indicated below. There are no right or wrong answers. This is a sample of *your own* beliefs and attitudes.

1	2	3	4	5	6	7
strongly disagree	moderately disagree	slightly disagree	uncertain	slightly agree	moderately agree	strongly agree

1.   The soul continues to exist though the body may die.

2.   Some individuals are able to levitate (lift) objects through mental forces.

3.   Black magic really exists.

4.   Black cats can bring bad luck.

5.   Your mind or soul can leave your body and travel (astral projection).

6.   The abominable snowman of Tibet exists.

7.   Astrology is a way to accurately predict the future.

8.   There is a devil.

9.   Psychokinesis, the movement of objects through psychic powers, does exist.

10.   Witches do exist.

11.   If you break a mirror, you will have bad luck.

12.   During altered states, such as sleep or trances, the spirit can leave the body.

13.   The Loch Ness monster of Scotland exists.

14.   The horoscope accurately tells a person's future.

15.   I believe in God.

16.   A person's thoughts can influence the movement of a physical object.

17.   Through the use of formulas and incantations, it is possible to cast spells on persons.

18.   The number '13' is unlucky.

19.   Reincarnation does occur.

20.   There is life on other planets.

21.   Some psychics can accurately predict the future.

22.   There is a heaven and a hell.

23.* Mind reading is *not* possible.

24.   There are actual cases of witchcraft.

25.   It is possible to communicate with the dead.

26.   Some people have an unexplained ability to predict the future.

*Item 23 is reversed for scoring.

Scoring (Tobacyk, 1988)
Traditional religious belief = mean of items 1, 8, 15, 22.
Psi = mean of items 2, 9, 16, 23.
Witchcraft = mean of items 3, 10, 17, 24.
Superstition = mean of items 4, 11, 18.
Spiritualism = mean of items 5, 12, 19, 25.
Extraordinary life forms = mean of items 6, 13, 20.
Precognition = mean of items 7, 14, 21, 26.

Scoring (Lange, Irwin and Houran, 2000)
First, recode each response (from 1 through 7) to 0 through 6.
New Age philosophy = sum of items 2, 3, 5, 7, 9, 12, 14, 16, 19, 21, 23.
Traditional paranormal beliefs = sum of items 8, 17, 22, 24, 26.
To recode these two factors with Rasch scaling, see the conversion table in Lange *et al.* (2000).

Appendix 10

Anomalous Experiences Inventory: Anomalous/Paranormal Belief Subscale
(originally developed in 1994; Kumar and Pekala, 2001)

For each statement below indicate whether the statement is true or false for you. Work quickly and give your first impression.

2.[†] I believe that mind can control matter.

9. I believe in life after death.

10. I believe I have great power and energy within me waiting to be awakened.

12. I want to understand the further reaches of my mind.

20. I believe that many paranormal occurrences are real.

22. I feel my mind can expand beyond its usual boundaries.

23. I believe in the unconscious.

26. I believe in reincarnation.

31. I have lived before.

34. I believe there is intelligent life on other planets.

44. I believe that people have energy (an aura) surrounding their bodies.

59. I practice witchcraft or sorcery.

[†]These item numbers correspond to those in the full AEI scale. For items in other subscales of the AEI, see Kumar and Pekala (2001). Note that the wording of some of the above items differs slightly from that originally reported by Gallagher, Kumar and Pekala (1994).

Scoring
Sum the number of 'True' responses over the twelve items.

Reproduced with permission of authors and publisher from:
Kumar, V. K. and Pekala, R. J. (2001). Relation of hypnosis-specific attitudes and behaviors to paranormal beliefs and experiences: A technical review. In J. Houran and R. Lange (Eds.), *Hauntings and poltergeists: multidisciplinary perspectives* (pp. 260–79). Jefferson, NC: McFarland. © McFarland 2001 and © Journal of Parapsychology 1994

Appendix 11

Australian Sheep–Goat Scale
(Thalbourne, 1995a)

For each item indicate your attitude using the following scale.

0 = false   1 = uncertain   2 = true

1. I believe in the existence of ESP.
2. I believe I have had personal experience of ESP.
3. I believe I am psychic.
4. I believe it is possible to gain information about the future before it happens, in ways that do not depend on rational prediction or normal sensory channels.
5. I have had at least one hunch that turned out to be correct and which (I believe) was not just a coincidence.
6. I have had at least one premonition about the future that came true and which (I believe) was not just a coincidence.
7. I have had at least one dream that came true and which (I believe) was not just a coincidence.
8. I have had at least one vision that was not an hallucination and from which I received information that I could not have otherwise gained at that time and place.
9. I believe in life after death.
10. I believe that some people can contact spirits of the dead.
11. I believe that it is possible to gain information about the thoughts, feelings or circumstances of another person, in a way that does not depend on rational prediction or normal sensory channels.
12. I believe that it is possible to send a 'mental message' to another person, or in some way influence them at a distance, by means other than the normal channels of communication.
13. I believe I have had at least one experience of telepathy between myself and another person.
14. I believe in the existence of psychokinesis (or 'PK'), that is, the direct influence of mind on a physical system, without the mediation of any known physical energy.
15. I believe I have personally exerted PK on at least one occasion.
16. I believe I have marked psychokinetic ability.
17. I believe that, on at least one occasion, an inexplicable (but nonrecurrent) physical event of an apparently psychokinetic origin has occurred in my presence.
18. I believe that persistent inexplicable physical disturbances, of an apparently psychokinetic origin, have occurred in my presence at some time in the past (as, for example, a poltergeist).

Scoring

Sum the responses over the eighteen items.

To recode the questionnaire responses with Rasch scaling, see the conversion table in Lange and Thalbourne (2002).

Reproduced with permission of author and publisher from:

Thalbourne, M. A. (1995a). Further studies of the measurement and correlates of belief in the paranormal. *Journal of the American Society for Psychical Research, 89,* 233–47. © American Society for Psychical Research 1995

Appendix 12

Paranormal Short Inventory
(Randall, 1997)

Listed below are a few statements containing opinions. Following each opinion please indicate *how strongly* you agree or disagree with that statement, using the following scale.

1	2	3	4	5	6
strongly disagree	disagree somewhat	disagree slightly	agree slightly	agree somewhat	agree strongly

1. It is probably true that certain people can predict the future quite accurately.

2.* For the most part, people who claim to be psychics are in reality very good actors.

3. It is quite possible for planetary forces to control personality traits.

4. Contrary to scientific opinion, there is some validity to fortune telling.

5. In spite of the laws of science, some people can use their psychic powers to make objects move.

6.* As a general rule, a fortune teller's predictions which come true are a result of coincidence.

7.* Regardless of what you might read in the magazines, people who actually believe in 'magical' ritual ceremonies are just wasting their time.

8. As a general rule, UFO sightings can best be explained as overreactions by people to naturally occurring events.

9.* For the most part, most fortune teller's predictions are general and vague. It is just the situation that makes them believable.

10. In spite of what many people think, card reading, for example, tarot cards, can tell a lot about a person and their future.

11. Cosmic forces (like astrology) can still influence people's lives even though they don't believe in it.

12.* Although some people believe there still are people who can actually put a hex on or cast a love spell on someone, such belief is only superstition.

13. Contrary to scientific belief, some people can make contact with the dead.

*These items are reversed for scoring.

Scoring
Sum the responses over the thirteen items.

Appendix 13

Exeter Superstitions Questionnaire
(Preece and Baxter, 2000)

What are your opinions?

We want to know your opinions about some things that many people believe. This is not a test — there are no right answers and we just want to know what you think.

For each item indicate your level of agreement using the following scale.

1 I believe that this is almost certainly untrue	2 I believe that this is quite likely to be untrue	3 I believe that this is quite likely to be true	4 I believe that this is almost certainly true

1. The positions of the stars and planets when you are born affect what will happen to you during your life.

2. Some houses are haunted by ghosts.

3. It is possible to tell what is going to happen to you in the future by studying the lines on the palms of your hands.

4. Wearing jewelry made out of certain crystals can help to keep you healthy.

5. Some men and women can find missing persons by swinging a pendulum over a map.

6. In the past aliens from some other planet have landed on Earth.

7. Breaking a mirror is likely to bring you some bad luck in the future.

8. [insert the date of the next scheduled 'Friday the 13th] is a Friday and people should be careful on that day as 'Friday the 13th' is unlucky.

Scoring

A skepticism score is computed as the sum of the responses over all items except 6; the data on item 6 can be analyzed separately.

Reproduced with permission of authors and publisher from:
Preece, P. F. W. and Baxter, J. H. (2000). Scepticism and gullibility: the superstitious and pseudo-scientific beliefs of secondary school students. *International Journal of Science Education, 22*, 1147–56.
© Taylor and Francis, P.O. Box 25, Abingdon OX14 3UE England 2000

Appendix 14

New Age Orientation Scale
(Granqvist and Hagekull, 2001)

Below are listed a number of statements describing different ideas in relation to issues such as spirituality, philosophy of life, knowledge and mental capacities. Please mark each statement by indicating the extent to which it corresponds to your opinion. Write *one* number in the space next to the statements. Use the following response scale.

1	2	3.	4	5	6
strongly disagree	disagree	partly disagree	partly agree	agree	strongly agree

1. I am convinced that thought transference and/or the ability to move things by mere thinking actually do work.

2. I've read some of the new, 'alternative' books that deal with how to reach spiritual or personal development (e.g., *The Celestine Prophecy, A Course in Miracles, The Scared Self, Out on a Limb*).

3. The position of the stars at birth affects how one will live one's life or how one's personality will develop.

4. I think that we are now approaching an entirely new age, that will *radically* change our view of science, spiritual knowledge, or the true nature of man.

5. To reach one's personal, spiritual insight, every individual should combine or mix the truths that are hidden within different old traditions (e.g., Shamanism, the religions of native people, astrology, Eastern wisdom, Kabbala).

6. There are some objects or places that have a special spiritual meaning, for instance by being surrounded by a certain type of energy.

7. I am convinced that at least two of the following phenomena occur: dreams reveal what will happen in the future, one receives premonitions of what is to occur, or there are people who can 'see' the future.

8. With the assistance of a 'medium', it is possible to get in touch with dead people or with life on other planets.

9. There are many 'alternative treatments' (e.g., Reiki healing, Rosen, Zone, Aura, Primal, Reincarnation, Crystal and Chakra therapy) that are at least as effective as the regular medical treatments for bringing about human well-being and health.

10. I regularly use some specific technique (e.g., Yoga, rebirthing, meditation, massage) to become a more harmonious human being or to reach spiritual development (do *not* include prayer as a technique).

11. Everything that happens in an individual's life has an underlying meaning that is important to try to comprehend.

12. The whole cosmos is an unbroken, living whole, that the modern man has lost contact with.

13. Things that happen (e.g., divorce, death) in a house or room leave a certain 'atmosphere' that affects the people who subsequently move in.

14. A problem with the established health care system is that science has priority over intuition or old wisdom.

15. I believe that a person's deeds are stored in his or her 'karma'.

16. People live more than one life, so that when they die they will be reborn after some time in another body ('reincarnation').

17. Compared to most religious and nonreligious people, I am probably somewhat of a spiritual seeker with an unusually open mind.

18. One's world around is mainly a mirror image of one's inner world, so that outer processes above all reflect one's inner processes.

19. Tarot cards, horoscopes, or fortune telling can be good starting points from which to develop oneself and one's possibilities.

20. Spirituality to me is above all about realising my true nature or becoming one with cosmos.

21. I am a vegetarian/vegan for one/some of the following reasons: meat eating impedes the functioning of the astral plane, the individual's karma is impaired by meat eating, or all living creatures have a holy place in the cosmos.

22. Several phenomena that are usually subsumed under the 'new age' label are personally valuable to me.

Scoring

Average the responses over the twenty-two items.

Reproduced with permission of authors and publisher from:
Granqvist, P. and Hagekull, B. (2001). Seeking security in the New Age: on attachment and emotional compensation. *Journal for the Scientific Study of Religion,* *40,* 527–45. © Blackwell Scientific, Osney Mead, Oxford OX2 0EL England 2001

Author Index

Subject Index